DEUTERONOMY

ABINGDON OLD TESTAMENT COMMENTARIES

DEUTERONOMY

WALTER BRUEGGEMANN

Abingdon Press
Nashville

ABINGDON OLD TESTAMENT COMMENTARIES
DEUTERONOMY

Copyright © 2001 by Abingdon Press

This book is printed on recycled, acid-free, elemental-chlorine–free paper.

Library of Congress Cataloging-in-Publication Data

Brueggemann, Walter.
   Deuteronomy / Walter Brueggemann.
      p. cm—(Abingdon Old Testament commentaries)
   Includes bibliographical references and index.
   ISBN 0-687-08471-7 (alk. paper)
   1. Bible. O.T. Deuteronomy—Commentaries. I. Title. II. Series.

BS1275.3 .B768 2001
222'.1507—dc21

2001033652

03 04 05 06 07 08 09 10—10 9 8 7 6 5 4 3 2

MANUFACTURED IN THE UNITED STATES OF AMERICA

For
Christiana Adair Brueggemann
and
James August Brueggemann

CONTENTS

FOREWORD

T*he Abingdon Old Testament Commentaries* are offered to the reader in hopes that they will aid in the study of Scripture and provoke a deeper understanding of the Bible in all its many facets. The texts of the Old Testament come out of a time, a language, and socio-historical and religious circumstances far different from the present. Yet Jewish and Christian communities have held to them as a sacred canon, significant for faith and life in each new time. Only as one engages these books in depth and with all the critical and intellectual faculties available to us, can the contemporary communities of faith and other interested readers continue to find them meaningful and instructive.

These volumes are designed and written to provide compact, critical commentaries on the books of the Old Testament for the use of theological students and pastors. It is hoped that they may be of service also to upper-level college or university students and to those responsible for teaching in congregational settings. In addition to providing basic information and insights into the Old Testament writings, these commentaries exemplify the tasks and procedures of careful interpretation.

The writers of the commentaries in this series come from a broad range of ecclesiastical affiliations, confessional stances, and educational backgrounds. They have experience as teachers and, in some instances, as pastors and preachers. In most cases, the authors are persons who have done significant research on the book that is their assignment. They take full account of the most important current scholarship and secondary literature, while not attempting to summarize that literature or to engage in technical academic debate. The fundamental concern of each volume is analysis and discussion of the literary, socio-historical, theological, and ethical dimensions of the biblical texts themselves.

The New Revised Standard Version of the Bible is the principal translation of reference for the series, though authors may draw upon other interpretations in their discussion. Each writer is attentive to the original Hebrew text in preparing the commentary. But the authors do not presuppose any knowledge of the biblical languages on the part of the reader. When some awareness of a grammatical, syntactical, or philological issue is necessary for an adequate understanding of a particular text, the issue is explained simply and concisely.

Each volume consists of four parts. An *introduction* looks at the book as a whole to identify *key issues* in the book, its *literary genre* and *structure*, the *occasion and situational context* of the book (including both social and historical contexts), and the *theological and ethical* significance of the book.

The *commentary* proper organizes the text by literary units and, insofar as is possible, divides the comment into three parts. The *literary analysis* serves to introduce the passage with particular attention to identification of the genre of speech or literature and the structure or outline of the literary unit under discussion. Here also, the author takes up significant stylistic features to help the reader understand the mode of communication and its impact on comprehension and reception of the text. The largest part of the comment is usually found in the *exegetical analysis*, which considers the leading concepts of the unit, the language of expression, and problematical words, phrases, and ideas in order to get at the aim or intent of the literary unit, as far as that can be uncovered. Attention is given here to particular historical and social situations of the writer(s) and reader(s) where that is discernible and relevant as well as to wider cultural (including religious) contexts. The analysis does not proceed phrase by phrase or verse by verse but deals with the various particulars in a way that keeps in view the overall structure and central focus of the passage and its relationship to the general line of thought or rhetorical argument of the book as a whole. The final section, *theological and ethical analysis* seeks to identify and clarify the theological and ethical matters with which the unit deals or to which it points. Though not aimed primarily at contemporary issues of faith and life, this section should provide readers a basis for reflection on them.

Each volume also contains a select bibliography of works cited in the commentary as well as major commentaries and other important works available in English. A subject index is provided to help the reader get at matters that cut across different texts.

The fundamental aim of this series will have been attained if readers are assisted, not only to understand more about the origins, character, and meaning of the Old Testament writings, but also to enter into their own informed and critical engagement with the texts themselves.

Patrick D. Miller
General Editor

PREFACE

I am grateful to the usual suspects for bringing my manuscript to the form of a book. This cast of characters includes first of all Tempie Alexander, without whom it would never happen. Tim Simpson has yet again prepared indices and done the final read of the manuscript. I am grateful to Carolyn Pressler and Patrick Miller for their editorial attentiveness to my work and for including it in the series, and to those who did the hard work at Abingdon Press.

I am pleased to dedicate the book to Ana and August who may grow to ask eventually, "What is the meaning of . . . ?" There are traces indicating that the tradition of Deuteronomy was focused on nurturing the next generation to faith. What better connection than to link my commentary to my next generation, which I do in gratitude and anticipation.

Walter Brueggemann

LIST OF ABBREVIATIONS

AB	Anchor Bible
BZAW	Beihefte zur ZAW
CBQ	*Catholic Biblical Quarterly*
JBL	*Journal of Biblical Literature*
JSOTSup	Journal for the Study of the Old Testament—Supplement Series
JTS	*Journal of Theological Studies*
OBT	Overtures to Biblical Theology
OTL	Old Testament Library
SBT	Studies in Biblical Theology
VT	*Vetus Testamentum*
ZAW	*Zeitschrift für die alttestamentliche Wissenschaft*

INTRODUCTION

It is impossible to overstate the importance of the book of Deuteronomy for the shape and substance of Israel's faith in the Old Testament. The book has given classic articulation to the main themes characteristic of Judaism and, derivatively, of Christianity. In broadest sweep, the book is a formulation of covenant theology, whereby YHWH and Israel are pledged to exclusive loyalty and fidelity to each other; YHWH is to assure the well-being of Israel, Israel is to live in trust in and obedience to YHWH.

The book is organized into three great speeches of Moses (1:1–4:40; 4:44–29:1; 29:2–32:47), together with concluding materials concerning the death of Moses, the leadership of Joshua, and the future of Israel (32:48–34:12). Primary attention is normally given to the long middle speech of 4:44–29:1 that constitutes the bulk of the book, is likely the oldest part of the book, and most pervasively voices the main Deuteronomic. Since the important work of Gerhard von Rad (1966:26-33), it is usual to notice that this second speech is organized around elements characteristic of covenant formulations:

—Historical prologue concerning YHWH's good actions for Israel (5–11),
—The statutes and ordinances of YHWH for Israel (12–25),
—Mutual oaths of fidelity (26:16-19), and
—Blessings and curses as covenant sanctions (27–28).

The material that constitutes this corpus contains sources that are diverse and have been gathered over a long period of time. In the final form of the text, however, these diverse materials come to be a unified whole that provides a theological statement that is available for repeated liturgical reenactment. Thus it is plausible that these materials are formed as they are for both periodic use in solemn worship and normative instruction, whereby Israel was periodically and in many different circumstances reconstituted as the people of YHWH.

Because Deuteronomy as a book reached its final form through a long editorial process designed to keep the book pertinent and responsive to different historical crises, it is not easy to date the book or to identify its origin. It is usual to suggest the following accent points in the formation and use of the book:

The book itself purports to be a series of addresses *by Moses* to Israel at the end of the long wilderness sojourn just before his death. In that context, Moses addresses Israel with a strong covenantal "either/or" made up of assurances and imperatives, for Moses knows that Israel in the new land of promise will have its faith in YHWH severely challenged by seductive alternatives of culture and religion. Attributing the book to Moses makes an important theological-canonical claim. However, a critical attempt to situate the origin of the book historically has made clear to scholarship that Mosaic authorship is a fictive claim assigned by a much later tradition. This fabrication is no historical deception, for the ancient world did not focus upon precise personal authorship in the same way the modern world does. The claim for Moses is rather a serious theological insistence that later interpreters of covenant continue to rely upon and extend the normative teaching tradition of Moses. Thus even though the book is not "historically" from Moses, it is indeed a formidable statement of what Israel came to accept as the substance of Mosaic faith authorized at Sinai and subsequently developed by an on-going stream of authorized interpreters.

The "historical" locus of the literature that became the book of Deuteronomy is likely to be situated in the eighth or seventh century, during *the period of Assyrian domination,* which is also the period of the great pre-exilic prophets in Israel. The "covenant structure" of the second speech, noted above, is parallel to and reflective of the form of the political treaties of the Assyrian empire in that period. A self-conscious Israelite community may have *borrowed* a covenant form deliberately to offer its covenant with YHWH as a radical *alternative* to alliance with Assyria. Frank Crüsemann (1996:201-75) has made a powerful case that the book of Deuteronomy is a radical assertion of "the people of the land," free agricultural landowners, who assert loyalty to YHWH as an alternative to loyalty to Assyria. Such a political movement in Judah was in deep conflict with the policies of the royal dynasty in Jerusalem that had come to rely upon Assyria. That royal loyalty to Assyria, so much opposed by the tradition reflected in Deuteronomy, is embodied by King Ahaz who is purported to have made deep covenantal commitments to the Assyrian king, Tiglath-pileser III (2 Kgs 16:7; see Isa 28:15, 18). This commitment of Israel to the empire was politically abhorrent, economically costly, and theologically repellent to those who were rooted in the radical Yahwism associated with the memory of Moses. The key reference point in this revolutionary theo-political alternative is the "Reform of Josiah" (2 Kgs 22–23) wherein the new king threw off the controls of the fading Assyrian authority in the interest of an independent Yahwistic, Torah-informed state.

Thus it would appear that the shapers of the tradition of Deuteronomy used old memories of Moses (or what purported to be old memories) in order to authorize a political resistance to imperial domination. While the political motives for such a maneuver are obvious, the theological claims behind the political maneuvers are serious and carry with them important ethical requirements. Thus in its primary casting, Deuteronomy is an articulation of "public theology."

The older eighth- to seventh-century materials were taken up and framed in the first speech (1:1–4:40) and the third speech (29:2–32:47) to serve the needs of *the exilic community* in the sixth century after Jerusalem had been lost and the opinion-makers in the community were deported out of the land. Scholars incline to regard chapters 1–3 and 29–32 as a literary theological introduction to the entire corpus of the Deuteronomic History that in its final form includes the books of Joshua, Judges, Samuel, and Kings.

Set in that subsequent context, it is evident that the fiction of entering the land from the "Plains of Moab" (1:5-8) is understood as the reentry into the land after the deportation. Accent upon "your little ones" (1:39) and "the next generation" (29:22) in this context has reference to the children and grandchildren of the generation of the deportees. It is this later generation, unburdened of the failures that led to exile (see 24:16), who can consider reentry into the land with a fresh resolve to be the obedient people of YHWH.

The older material was reused yet again in the fifth century by the Ezra movement. Ezra and his followers may well have played a key role in the formation of the canon. The Ezra movement became the primary impetus for the shaping of emerging Judaism. This reuse by Ezra the scribe enabled the older materials of Deuteronomy to become enormously influential in the shape and cast of Judaism as a people of the Torah (see especially Neh 8:1-8).

Through *Josiah* as representative of the older revolutionary movement (2 Kgs 22–23) and *Ezra* as the decisive force in early Judaism (Neh 8:1-8), along with other unknown traditionists, the corpus of Deuteronomy became *a canonical book*. As canonical literature, it voices for ongoing generations of Jews and Christians the primal claims of covenant faith, and a radical social ethic that envisions a different mode of social relationships in a distinct, self-conscious community.

These reference points of *Moses, Josiah,* and *Ezra* point to a process of many traditioning agents who generated the book. It is not possible to prefer one of these points as decisive, for the book is an outcome of a process of faithful interpretation done over a long period of time.

Biblical scholars tend to identify the participants in that formative process:

1. The older parts of the tradition pay particular attention to *the Levitical priests* who are understood as the heirs to Moses and the designated keepers and teachers of the Torah. There is a strong scholarly hypothesis that these Levitical teachers are

the force behind the book. This makes particular sense if one focuses upon the book backward to the memory of Moses.

2. The traditioning process in the eighth and seventh centuries is alive to *the prophetic movement* with reference to Amos, Isaiah, Micah, Hosea, and later, Jeremiah. It is not possible to determine if the primary influence is from Deuteronomy to the prophets or from the prophets to Deuteronomy. It is sufficient to say that the same interpretive matrix was important for both enterprises, "Torah" and "prophets." Both literatures insisted upon Israel's answerability to YHWH, who presides over the public processes of history.

3. A strong case has been made that *the scribal tradition* with its sapiential focus is generative for developments in Deuteronomy from Josiah to Ezra. The scribes are the self-conscious "scroll makers" who generate the canonizing process, on which see, for example, Baruch the scribe in Jeremiah 36.

While scholars have used great energy on these several hypotheses concerning *Levitical, prophetic,* and *scribal* sources for Deuteronomy, it is likely that no single hypothesis can account for everything in the book. More likely, the book of Deuteronomy emerged from the best efforts of many interpretive enterprises in Israel; it represents a hard-fought consensus in Israel about the key claims of Yahwistic faith. In general those sources converge in a "YHWH alone" perspective on faith and life.

The key claim concerns the exclusive gift and demand of YHWH and the insistence that this single covenantal loyalty should be decisive in every aspect of Israel's social relationships. In the body of statutes and ordinances (12–25), it is possible to see the ongoing work of covenantal interpretation as the community seeks to discern the implications of Yahweh's exclusive sovereignty for the several dimensions of Israel's public life: right worship, just economics, viable public power, faithful conduct of war, and the sustainable ordering of family life.

A study of the details of the laws indicates tension between generosity that is rooted in neighborly *mutuality* and harsh *authoritarianism* that appears to be an anxious response to the threat of social disorder. In recognizing this pervasive tension one ought not to claim more than the evidence permits for a genuine ethical mutuality. At the same time, it is correct to insist that Deuteronomy has set in motion a covenantal ethic that has continued to be a generative force in the revolutionary ethical convictions of Judaism and Christianity. Deuteronomy has in purview a profoundly neighborly ethic that understands the formation and maintenance of a communal infrastructure as a primal mode of obedience to the God of covenant.

Given its generative and imaginative character, Deuteronomy characteristically evokes attention to the canonical location and context of the book. As the book of Deuteronomy completes the "Torah," Judaism's most sacred scripture (the Pentateuch), its relation to Genesis through Numbers is important. Deuteronomy is mindful of Genesis through Numbers, but also stands apart from them. It looks back to the normative memory of the Genesis ancestors and the traditions of Moses; but then it turns from them forward. Deuteronomy has important links to the "canonical" history of Joshua, Judges, Samuel, and Kings. It provides the vision that guides the presentation of that royal history of Joshua through Kings that ends in deportation (Noth 1991). Thus Deuteronomy stands at midpoint between the ancient memory of Genesis through Numbers and the sorry history of Joshua through Kings. Deuteronomy looks both *backward to rootage* and *forward to crisis,* and interprets at the precise place where *rootage* and *crisis* intersect. The book makes a case that the rootage of the past is the clue to understanding and faithfully living in the crisis.

Located at that precise intersection, Deuteronomy voices a remarkable dynamic for faithful, imaginative interpretation. The book received its familiar name from 17:18; the Greek term rendered in NRSV as "copy" is *deuteros,* a second version (of Torah), thus *deutero nomos,* "second law." It is clear that Deuteronomy is not the "original version" of Torah from Sinai, but is and intends to be a derivative interpretive tradition that comments on the Sinai materials in ways that keep the remembered tradition pertinent. As important as are the materials that constitute the *substance* of Deuteronomy, it is equally important to take into serious account its *process* of interpretation whereby "Moses," in each new generation, restates Torah in fresh ways.

This vitality in the interpretive process is a primal contribution of Deuteronomy to Judaism and to Christianity. That vitality means that there is no final, settled interpretation, no "strict construction," but always another reading of the tradition that must be done afresh. In Judaism this openness is to be found in "the oral Torah" that runs beyond what is written. In Christianity it is the "apostolic tradition" that becomes the "fuller sense" of the text that is always again to be reappropriated (Brown 1995). Thus the text itself, with its full canonical authority, is not the last word in the interpretive process. It is a model word that invites and authorizes "Moses," in always a new circumstance, to interpret again.

Such an understanding of the dynamic process—that is "not with our ancestors . . . but with us, who are all of us here alive today" (5:3), for those who are "not here with us today" (29:15)—alerts us to the openness of this interpretive tradition and warns against any settled literalism. In the hands of imaginative, faithful interpreters, the text always "means again" and "means differently." In a sense then, Deuteronomy is a model commentary that becomes the warrant for the endless flow of commentaries that continue even to this present series, each of which has the task of reiterating the tradition afresh.

Such an enterprise suggests that the text of Deuteronomy may be expected to say more than it says and to say differently from what it says. This requires that one must allow Deuteronomy to be a literary-theological "trope," a use of words in other than their literal sense. Such an awareness does not give license for the text to mean just anything, but it means to listen attentively for what may be present in the text beyond what is obvious. This may be particularly important in Deuteronomy given the harshness that borders on brutality and the exclusionary spirit of some statutes. The patriarchal casting of family statutes or the brutality of holy war or the death formula, "shall surely die," leads one to think again about the intent of the present canonical text. These statutes seem to be a measure of anxiety about the maintenance of the community, and an attempt to draw boundaries of membership in order to delineate the integrity of the community (Stulman 1990; Mullen 1993). Without any attempt to "explain away" the harshness so clearly present in the text, it may be useful to see that the harshness reflects a felt anxiety for which the statute becomes a vehicle.

The tradition of Deuteronomy has the recurrent problem of a generous ethic in a community that must maintain itself in the face of threatened disintegration. More simply, it must struggle with the difficult issue of who is in and who is out. Israel is "in the world" ("in Canaan") but not "of the world" ("Canaanite"). Some of its responses to this issue are clumsy and awkward, but the issue is for that reason no less important and tricky.

The theological accent point of this text, then, is what is called in Christian theology "ecclesiology." That is, a sense of the community that must always be redefined in terms of its origin, purpose, and destiny. The "land" may then be understood as hope for the promised well-being that comes to be called "Kingdom of God." In Deuteronomy Israel is not yet in the land. It is on the way there. How it arrives there is the overriding issue. It takes Moses, always again Moses, no less than Moses, to insist that this covenant community, responsive to YHWH, understand the terms upon which its future may be viably occupied. Moses knows that the future is gift, but it is a gift that can be readily forfeited. Israel must always again rechoose that future in the form of present-tense obedience. It is no wonder that the book of Deuteronomy worries about the "children," for the future is always the task of the next generation that, hopefully, has listened long enough and well enough to choose wisely.

COMMENTARY

MEMORY AS CONTEXT FOR INTERPRETATION (1:1–3:29)

These introductory chapters to the book of Deuteronomy are a mixture of speech by Moses and *narrative* memory. The speech of Moses is the voice of the tradition that summons Israel to enact its peculiar destiny as the object of YHWH's special promise, presence, and demand. Here as for all of the book of Deuteronomy, it is impossible to overstate the importance of Moses as the deepest human authority this tradition can know, as the authorizing human voice that is taken as YHWH's own word.

The narrative memory is laid out as a travel report, tracing the way in which Israel moved from Sinai—the mountain of command—to the goal of the promised land, just beyond the Jordan. The selective, stylized narrative memory appeals to what may be older narrative sources in the book of Numbers. The text assumes the foundational reliability of that memory. The narrative memory serves as a matrix out of which Moses may address Israel in a compelling and didactic way. From the *context of memory* the voice insists that Israel must ponder its past in order that in the present, it may be more fully, obediently, and responsibly the people of YHWH. The intention of the retrospect is to make cogent and palpable Israel's distinct identity in the present, an identity rooted in loyalty to YHWH.

Exegetical Analysis

1:1-5: The initial paragraph of this introduction quickly locates Moses in a particular time and place (1:1-5). The time is specific: first day, eleventh month, fortieth year from Sinai. The reference point is Sinai; what counts is how far removed from Sinai is this speech of Moses. The statement at the same time links these words of Moses to Sinai and distances them from Sinai. These are not Sinai words. These are derivative. The place is equally specific: it is by the Jordan, that is, near the land of promise but not in the land. The time and place locate Moses, who dominates this opening account as he will dominate the entire book of Deuteronomy. He will speak, and his words will be remembered. He needs no introduction or further authorization. His voice is a decisive given in Israel. It has been so since Sinai. In Exodus 20:18-21, Moses was accepted as the mediator, the one who will "relay" the word of YHWH to Israel.

This two-step, relayed utterance from YHWH-to-Moses-to Israel is crucial for the revelatory process of Deuteronomy and for the way in which the Old Testament understands the gift of YHWH's disclosure of Torah. This is divine word; but it is human speech.

Israel received the divine word directly only in Exod 20:1-17. Such direct address is too ominous for Israel to bear. From that moment at Sinai, Israel is prepared for the human speech of Moses. The word of Moses is reliably the command of YHWH. This stratagem places Israel's high confidence in this particular human utterance, but acknowledges that it is *human*. The text gives no hint and expresses no curiosity about *how* Moses is commanded by YHWH. Everything that follows in Deuteronomy relies upon this shrewd interpretive "two-step."

The work of Moses is to "expound" Torah. The phrase "this Torah" suggests that there is a recognizable corpus of teaching that is known to be authoritative in Israel. The corpus that follows here "expounds" "this Torah," that is, the Torah of Sinai. The term "expound" *(b'r)* means to "make plain, make clear" (see Deut 27:8; Hab 2:2), that is, to say it so that it can be understood. While the other uses of the term suggest writing more legibly or larger, in 1:5 the word means to explain or exposit, that is, to extrapolate meanings. Deuteronomy is Israel's great book of exegetical extrapolation; thus it is commanded that Torah be made more explicit in terms of particular circumstance. The

Torah of Sinai is always in need of such interpretive extension in new circumstance.

1:6-8: When Moses begins his "clarification" of Torah, the first utterance concerns a departure from Sinai at the command of YHWH, alluding to the memory of Num 10:11-13 (1:6-8). YHWH does not intend Israel to remain forever at Sinai, and certainly the community here addressed is far removed in time, in place, and in circumstance from Sinai. YHWH wills for Israel a future elsewhere, in the land.

The *command* is in the service of the *promise* of the land already pronounced in Genesis to the ancestors. Thus the final book of Torah complements the first book of Torah, pairing Genesis and Deuteronomy as "land documents," focused on Israel's promised inheritance. The promise brackets the emphasis on Torah found in Exodus, Leviticus, and Numbers. Moses' first utterance quickly accomplishes two matters. First, it asserts that the present generation is yet again a generation under promise whom YHWH intends to be recipients of the land. Second, the promissory utterance specifies the boundaries of the land in the most sweeping scope, thus echoing the promise to Abraham in Gen 15:18-21 (see Deut 1:24; Josh 1:4). Note well: the first utterance in this book of commands is a promise for what is not yet given to Israel. All of the commands to follow are in the service of that promise that is YHWH's primal intent for the present generation of Israel.

1:9-18: Moses' initial recital perhaps looks back to Exod 18:13-37 (1:9-18). Here the memory of that administrative initiative is prefaced in two ways. In verse 10, it is affirmed that God has multiplied Israel as promised. Indeed it is the fruitfulness of Israel that creates the need for a more complex judicial system. The promise of "many heirs" was made to Abraham (Gen 15:6); its actualization was acknowledged at the beginning of the Exodus narrative (Exod 1:7). The verbs "multiply" and "bless" recall the creation account (Gen 1:28); God's initial words of blessing are enacted in Israel, who is the carrier of YHWH's will for all creation. The celebrative retrospect of verse 10 is matched by the future hope of verse 11. Moses expects that in time to come there will be even more sons and daughters, more heirs to occupy the huge expanse of the land of promise now envisioned. YHWH's generative promise marks this community even in the wilderness.

What counts, however, in the context of such fecundity is the proper management of the community. From the outset, Israel needs a procedure to ensure reliable justice. Here it is Moses, not Jethro, who has devised a judicial system accepted by the community. There must be good judges who are impartial and unintimidated, for what they administer is the justice of God (v. 17). The charge to the new judicial appointees is decisive for Israel (see Exod 18:21; Deut 16:19-20; 2 Chron 19:7). From the outset Moses understands that the land of promise must be ordered justly. A trustworthy judiciary is a *sine qua non* for a covenant community. It is the judges' task to ensure that the land given in *promise* will be a land kept in *Torah*. Moses melds together the key traditions of Israel, traditions of *promise* and of *demand*.

The actual content of this "justice" is to be equitable to "small and great," with no advantage to the powerful. Furthermore, this justice is to be equitable for covenant members and outsiders ("resident aliens"), that is, for all parties to any social dispute. In the prophetic tradition, it is precisely the failure of justice that causes the loss of land (Amos 5:7, 10-11, 14-17; Isa 5:8-10, 24-25; Jer 7:5-7). The land of promise must be ordered by justice, or the promise will evaporate. Anticipating Deut 17:8-13, verse 17 foresees a court of appeal to the central authority of Moses atop the pyramid of judicial power (Wildavsky 1984:146).

1:19-25b: After the "pause for justice" in verses 9-18, the text returns to the theme of verses (6-8) (1:19-25). The initial part of the journey from Sinai is to Kadesh Barnea, a major oasis in the arid south, apparently a place prominent in Israel's memory as a way station on its journey (see Num 13:23-27; 32:8-15). According to tradition, Israel was poised to enter the land of promise from the south. The tribes sojourn to the very edge of the land, and are ready to enter. In verse 21, Moses authorizes Israel to "take possession" of the land. The wording is worthy of note. Tradition knows that finally the land is not *given*, but is *taken*. The land for Israel is indeed willed and authorized by YHWH, but Israel must act. The verb "take possession" signifies forceful military action.

Perhaps ironically, the mandate is followed immediately by a salvation oracle: "Do not fear." This form of affirmation is a characteristic assurance given to the army that is about to undertake a risky enterprise (see Deut 20:3). There is no doubt in the utterance of Moses that the venture will succeed, for it is authorized and overseen by YHWH. The anticipation of conflict, however, is reason enough for fear and anxiety. The success of the troops' *mission* cannot be sure, apart from this utterance. Moses utters an assurance that makes YHWH a partner in the venture, thus weighing the odds of success heavily in favor of Israel.

Moses is immediately ready for an assault on the inhabitants of the land. The community of Israel, however, is more cautious and wants to reconnoiter in order to determine strategy and to assess risks (v. 22). Moses approves the mission. There is no hint here that such a maneuver is a fearful delay nor is it reckoned to be an act of faithfulness; it is simply prudence. The exploration party is sent and returned quickly, all within the scope of verses 22-25. Their report is unreservedly positive. The land is good! The produce is fabulous. No wonder, for they had witnessed "the Valley of Eshcol" (see Num 13:23-24).

1:26-45: By verse 25, all seems in readiness for entry into the land in pursuit of which Moses and Israel have come so far. All are agreed about the desirability of the land. None doubt Israel's entitlement to the land from YHWH. Moses' work in remembering, however, is also to recall that the past concerning the land has been problematic. These present verses function as a negative counterpoint to the celebrative tone of verses 19-25. Verses 26-27 are sober in their alarm. Moses accuses Israel with a threefold indictment: "You were unwilling . . . you rebelled . . . you grumbled." This speech of Moses appeals to the "murmur tradition" of the wilderness sojourn prominent before (Exod 15:22-26; 16:1-3;

17:1-7) and after (Num 11:1-15; 14:1-4) Sinai (Coats 1968, 47-127). That is, in the remembered tradition Sinai is situated in the midst of complaint.

Whereas the Torah of Sinai is YHWH's command to Israel, the murmur tradition that frames Sinai is about Israel's challenge to and dissatisfaction with YHWH. In the older tradition, the murmuring complaint against YHWH and against Moses is grounded in the risk of *the wilderness* where there are no visible means of life support. But here, as in Num 14:1-4, based on the data of Num 13:28-29, the murmur is *at the brink of the land*. The threat protested now is not lack of resources in the wilderness but dangers in the land entry. The complainers looked back to Egypt with an imagined preference for the conditions of slavery. They looked forward to the land ahead and saw formidable resistance to their coming.

The murmuring Israelites took stock of the God of promise and concluded that YHWH was in fact their enemy who willed to destroy them. The entire journey to the land of abundance is seen as a grand plot to destroy. Israel has completely misconstrued YHWH's leadership in its life. That, of course, is the point of the indictment against Israel: Israel's pervasive misconstrual of YHWH.

The ground for Israel's remembered refusal to enact the promise of YHWH and receive the land is that Israel will be at risk. They were scared! The cities—surely formidable Canaanite city-states—with their mind-boggling fortifications were too much for this resourceless company fresh off the wilderness. Moreover, there had been reported sightings of the residue of old "giants" who were too big and strong to be taken. The children of promise are wholly immobilized. They are unwilling to continue the venture on which their faith had started them.

Moses, however, remembers not only the recalcitrance of Israel. He also recalls his own vigorous response to their cowardice. He had addressed them with an imperative that was designed to stiffen their spines. The assurance remembered in verse 21 is here remembered as a demanding imperative. The wording of verse 29 echoes that of verse 21. But while verse 21 is phrased as an assurance, verse 29 is worded as an imperative. Israel is a people of faith, and so cannot be a people of fear. The immobilizing fear comes because they no longer trust YHWH as an adequate force on their behalf. Moses asserts the defining mark of Israel that the tribes had forgotten in their fear. Israel is accompanied by YHWH, who can meet any threat awaiting them in the new land. YHWH is the key agent in the land-taking maneuver; Israel is completely misinformed if it imagines that success depends upon its own prowess. It is YHWH who will make the decisive difference, who will be the leader in the violent dispute over the land. The ground for the assurance concerning the land ahead is the memory of the Exodus, when Israel had been hopelessly defeated by the Egyptian powers—except YHWH was engaged (Exod 14:13-14).

What happened then will happen again, now. *This* will be "just as" *that* (v. 30). The "just as" (= "according to all") is parallel to the "just as" of verse 3. The Exodus, so far as this tradition is concerned, is not in doubt. It becomes the ground for trust in the future. What YHWH did in Egypt, moreover, is matched by what YHWH has done in the wilderness. In the wilderness, when Israel was in despair,

> the LORD your God carried you, just as one carries a child, all the way that you traveled until you reached this place. (v. 31)

Indeed, YHWH carried a people that could not travel under its own power. YHWH has been and will be utterly reliable. There is no reason to back down at the brink of the land, no ground for fearing the giants and the fortresses in the new land; YHWH is more than a match for any such threat.

After Moses' remembered appeal for trust in YHWH, however, Israel's squeamish response is also recalled. The verdict of verse 32 is terse: "You have no trust" (*amen*). The term means to have complete confidence in YHWH in a situation of threat when Israel has, on its own, less than adequate resources to cope. The episode of the Exodus was a time of trust (see Exod 14:30-31). In this analogous circumstance, however, Israel showed no confidence in YHWH (see a parallel negation in Isa 7:9). YHWH is characteristically willing and able; Israel is characteristically frightened and refuses to act on that assurance. Israel prefers to count on its own inadequate resources.

YHWH, Moses asserts, is indeed faithful and trustworthy; but YHWH will not be mocked. Israel's refusal to "trust and obey," so says Moses, evokes YHWH's harsh judgment. The condition of the new land is complete trust in YHWH; thus, no trust equals no land. None who doubts YHWH will receive the land.

The only exceptions in the present community are Caleb and Joshua. In the memory of Israel, Caleb and Joshua stand firm in faith against the community of doubters (Num 14:6-9). These two have complete confidence that YHWH is reliable and adequate in the face of even this great threat. Because of their readiness to risk all for the sake of the promise and because of their complete confidence in YHWH, Caleb and Joshua are exceptions to the death verdict issued upon the entire generation of Israel in verses 35-40 (Olson 1985). In the book of Numbers Caleb and Joshua symbolize the new generation that is unmarked by faithlessness who will receive the land of promise. The contrast between these two and all the others is the contrast between *faith* and *faithlessness* and consequently, between those who receive land and those who do not.

This simple contrast is further enhanced by two surprises the narrative reports in its conclusion (vv. 37-39). First, who would have suspected that Moses would be identified with the disbelieving community and included in their exclusion from the land? Moses is not charged with faithlessness but is contaminated by the community of unfaith, and so suffers exclusion along with the others. The text in verse 37 provides a nice bracket with 34:1-8 where the verdict of exclusion of Moses from the land is enacted. Second, "the little ones," whom those without faith thought would be lost as spoil in defeat, turn out to be the wave of the future; the vulnerable ones who will receive the land. The contrast between the hard-hearted doubters and the innocent children is complete. The ones most at risk will receive the promised land. Everything, asserts Moses, depends upon trust. The speech of Moses makes a characteristically sharp contrast between *old and new*, between *faithlessness and faith*, between *loss and gift*.

After the harsh and uncompromising rebuke of verses 35-40, so Moses remembers, Israel "repents" (vv. 41-45). It does so at the thirteenth hour (not the eleventh hour), when it is too late. Having been turned away from the land of promise, Israel now confesses its sin and prepares to fight its way into the new land. It is clear that even in its confession of sin, Israel does not yet understand at all its sinful lack of faith. Its new *willingness to fight* is an act of disbelief fully commensurate with its earlier *refusal to fight*. Both refusal and willingness, without YHWH, are hopeless acts of self-destruction.

Moses' characterization of Israel's belated willingness to fight portrays a ludicrous picture of Israel, dressing up in army fatigues, rather casually, perhaps excessively confident. Their attitude is odd, given how intimidated they have been only a few verses earlier (v. 32). The scene may anticipate the urgency with which Saul equips David in order to face the Philistine giant (1 Sam 17:38-45). Israel in our text suits up in its autonomy, without reference to the God whom David trusted completely.

In response to this blasé, overconfident act of autonomy, the same God who promised in verse 30 to "fight for you" now declares, "I am not in the midst of you" (v. 42). The reason for YHWH's absence from Israel is that Israel did not "listen." The term *listen (shema)*, is decisive for Deuteronomy. It implies ceding one's life over to another in obedience. But Israel here in its autonomy does not obey and therefore cannot succeed.

To fight without YHWH is an act of disbelief. The outcome is predictable. The hill country people swarm like bees, chasing Israel south to "Hormah." The name "Hormah" is linked to the term *herem*, that is, wholesale destruction. If faith is the condition of the land, then faithlessness leads to prompt, harsh defeat. Beyond the military defeat, moreover, in its disbelief Israel is cut off from YHWH. YHWH will not listen to their cries of need. Israel had not listened (v. 43); now YHWH responds in kind. Israel has chosen a future without YHWH, and now it has that future for itself. The promise to the ancestors (v. 8), reiterated by Moses (v. 21), is now remote, if not forfeited. God is not likely to reactivate the promise among this people any time soon.

In this geographical representation, Kadesh-Barnea is the midpoint between *Horeb* (Sinai) and the *wilderness* opposite the Jordan River. Kadesh-Barnea is a major oasis in the south (1:46–2:23). The Israelites had arrived at the oasis prepared to enter the land (1:19). In their faithlessness, however, they were repelled and defeated. While the narrative of defeat in 1:44 situates Israel at "Hormah," the positive and therefore durable reference point in this memory is Kadesh-Barnea. The narrative of chapter 2 takes Kadesh-Barnea as its launching pad.

1:46-2:23: The narrative is not interested in chronology but in a demanding, defining relationship with YHWH. In anger the older, disobedient generation had been commanded "back into the wilderness in the direction of the Red Sea" (1:40; 1:46–2:1). "Back into the wilderness" and "toward the Red Sea" are theological rather than geographical reference points. Disobedience had earned Israel more time in the wilderness. If proximity to the land of promise bespeaks anticipated well-being, this regression "toward the Red Sea" in parallel fashion signifies regression to Egypt and slavery. Thus the command of 1:40 and the report of 1:46–2:1 indicate a sentence of jeopardized life that happens when Israel refuses to trust and obey YHWH.

What follows in these verses is the second, more successful approach to the land of promise. Whereas the attempt to enter the land from the south had been an unmitigated disaster due to Israel's lack of trust in YHWH, this account brings Israel to a second effort at the land of promise approached from the east. The narrative reports on a conflict-free and successful advance toward the land. After the introductory comment of 1:14–2:4a, the narrative traces a peaceful procession through the territories of three related communities, the Edomites (2:4a-8a), the Moabites (2:8a-9), and the Ammonites (vv. 17-23). This pattern of peaceful sojourn is interrupted by two other comments in verses 10-16.

The introductory report of 1:46–2:4a reiterates the command of 1:40, "in the direction of the Red Sea." Thus there is narrative continuity. Given that, however, two elements in this introduction are surprising. First, YHWH's invitation to "head north," parallel to the command of 1:7, carries none of the strong rebuke of chapter 1. The new initiative suggests that YHWH "remembers their sin no more" (Jer 31:34). In any case, this introduction is unburdened by any negative memory.

Commensurate with YHWH's new, positive initiative is the fact that here Israel indicates none of the distrust that defined the preceding episode. Now Israel is able to undertake the journey in scrupulous obedience to YHWH's conditions, and apparently in complete confidence in YHWH's rule. Both parties are here presented positively, so that the venture toward the land may now succeed; YHWH is free of anger, Israel is free of doubt. This is indeed a new beginning!

In the first maneuver of the new initiative, Israel passes through the territory of Edom, from the south, in the ravine of the Arabah south of the Dead Sea (vv. 4a-8a). The land is described as that of "your kindred, heirs of Esau." The directive appeals to the Genesis account of conflicted relationship between the ancestral twins Jacob and Esau (Gen 25:23-26). That Esau is now "afraid of you" echoes the blessing given to Esau in Gen 27:39-40. Esau is destined to be subordinate to Jacob. This narrative report of Deut 2:4a-8a is sharply contrasted with the unfriendly encounter of Num 14:14-21 in which Edom refused to permit Israel to cross its territory and Israel subsequently "turned away." The present narrative, by contrast, presents a benign picture in which Israel is careful not to offend and Edom grants passage without comment.

Israel is not to exploit this advantage, but to respect the host country scrupulously. Perhaps Israel in its power could have raided and usurped what it needed, but that is prohibited by YHWH. There are two reasons for the prohibition. First, the land Edom holds was also the gift of YHWH, as precious and guaranteed to them as will be Israel's own land. This is an important motif, to be reiterated with reference to Moab and Ammon, for it affirms that there is more than one promised land that is assured to more than one people. It is remarkable in this tradition so preoccupied with Israel's exceptional character as the community of YHWH that there are other communities also on the horizon of YHWH's specific beneficence. Israelite entitlement gives it no permit to disrupt the entitlement of another people by YHWH; for that reason all provisions for the journey must be purchased and not seized, in a show of meticulous respect for a kindred people.

The second reason for the prohibition against usurpation is that it is unnecessary. Israel does not need to confiscate food and water from its "host community, "because everything it needs is provided by YHWH (v. 7). YHWH has been attentive to Israel all these forty years of the wilderness sojourn. Indeed, not only attentive and aware of need, but unfailing in giving blessing. The power of YHWH's blessing has had the capacity to transform the deadliness of the wilderness into a life-giving place. All this time in the wilderness when Israel might have expected deep risk, hardship, and scarcity, it "lacked nothing" (see Pss 23:1; 78:19). The affirmation of "lacked nothing" is astonishing, for in the wilderness one may expect to lack everything.

The second phase of Israel's successful sojourn toward the land is through Moab, a kingdom that borders Edom (vv. 8b-9, 13). This report is an abbreviated parallel to the narrative concerning Edom, with the same accents. Israel is not to engage in conflict with Moab, because the land held by Moab is also a grant from YHWH that Israel is not to challenge. Again it is affirmed that the land-granting God has more than one client. The kinship of Israel to Moab is older than that with Edom, for it reaches back into the Abraham narrative (Gen 19:30-38). The narrative does not pause over the duplicitous, incestuous origin of Moab in that narrative, but simply acknowledges the relationship that curbs the potential for conflict and violence.

The third encounter of this positive report concerns the territory of Ammon (vv. 17-19). There is no variation here from the Moab narrative; again the territory of a "kinsman" is to be honored as a gift from YHWH, again with reference to the birth narrative of Gen 19:30-38. Thus the three episodes, with slight variations, portray the guidance of YHWH that protects both Israel from hostile action and the host territories from unwarranted assault. In each case the obedient responsiveness of the new generation of Israel exercises the discipline and restraint required by

YHWH. Perhaps YHWH's deferential protection of other peoples was not a welcome restraint upon Israel. Israel nonetheless was confident enough of its own land grant from YHWH that it did not need to violate the land grants given by YHWH to others.

This threefold advance toward the land of promise is interrupted by two other motifs in the narrative. First, the narrative acknowledges that prior to the allotment of territory respectively to Edom, Moab, and Ammon, the land was already occupied by inhabitants who were tall and ominous (vv. 10-12, 20-22). While the naming of the threatening populations is not nicely ordered according to the three phases of the narrative, the report affirms that these ominous precedents concerned all three peoples prior to Israel—Edom, Moab, Ammon. These threatening enemy peoples go by many names—Emim, Anakim, Rephaim, Horim, Zamzummim. (The Avvim are mentioned in v. 23 as a preceding occupant of the land, but are not noted as "strong and numerous.") The narrative has no special interest in further delineating or characterizing these peoples. What counts is that they were there in the land and now they are gone. They were there in all their power and intimidation, but they were not able to resist any of the peoples given entitlement by YHWH.

Thus even the acknowledgment of the previous threat is turned to an affirmation of the fidelity of YHWH whose land grants cannot be withstood, even by powerful peoples. Such a sweeping claim is in contrast to 1:26-29 where Israel shrinks from its own entitlement in fear and disbelief. It is clear that the defeat of the ancient, giantlike populations is an assertion of YHWH's fidelity and an assurance that in the face of any threat, with YHWH Israel is safe and will be victorious. Thus the experience of the other peoples is presented as both an *affirmation* of YHWH and an *assurance* to Israel.

Caphtor also receives land in verse 23. This notation is remarkably lean. The statement does not claim any kinship for Israel with Caphtor, nor does it credit the land as a gift of YHWH. It may however be implied from Amos 9:7, the only other citation of Caphtor in the Old Testament—that Caphtor is reckoned to be the beneficiary of YHWH's Exodus activity and perhaps YHWH's land-granting authority. Given the fact that no kinship of Israel to Caphtor is suggested, this affirmation in Amos is striking indeed, for it affirms that YHWH performs exodus for a people wholly unrelated to Israel (see Brueggemann 1998).

Thus the defeat of the antecedent populations is a most positive interruption to the threefold narrative of journey. That positive interruption is matched in verses 14-15 by a second, negative interruption. Here the narrative comments on why Israel waited at Kadesh-Barnea for thirty-eight years. The long time lapse was to wait until all of the old, disobedient generation had died (see 1:35-40). These verses create a hiatus between the old faithless generation and the new generation of trust and obedience that will be important in subsequent use of this material. The gap in generations imagined by the narrative permits a new generation to emerge from "your little ones" that is unburdened by old failures and free of old fears (1:39). This hiatus illuminates both YHWH's new readiness to proceed in verses 3-4 and Israel's new readiness to engage in trustful obedience. This is indeed a new beginning that stands in complete contrast to the recalcitrance, failure, and defeat of chapter 1.

The insistence of the tradition concerning the relation of Israel to these three kin-states is well worth noting. The instability of the tradition permits some very particular judgments concerning future interactions (see 23:3-7). The relationships are complex and admit of no single telling. In our text, however, Israel is made aware that there are others with land entitlements from YHWH that must be respected. The God who gives land to Israel is not to be claimed too closely as "the God of Israel," but is positively engaged with and for other peoples as well.

2:24–3:11: After the memory of the defeat of the old generation in its faithlessness (1:19-45) and after the memory of the irenic passage through friendly territory by the new generation, a faith-filled movement on the part of Israel (2:1-23), the narrative now enters a third phase, namely, an aggressive and successful military campaign east of the Jordan (2:24–3:11). The two adversaries who were defeated are Sihon the Amorite (2:24-36 [37]), and Og of Bashan (3:1-11).

Og is identified as the last of the *Rephaim*, and Sihon by indirection is also linked with the *Rephaim*, since he is a likeness of Og. Thus the narrative reports on the decisive defeat of the "giants in the land" by the power and will of YHWH. The importance of the "Rephaim-connection" is that Israel is reminded that YHWH has already defeated the Rephaim, or their equivalents, the Emim, the Anakim, the Horites, and the Zamzummim (2:10-12, 20-21; see 1:18). None of these was a match for YHWH in earlier times. The inference is that neither Sihon nor Og in his turn can resist Israel when Israel is guaranteed by YHWH. As Israel can remember these ancient victories against seemingly great odds, so Israel can legitimately anticipate victories in the forthcoming disputes with occupants of the land. None of the enemies is a match for the power of YHWH, the very assurance that Israel in 1:26-33 was unable or unwilling to trust.

The more extended report concerns confrontation with Sihon the Amorite (vv. 24-37, 38). The initial word of YHWH to Israel, with the declarative "see," is an assurance of victory as Israel begins to occupy the land of promise (vv. 24-25). Although there will follow an attempt at negotiations, YHWH and the narrator already know that the negotiations cannot succeed. As the negotiations cannot succeed, so the battle cannot fail, because YHWH has already decreed victory. The assurance of victory is not so much based on Israel's military prowess as upon the reputation of Israel that is spread about in what looks like war propaganda (v. 25). Indeed the battle is half won before it begins, for the enemy is already immobilized in its fear.

Israel seeks to negotiate safe passage through the territory of Sihon, offering the same terms that were successfully offered to Edom (2:4-6) and Moab (2:8b-9, 13). Israel proposes to pass through peaceably on the way to territory across the Jordan. The exchange between the two powers is curious. The Sihonites are said to be trembling in anguish before Israel. And yet they do not accept what seem like favorable terms from Israel. The narrative exhibits no curiosity about the matter and does not speculate about what might have been the Sihonites' reasons for resistance.

In the end, the reason that Sihon embraces combat is that

YHWH has created in Sihon the urge to resist. This was not a freely made human policy decision, by Sihon, but an act willed by YHWH before which Sihon could exercise no free will. The entire matter is being staged by YHWH, perhaps so that YHWH may "get glory" (see Exod 14:4, 17). The report of YHWH's act upon Sihon is in a double phrase, "hardened his spirit," "made his heart defiant" (v. 30). The purpose is to "hand him over," that is, to bring him to defeat.

In addition to asserting YHWH's presiding governance over the entire exchange, the phrasing is intentionally reminiscent of the Exodus narrative. It was YHWH who made Pharaoh a hard-hearted resister, in order that the deliverance should be glorious for both Israel and YHWH (see Exod 10:1-2). Thus Sihon is here cast in the role of Pharaoh, in order to suggest that the battle is to be understood as another Exodus, the dramatic rescue of YHWH's people from the grip of an enemy before whom Israel could not stand alone.

The actual battle report consists in two parts. First is a brief declaration and assurance by YHWH that initiates the assault (v. 31). The phrasing parallels the earlier declaration of verse 24. YHWH's role in the matter is to authorize and assure, and to guarantee the outcome in hidden ways. The second part is the actual carefully crafted battle report (vv. 32-36). The report is framed by two affirmations about YHWH:

"The LORD our God gave him over to us" (v. 33a).

"The LORD our God gave everything to us" (v. 36b).

There is no doubt that YHWH is the decisive agent in the outcome.

Between these two affirmations, however, the battle report concerns only the courageous action of Israel (vv. 33b-36a). The report is dominated by the pronoun "we":

We struck down;

we captured;

we utterly destroyed;

we left;

we kept.

In its memory Israel celebrates how much was accomplished by its own actions.

This characteristic and highly stylized battle report suggests three comments. First, the coupling of *YHWH's actions* and *Israel's actions* is a characteristic Israelite statement of theological synergism in which the two actions by two agents are connected and intertwined. Theologically, such a claim tells against any simple assertion of "God's mighty deeds," and recognizes that on the ground, real people must fight real battles. What YHWH seems to do is to authorize, assure, and guarantee.

Second, it is asserted that Israel "utterly destroyed" the Sihonites and left no survivors (v. 34). This is a simple case of *herem*, the Hebrew term for the total annihilation of the enemy as a burnt offering in devotion to YHWH (see Deut 20:10-18). Such a usage suggests both that Israel was completely faithful and single-minded in its obedience to YHWH, and that the narrative appeals to the most primitive and elemental tradition of the wars of YHWH. However, the following detail severely qualifies the requirements of *herem*. That harsh and absolutist theory of war allows for the killing of the enemy, but the rescue of rich spoil. Indeed the narrative of Sihon would seem to be the best illustration of the instructions of Deut 20:10-14. The narrative of 1 Sam 15, however, suggests that while the theory of *herem* is absolute, it admits of more than one reading with various degrees of realism in its enactment (Stern 1991). The report of the battle against Sihon gives no hint of disapproval for the rescue of booty by Israel. In the slaughter of the men, YHWH has received, according to the harsh demands of faith, a gesture of acknowledgment that the victory belongs only to YHWH.

Third, the concluding formula, "No citadel was too high for us," perhaps permits a sociological observation. As a movement of people completely dependent upon YHWH's leadership, Israel is always laboring and fighting against great odds, against adversaries who are stronger and better equipped. If there is in this narrative report any authentic ancient memory, the rhetoric suggests the mood of vulnerable, ill-equipped peasants who had, in practical reality, no chance of success against established military power, against Canaanite concentrations of sociopolitical power.

Whatever may be the historical rootage of this textual memory, the theological point is that no human mechanism, no matter how powerful, can stand against the inscrutable but decisive power of YHWH. The gift and seizure of the land completely disrupted all ordinary and commonly relied upon power arrangements. This turn of affairs is of course beyond Israel's understanding or Israel's design. The seizure of the land is "a new thing" wrought by YHWH. The tradition, in the mouth of Moses, can only attest what it has seen and knows.

Verse 37 is a curiously placed report, lodged between the two episodes concerning Sihon and Og. The verse looks back to verse 19 and confirms that action. While the verse seems to be out of place in its present locus, it may be an important affirmation of peaceful family relations sandwiched between two war reports. Not everything about the land concerns war. As YHWH wins battles, so also YHWH commands peace.

Israel's conflict with Og of Bashan is closely paralleled to the Sihon episode, though with some interesting rhetorical variations (3:1-6). Here there is no initial offer of negotiation; the report moves promptly to the battle. The rhetoric of battle begins with an oracle of assurance, echoing 1:21, 29. Only this time, in contrast to chapter 1, the assurance is accepted by Israel. As before, the accomplishment of victory combines YHWH's "handing over" the enemy and Israel's violent onslaught. Again the killing in *herem* is total, without survivor (vv. 3, 6); again the spoils of battle are acknowledged. The single development that has no parallel in the Sihon episode is the description of the conquest. Not only were sixty towns taken, but the towns were massively fortified (3:5). The escalated rhetoric concerning fortifications of course greatly enhances the victory of YHWH. The victory is again total, causing a magnification of YHWH's magisterial claim, and vindicating Israel's complete trust in God.

The battle report concludes with a summary statement in verses 8-11. Now the accent is not on the persons of the defeated kings, but upon their territory. The claim is made for all of the traditional Israelite land east of the Jordan, in Gilead and Bashan. The conquest matches the entitlement that the entire narrative takes for granted (see 1:7-8). The narrator cannot resist a final note concerning Og, who has just been routed by the armies of YHWH. Og is no mean or trivial adversary. He belongs to the earlier fearsome population that had immobilized Israel in 1:26-33. Attestation of his dread-filled person and appearance is his iron bed, still, so the narrator claims, retained as a trophy in the capitol of the Ammonites, a friendly kin-group of Israel. The bed, nine by four cubits, gives evidence that Og was a giant, a formidable enemy. (The length of a cubit is not certain, but the intended rhetorical effect of the statement is clear.) He is, however, a massively *defeated* giant, as anyone who resists Israel surely will be. There was then no cause for fear; there is now no cause for fear. There is no giant so large, no force so powerful that it can stand against YHWH's assurances or that can undermine Israel's faith. The bed is an *empty* bed. It witnesses to a total defeat, that is, a total victory for "our side." YHWH is faithful, and can be trusted in any circumstance!

3:12-29: The land to the east of the Jordan to which Israel claims title is now militarily secure (3:12-29). It has been won for Israel by a combination of YHWH's authorizing declaration and Israel's military courage. The success indicates, in contrast to the faithlessness of the older generation in 1:26-33, that the new generation has acted in full obedience to and trust in YHWH, the condition of all such success.

With the successful occupation, Moses reports on two characteristic postwar actions. First, the land must be judiciously and carefully parceled out among the victorious tribes (vv. 12-17). According to stylized Israelite tradition, the land to the east of the Jordan was assigned to two and a half tribes—Reuben, Gad, and the half tribe of Manasseh. There are perhaps traditional tribal claims reflected in this allotment, reiterated in Joshua 13:15-32. It is especially important that Machir is mentioned independently (v. 15). This mention may suggest that at one time Machir constituted a major tribal grouping, a possibility that in turn indicates that the actual list of the tribal configuration may be a good deal less stable than the stylized list itself suggests. In any case, the action of allotment has the effect of tracing in considerable detail the boundaries and limitations of what constitutes Israel's envisioned inheritance of land.

It is, moreover, noteworthy that it is Moses who allots, even as Joshua conducts the distribution of land to the west in Josh 14:6–19:51. That is, the land is distributed by human agents, not by YHWH, for the distribution is only a secondary action after the primary action of conquest is accomplished by YHWH. The achievement of this distribution in our verses evokes no lyrical assertion, because the narrative recognizes that the great effort across the Jordan is still to come. This is a half-finished job with no immediate cause for celebration.

Because it has been known since 1:37 that even Moses of the older generation will not cross the Jordan into the land of promise, verses 18-22 mark an important transition in the narrative. The transition is in two parts. First, the two and a half tribes, now secure in their newly occupied land, are tempted to settle into their land without assisting the other tribes who still awaited their land. Thus the text remembers Moses strongly urging the settled tribes to act in solidarity with the tribes still awaiting their entitlement. Moses summons the Eastern tribes to action: none shall rest until all rest (v. 20). The term "rest" is clearly a special word in the tradition that signifies full, settled security in the land as a gift of YHWH (see Deut 12:10; 25:19; Josh 21:44; 2 Sam 7:1). A command is fulfilled in Josh 22:1-9 when the tribes to the east return to their inheritance, because now all are "at rest" (Josh 21:43-45).

The second piece of unfinished business is that Joshua will succeed Moses as leader of the land occupation (see Deut 31:1-8, 23; 34:9). The launching of the attack on the territory west of the Jordan is apparently as dangerous as the aggression in the east. The text approaches the matter carefully and dramatically (vv. 21-22). Moses' charge to Joshua appeals to the recent defeat of Sihon and Og: as attestations that YHWH can indeed defeat any enemy of Israel. As God has been victorious in the east, so Joshua may be certain of YHWH's victory in the west in time to come. On that basis, Moses issues a summons of faith to Joshua (v. 22). The rhetoric is the same that Moses had issued to the recalcitrant older generation in 1:30 that in turn had echoed the older utterance of Moses in Exod 14:13-14. In contrast to the resistance of 1:32, now Joshua and Israel are faithful and are prepared to move in confidence and trust (see Josh 1:5-9, 16-18). The transition from the *older generation of Moses to the newer generation of Joshua* is completed in verses 23-29, with the final, decisive exclusion of Moses from the future. These verses are framed as narrative in verses 23 and 20. Between these notations, the text consists in a petitionary prayer of Moses (vv. 24-25) and an unwelcome response to that petition on the part of YHWH (vv. 26-28).

The prayer on the lips of Moses is that he may cross the Jordan to see the good land, and to witness the continuing "mighty acts" of YHWH. The prayer sounds like the prayer of every older generation that it be permitted one more season of leadership and control. The prayer of course is not unaware of YHWH's verdict in 1:37 that had already precluded Moses' entrance into the land. Moses is excluded "on your account," on the basis of the recalcitrance of the older generation. Moses prays to have the exclusion revoked.

But the prayer is to no avail. YHWH is adamant. The exclusion stands "on your account." The narrative manages to use the exclusion as yet another opportunity to rebuke resistance to YHWH. YHWH sharply refuses to discuss the matter. Instead of granting the request of Moses, YHWH makes two alternative provisions. First, Moses may see the land, but not enter it (see 34:1-4). It has been suggested that to see the land is an act of entitlement whereby possession is asserted (Daube 1947:24-39). Perhaps. But the second provision is to refer the entry to Joshua who will need all the encouragement with which Moses can endow him. The narrator goes to great pains to mark the Jordan as the boundary of old and new; not even Moses may violate that demarcation.

The account comes to an end with what may be a geographical note about Beth-peor (v. 29). Characteristically, however, the narrative is much too dense to settle for a simple geographical note. Peor is the last stopping place before crossing the Jordan and is linked to Shittim on the other side of the Jordan. In the decisive reference to "Beth-peor . . . Shittim," Israel, it is reported in Num 25:1-4, "yoked itself to the Baal of Peor" and acted faithlessly toward YHWH. None of this is expressed in verse 29, of course. Given the covenantal urgency of Deuteronomy, however, it is plausible that this geographical note intends to mark land entry as an exceedingly dangerous and tempting moment when Israel is seduced to faithlessness. It is no wonder that Joshua needs all the assurance of verse 28, not in order to have military success, but in order to remain constant toward YHWH and resistant to the religious alternatives with which Israel is confronted in the land. It is indeed remarkable, in chapter 3, how assiduously the narrator attends to this transitional moment upon which the whole of the future of Israel appears to rest.

Theological and Ethical Analysis

This defining memory in the mouth of Moses is cast as a severe *either/or* for the listening community. Indeed the either/or of obedience or disobedience, life or death, land or landlessness is the defining choice endlessly and urgently voiced by Deuteronomy (see Deut 30:15-20). In these introductory chapters, the whole of Israel's future is voiced as a non-negotiable either/or decision upon which everything depends. How Israel decides determines the shape of Israel's future. That urgent choice involves a number of facets, some of which are obvious but for that no less important:

1. There is a deep contrast between *old generation* and *new generation*, and the listening community must decide (always again) with which generation it will align itself, looking backward or forward. The old generation is deeply and hopelessly mired in disobedience and has no future. Indeed that mire is so deep that Moses, the faithful leader of that older generation, is taken down with it "for your sake" (1:37; 3:26). Moses himself is not indicted in the text, but he must pay for the recalcitrance of his generation. In contrast is the new generation led by Joshua, unmarked by disobedience, fully prepared to run all the risks of glad obedience, on the basis of YHWH's assurances.

The new generation in its trust and obedience will receive the land. The same generosity to a vulnerable community is echoed by Paul:

Consider your own call, brothers and sisters: not many of you were wise by human standards, not many were powerful, not many were of noble birth. But God chose what is foolish in the world to shame the wise; God chose what is weak in the world to shame the strong; God chose what is low and despised in the world, things that are not, to reduce to nothing things that are. (1 Cor 1:26-28)

2. The pivotal contrast between the old and new is reenforced by the contrast of *faith and faithlessness*. The older generation's lack of faith is explicit in 1:32, "you have no trust in the LORD your God." It is a faithlessness that eventuates first in a refusal to go to the land of promise (1:26-33) and then a disastrous defeat in an autonomous pursuit of the land (1:41-45). The new generation is portrayed as fully trusting and obedient, though that positive verdict is not explicit but given only in narrative examples. The consequence of such trust is a capacity to move successfully and effectively toward the land and a readiness to receive what YHWH will give. "Faith" and "faithlessness" are alternative decisions about whether YHWH is an adequate resource for contexts of danger and threat. Everything, so the tradition insists, depends upon that decision.

3. The focus of the contrast of *old generation/new generation* and of *faith and unfaith* is the good land. The land is characterized as rich, abundant, and prosperous (1:24-25; see Num 13:23-24). The hyperbolic rhetoric indicates that this is a gift of YHWH's generosity that surpasses Israel's rhetorical capacity. Indeed, it is evident that the land is "good," "very good"; in the rhetoric of Israel, this is the "new creation" of Gen 1:31, where the fullness of all YHWH's abundance comes to fruition. Israel is to be the singular recipient of that unspeakable generosity that requires, in Israel's praise, the lyrical language of doxology by which to respond to "very good."

4. The provision for judges in 1:9-18 is a crucial insistence in

this tradition about the either/or of *justice and injustice*. The ethical insistence of these verses is that Israel must diligently practice justice that takes into account the claims and needs of every member of the community, each of whom is bound in neighborliness to every other. The practice of such a neighborly connectedness will make the land livable. Economic and judicial practices to the contrary, however, will jeopardize the land and put the community at risk. Of all the choices Israel must make, the decision for justice is the most elemental in the Torah tradition of Deuteronomy.

5. The sorting out of *peace and war* is a derivative issue in these chapters. The memory offered here has no uncertainty that peace is to be extended to Edom, Moab, and Ammon, kindred tribes who are also recipients of God's promised land. By contrast, the "Amorite" kingdoms of Sihon and Og are appropriately objects of military attack, though even with Sihon, peaceable terms are offered (2:26). The tradition of Deuteronomy is not absolutist about either pacifism or about aggressiveness, but requires a succession of decisions about when and where and with whom there may be peace or war. The fact that even Sihon (but not Og) is offered peaceable terms suggests that the tradition tilts toward neighborliness, even toward those seen to be adversaries. While the vision of peace is not endlessly extensive here, the fact that peaceable terms are to be given to "kindred" suggests a vision that is open to enlarged scope. Thus when the question is subsequently put, "Who is my neighbor?" (Luke 10:29), this tradition is open to expanding the scope of neighborliness to include those previously taken to be enemies.

6. The demand that the two and a half tribes who have secured land east of the Jordan River must participate in the western campaign is a choice *for unity rather fragmentation* (3:18-22). The tradition strongly urges unity among the parts of Israel and disavows any limitation of common responsibility in the service of separatist interests. In these last three points, one sees an emerging vision of Israel as a *peaceable, just,* and *unified* community. The text vigorously resists *war* where it is not

48

necessary, *injustice* rooted in private, exploitative interest, and *separation* that neglects common responsibility.

It is possible to take all of these several elements of choice as a large and commanding either/or. On the face of it, the either/or is fictively addressed to the *early community of Israel* in transition from Moses to Joshua, from old to new, at the highly symbolic point of the Jordan River. According to common critical opinion, this summons to decision is addressed to *an exilic community of faith* that is, at least in the imagination of the authors of this document, about to reenter the land of promise after having been displaced from that land. If that is indeed the sixth-century context of address, then the text in its urgency bids the new generation of the faithful to accept the freshness of its new beginning as a gift from God and not be governed by or committed to what is old and failed. The new Israel after exile, evoked and imagined in this summons, is to be a community *unified, just,* and *peaceable,* and above all, *trusting,* all contrasts to the status of the old community that had ended in displacement and death.

Such an understanding of the urgency of the text brings this summons into close proximity to two other textual presentations. First, Ezek 18 is concerned to liberate the new generation from the guilt and judgment of the old:

> It is only the person who sins that shall die. . . . Cast away from you all the transgressions that you have committed against me, and get yourselves a new heart and a new spirit! Why will you die, O house of Israel? For I have no pleasure in the death of anyone, says the Lord GOD. Turn, then, and live. (Ezek 18:4, 31-32) (Joyce 1989:35-60)

Second, Isaiah in the exile witnesses to a "new thing" that is no longer derivative from or in hock to what is old:

> Do not remember the former things,
>   or consider the things of old.
> I am about to do a new thing;
>   now it springs forth, do you not perceive it? (Isa 43:18-19)

When the Deuteronomic summons is placed alongside these sixth-century statements, one may observe a convergence of declarations, demands, and expectations about a new beginning.

Taken as a canonical text, this summons to displaced people becomes, *in many times and places*, a summons to intense trust in YHWH that emancipates from what is old and failed. The voice of scripture that speaks here is an insistent invitation that the community of faith should be defined neither by its past, which is strewn with bad choices, nor by its context that breeds despair, but by its deep and elemental linkage to a God who can be trusted in every risky circumstance to give new gifts. The voice of Moses sounds among the faithful over and over, to assert that new choices are being offered by YHWH, and that those choices will determine the shape of the future. The faithful are not fated by what is over and done. When the faithful choose afresh, new futures become possible:

> There is a new creation: everything old has passed away; see, everything has become new! All this is from God. (2 Cor 5:17-18)

What Paul frames with reference to Christ, Moses has already envisioned in an invitation, assurance, and summons to the rising generation of Joshua.

AN URGENT, LAND-SECURING DECISION (4:1-43)

The retrospective speech of Moses in chapters 1–3 has brought Israel—the new post–Moses generation—to the brink of the land and to the moment of life-or-death decision. In verses 1-40, the present chapter offers, as a speech of Moses, the fullest, perhaps most mature covenant theology of the tradition of Deuteronomy. While this chapter is rhetorically a continuation of chapters 1-3, most scholars believe it is a distinct and later piece governed by the urgency of "so now" (v. 1). Because it is a later piece, the chapter is taken to be addressed to the community of exiles in the sixth century (see especially vv. 27-31), and so is intended as an introduction to the long narrative account of land loss in the corpus of Joshua–Kings.

Exegetical Analysis

4:1-8: The first two verses articulate the thesis of the chapter and indeed the thesis of the historical narrative to follow after the book of Deuteronomy in Joshua–Kings. Israel may now receive (re-receive) the land promised to the ancestors in Genesis; but its continuing occupation of the land is dependent upon full obedience to the commandments Moses is about to utter. Thus verse 1 deftly holds together the *free gift of land* and the *conditions of commandment* for receiving the land. This juxtaposition is definitional for all that follows; the verse brings together the Genesis memories of promise and the Sinai announcement of commandments. Thus the land is characteristically understood in connection to obedience. The remainder of the speech in this chapter presents both the substance of that required obedience and the urgency of that obedience.

The second verse makes clear and specific the intention of verse 1. The commandments to be embraced are the ones taught and authorized by Moses. It is *Mosaic* commandments that matter. The tradition self-consciously enunciates a normative "orthodoxy" that excludes variant commandments. For all generations to come, including that of the sixth-century exiles, the condition of land entry and retention is Mosaic teaching.

By way of illustration, the speech cites the remembered story of the "Baal of Peor" (Num 25:1-4; see Num 31:16). That particular "Baal," of whom we know nothing, was a Moabite alternative to YHWH. When the people of Israel confronted this religious alternative, some "yoked themselves to Baal" and were destroyed by YHWH, who will tolerate no rival. In that ancient confrontation, Israel had come to a moment of great decision. It chose badly and received death, as Israel always receives death when it chooses against YHWH. But not all chose wrongly on that occasion. Some adhered to YHWH and were kept alive.

The narrative of Peor as such holds no interest for Deuteronomy. It is cited only as illustration of the high stakes at play in a decision for obedience or disobedience. The concluding phrase of verse 4, "all alive today," indicates that the text addresses and is concerned for the present generation of Israelites, those who have been in the wilderness of exile and are about to reenter the land. Like the ancient generation at Peor, the present generation faces a dangerous, life-or-death decision about loyalty. Israel has a precedent for "choosing life," but is on notice about its choosing.

The remainder of this speech of Moses exposits the radical either/or just enunciated. Verses 5-8 offer a remarkable argument about the distinctive identity and vocation of Israel in the world of the nations. It is not enough that Israel should be obedient, as already enjoined in verses 1-2 (v. 5). Moses is here doing "public theology," aware that Israel's radical and intentional choice of obedience takes place in broad daylight before the eyes of all the watching nations. What is proposed is the ordering of a "contrast society," quite unlike the other nations, a contrast that is lived out in ways that are inimical to the watching nations. It is as though Moses intends that Israel should be "bragged upon" by the other nations who will be dazzled by what they see lived out in Israel's existence.

Two times the speech uses the phrase "wise and discerning." This is remarkable rhetoric to find in Deuteronomy, for it is not language associated with the Sinai covenant. It is rather the phrasing of pragmatic, prudential ethics, the ethics of those who are wise in the use of power. A familiar usage of the phrase is in the nomination of Joseph to protect the imperial interests of Pharaoh (Gen 41:33, 39; see 1 Kgs 3:12). Joseph is celebrated not for being pious or orthodox, but for being effective in the ways of the world. For this text it is important that the celebration of Israel is not for some narrow, ghettoized religious passion, but for effectiveness by the norms of the nations. In verses 32-40, the speech of Moses situates Israel not only in *the covenant of Sinai*, but also in the context of *creation theology*. When it is obedient, Israel will be effective, prosperous, and successful. Moses makes the claim that obedience "really works" in the world. The nations will be able to see its decisive difference.

After this pragmatic claim, the speech specifies in two ways—through rhetorical questions—what it is that makes Israel dazzling in the eyes of the nations. First, Israel distinctively has "a God so near." This is the people among whom YHWH is effectively present to protect and bless. The several traditions of the Old Testament work in a variety of ways to speak of YHWH's presence in and with and for Israel—name, glory, tent, tabernacle, temple—but all are agreed that YHWH is definitively and decisively *with Israel;* the nations, moreover, can see as much!

The second "dazzling" characteristic of Israel is that it has "statutes so just," laws, commandments, and procedures that assume a community of neighborly economic and political practices. The watching nations can see that the socially powerless in Israel—widows, orphans, aliens—are treated according to social policies and practices that curb oppression and exploitation. It is impossible to overstate the importance of these two marks: the nearness of God and just social practice. The contrast between Israel and the nations is not merely religious, but concerns economic and political matters. But Israel as contrast society is not flatly concerned for social policy, for it is the God present to Israel who matters decisively. All through the book of Deuteronomy, the tradition is at pains to hold together *holy presence* and *social practice,* for either alone is inadequate and will not grasp the attention of the nations.

The concluding verse of this unit makes the claim that "all this Torah," with its promise of YHWH's presence and its guarantee of neighborly justice, is what makes Israel unlike all other peoples. The phrasing refers to the formation and identification of a fixed Torah, suggesting a late form of Deuteronomic theology with its scroll-consciousness (see 2 Kgs 22:8). That there is a known, identifiable, Mosaic scroll marks Israel in a peculiar way. Moreover, because the nations see and are dazzled, the Torah-identity of Israel is a draw for the other nations as well. This peculiar Deuteronomic celebration of the Torah may lie behind the prophetic vision of the nations attracted to the place of Israel's scroll in the vision of Isa 2:3; Mic 4:2 (Sweeney 1996:65).

4:9-31: After these more general statements, the speech of Moses now draws the listening community closer to the intense founding event of Sinai (vv. 9-24). The great threat to Israel is amnesia (v. 9). Israel may lose contact with the founding events, forget its own peculiar identity, and so cease to enact the "wisdom and discernment" entrusted to it. It is entirely likely that later generations will have no lively contact with the founding generation, and so not embrace its sense of urgency. To address the problem of long-term, intergenerational amnesia, this speech seeks to bring the present generation of would-be returnees immediately to the ancient, still defining event. It is *by utterance* that later generations of Israel are always again brought to Sinai and the drama of covenant making. By utterance, this generation is invited to the awesome assembly, whereby Israel is entrusted its peculiar identity in the world. By utterance this generation hears a voice but sees no form. That voice of Sinai keeps sounding into all subsequent generations of Israel. That voice speaks covenant, binding Israel in all generations and in each generation to the life and will of YHWH. The voice continuing to sound gives ten commandments. The reference to "ten" in "stone" suggests a finished, identifiable, covenantal ethic. All of this happened once decisively; all of this happens yet again decisively in this text and in every reuse of this text. It is the commanding voice of Sinai that makes its bid to this generation about to reenter the land, insisting that its reentry is possible only by intense commitment to Torah.

Now the general appeal to Sinai and its commandments is made quite pointed and specific (vv. 15-20). Perhaps surprisingly, the focus of urgent appeal here is to the second of the ten commandments (see Deut 5:8). This speech regards *idol*, the graphic, visual representation of God, as the deepest threat to covenant. It is definitive that YHWH at Sinai appeared not in a form but through a voice, not image but utterance. This does not suggest that YHWH has no form, but that the divine form—whatever it is—remains inaccessible (see Exod 33:20-23). Israel is given nothing to go on but utterance, and must learn to trust that reliable utterance. Form is a device for making things more certain, more controlled, more palpably available. Thus the great temptation to Israel is an attempt to domesticate YHWH by drawing YHWH into an already known world, and thinking thereby to overcome the risky strangeness that is inherent in covenantal relationship.

There are many candidates for such domestication, human likeness, animal likeness, bird likeness, creeping thing likeness, fish likeness; none of these "logos" will do. None in principle will do, because YHWH is *unlike* any other, not to be categorized or schematized into what is known and controllable. YHWH is incomparable; to deal with YHWH at all, Israel must accept the risky givenness of strangeness and freedom that yield nothing at Sinai but a voice of command and promise.

The profound contrast between *covenant obedience* and *idol* is further explicated in verses 19-20. While the voice at Sinai will tolerate no idols, here it is allowed that idols are "allotted" by YHWH to the nations, but prohibited to Israel. The allowance is made in order to assert the peculiar identity of Israel, rooted in the peculiar relation Israel has to YHWH, in turn rooted in deliverance from the hardships of Egypt. In these verses idols are not in principle condemned, but are simply inimical to Israel's identity as YHWH's special inheritance. The verses closely parallel the poetry of 32:8-9 wherein all other gods are entrusted by "the most high God" with other peoples, but Israel is YHWH's own. The two terms "allot" and "inheritance" are used again, so that 4:19-20 and 32:8-9 form something of an envelope concerning Israel's peculiar identity, specified in the commands that these two terse statements bracket.

The interlude of verses 21-22 returns to the recognition that Moses cannot enter the land of promise "because of you" (see 1:37; 3:26). The function of the statement is to contrast Moses, along with all the disobedient generation, with the new generation that now can decide to receive the land obediently, presumably after exile. Thus the sharp contrast "I . . . but you" pertains not only to Moses, but to all the failed generation that he leads and represents.

The general contrast of *covenant obedience* and *disobedient idolatry* that constitutes the great decision Israel faces is now given historical specificity (vv. 2e-32). The injunction of verse 23 again contrasts covenant and idol. Verse 24, when linked to verse

31, concerns the character of YHWH who is "devouring fire, jealous God" (v. 24) and then "merciful God" (v. 31). The verses focus on the alternative ways in which YHWH may be inclined toward Israel, inclinations that match Israel's propensity toward YHWH, and that are connected with concrete moments in Israel's life.

The *jealous God* is a God who will tolerate no disobedience and who will severely punish disobedient Israel (vv. 24-26). These verses are a quick retrospective upon the life of Israel in the land that produced the punishment of land loss and deportation. The outcome of YHWH's jealousy is "scattering" (exile) where Israel will be recruited into false worship, an unbearable fate for a community belonging to YHWH. The "there" of verse 28 may be any deportation, but surely pertains specifically to the deportation to Babylon in the sixth century. Thus the disobedience of Israel leads to land loss in a harsh manner that abrasively subverts Israel's true character. The simple calculus of disobedience/displacement, by appeal to the jealous God, constitutes the spine of Deuteronomic theology.

In verses 29-31, the anticipatory speech of Moses abruptly changes direction: "from there," that is, from Babylon. The speech changes because the attitude and practice of Israel will change in exile. The community that had acted corruptly now seeks YHWH, *turns to* YHWH, and *hears* YHWH. Israel resolves to be a fully obedient, responsive people. The good news is that YHWH will be found and is available to Israel. It might have been concluded in verse 26 that the relation of Israel to YHWH had reached the point of no return, and was terminated. But no . . . YHWH will be found! Indeed, YHWH is *merciful*, will not *abandon*, not *destroy*, not *forget*. While the calculus of verses 24-26 is commonly taken to be the core of Deuteronomic theology, here it is insisted that YHWH is indeed a God of mercy whose attentiveness to Israel and inclination toward Israel endure through and beyond the alienation of exile. In the end, Deuteronomy proclaims a God of mercy!

These verses sketch an overview of faith midst the deep disruption of Israel's deportation:

circumstance:	into exile	→	out of exile
Israel's propensity:	corruption	→	return
YHWH's response:	jealousy	→	mercy.

The speech in these verses is a *retrospect* on *disobedience/deportation/jealousy* and a *prospect on turning/restoration/mercy*. The speaker is situated just at the pivot point between "there" (Babylon) and "from there." The text addresses Israel, who is situated (at the Jordan) between remembered disobedience and anticipated mercy, and now must decide. There is more than one way in which Israel can receive YHWH, jealous or merciful. The theological affirmation is that *how YHWH is* responds to *how Israel is.* YHWH will be *jealous or merciful* in response to Israel as *corrupt or repentant.* It is evident that this unit of text is designed with "mercy" as the last word. Mercy and jealousy are both possible responses on the part of YHWH. How it will be with YHWH depends entirely upon Israel's readiness to accept its identity as YHWH's "very own possession" (v. 20). Accepting this vocation in obedience, Israel in exile receives remarkable assurance from the God of all mercy: not abandoned, not destroyed, not forgotten!

4:32-40: The primary summons to obedience, grounded in a sweeping theological claim, is reiterated once more in verses 32-40, only now the theological grounding is more expansive, as large as creation. Israel is asked a series of three questions that require a negative answer and that invite Israel to be amazed at its own peculiar status in all of creation (vv. 32-34):

Has anything (like Exodus-Sinai) ever happened elsewhere? *No!*
Has any other people experienced anything like Sinai? *No!*
Has any God made such a people in such a way? *No!*

No such event! *No* such people! *No* such God! None, not in all of creation. These verses may be productively linked to verses 5-8, where the same mode of question with an implied negative answer is also used with the same expansive horizon: No other nation with a God so near, no other nation with a Torah so just. The text

Deut 4:32-34 scans all of creation from one end to the other, for all times since the creation of humankind. There are no parallel cases anywhere, ever. Only Israel has such a chance and a choice.

The rhetoric moves sharply from the universal to the concrete in verse 35: *to you*, to Israel, only to Israel. Israel is to "know" (acknowledge) what it has been shown. What it has seen in its own life is that there is no other God. The reason there are no parallel miracles and no parallel peoples is that there is no other god capable of such wonders, no god so powerful and willing . . . which fact leads to the conclusion, "there is no other." In this statement, reiterated in verse 39, the tradition of Deuteronomy reaches one of the most complete statements of "monotheism" in all of the Old Testament, a statement reached in exile as Israel reflected upon its own existence as a gift of YHWH's powerful commitment. Israel is to know (acknowledge), to trust, to decide, to accept its peculiarity. This "monotheism" is a practical, ecclesial statement that has to do with the character of YHWH's people even as it has to do with YHWH's own life.

The concreteness of "to you" in verse 35 is matched by the concluding parallel formulation in verse 39. Between the two bids for theological affirmation, verses 36-38 offer a recital of what has been distinctively given by YHWH in the life of Israel:

> He caused Israel to hear;
> he showed his great fire;
> he loved your ancestors;
> he brought you out . . . to bring you in, giving land.

The recital is the conventional naming of the miracles that constitute Israel's identity-giving memory. This is what Israel has witnessed. In response to the "showing," Israel is to acknowledge both YHWH's incomparability and distinctiveness and Israel's derivative incomparability and distinctiveness. (This same parallelism is stated in the prayer of David, perhaps also a Deuteronomic voice, 2 Sam 7:22-23.)

Finally the text ends in verse 40 with a reiteration of the basic thesis of verse 1. Land depends upon obedience. The community addressed knows about "there" (= exile, v. 28) and now is about to move "from there" (= out of exile and back to the land, v. 29). Israel stands before a great decision, to accept its vocation as a people of Torah obedience or not. The "acknowledgment" to which Israel is summoned (vv. 35, 39) is a quite practical one that concerns the daily, concrete enactment of a different life in the land. The land is given—re-given— by the God of mercy. The urgency of the summons rests in the awareness that a wrong choice and a rejection of destiny as the people of Torah will cause the God of mercy to reappear in the life of Israel as a devouring fire.

4:41-43: This is a curious addendum to the long speech. It is not at all evident why this reference to cities of refuge should occur here. The verses may suggest quite concretely how Israel may enact its vocation as a "contrast society." Whereas aggression and violence are characteristically uncurbed in other societies, Israel as a community of covenantal obedience has a stake in the protection of the neighborhood from such violence. Thus the purpose of the cities of refuge is that people facing certain circumstances may "live" (v. 32). *Obedience to YHWH* is characteristically enacted as *concern for neighbor.* Cities of refuge were no doubt an "economic inconvenience" in an acquisitive society. Israel, however, is unlike any other community; it is committed to inconveniences that foster life.

Theological and Ethical Analysis

Deuteronomy voices a theology of the land of promise; it reflects upon the generosity of YHWH's gift of the land, the crisis of land loss, and the wonder of land restoration. It speaks urgently about the costly attentiveness required for land retention. In an interpretive situation at the beginning of the twenty-first century that is postagrarian, one may take land as a metaphor for an arena for a viable communal existence that protects and enhances a shared humanity. (To take land as metaphor is not at all to lose the specificity that belongs to land as a concrete historical placement, but it is to observe that concrete historical placement may take various forms in a postagrarian society.) The free gift of land, so Deuteronomy asserts, is held only in Torah-based obedience that is to take the form of an economy of proportion, a politics of discipline and compassion, and a faith that cedes authority beyond self-aggrandizement.

It is the simple and nonnegotiable linkage of *land* and *obedience* that constitutes the claim of this text. Deuteronomy however, does not articulate universal principles; it addresses a concrete crisis of a community that stands precisely at the moment between land loss and land restoration. In order to hear this text addressed to itself, each successive community must situate itself in that peculiar and specific crisis moment of decision making.

The address aims at evoking (or re-evoking) a distinct community that understands its life as a "contrast society" that is to order its public practice differently, quite unlike the nations around it. Land loss had occurred because Israel had sought to be "like the nations" in its community practice (see 1 Sam 8:5, 20). Now Israel is summoned back to its true life in the world. That requires a "return" to YHWH, with all of the Torah disciplines and practices entailed in such a return. Thus the text has a primary "ecclesial" accent aimed at summoning the community to a different sense of itself in the world. The text clearly believes that such an alternative public way in the world is not only urgent but also practical.

The ecclesial concern to refashion a "contrast society" is oriented to the reality of the God uttered by Moses. That YHWH has done this unparalleled wonder in the world, and that YHWH is the only God means that Israel has no alternative choice for life. In coming to terms with its identity, Israel must come to terms with the reality of YHWH who is known in and through the events of Exodus and Sinai. God, however, has more than one way to relate to Israel. In its suffering and dislocation, Israel has known YHWH as a devouring fire. Now Israel stands at a moment of redeciding, when it may come to terms with YHWH who is a God of mercy. How YHWH shall be present in the life of Israel depends upon Israel's decision about how to live in the world.

Deuteronomy is characteristically focused upon the life of

Israel. In verses 5-8, Moses' speech is aware of the other nations. Even though they have been "allotted" other objects of worship (v. 19), Moses knows that the other nations are watching Israel and are noticing (v. 6). They are attentive enough to notice the difference embodied in Israel and are able to recognize, on their own worldly terms, that Israel is "wise and discerning." In the purview of non-Israelites, the appeal of Israel's alternative way in the world does not depend upon the Torah of Sinai, but can be judged by the norms of the world. Of course this text makes no address to other nations, and has no direct impetus to invite them into Israel's way of life. That alternative way of life, however, is discernible (and therefore available) to the other nations.

The decisive choice offered Israel is "covenant" or "idols." This may, at first glance, seem an odd and incommensurate pairing. Upon reflection, however, these alternative choices prove to be poignant in a modern (postmodern?), image-propelled society. Karl Marx had already seen in the modern world the power of "commodity" to become a fetish that commands inordinate loyalty and that is assigned inordinate authority. Since Marx, with the emergence of electronic media, there can be no doubt of the power of image to create a "virtual reality" that is variously remote from lived reality. It is not a great leap from Moses' idols that are "visual forms" through Marxian "commodity fetishism" to the power of "logo" and "icon" in film, propaganda, and advertising that redefine human existence.

The point is well made by two critical commentators on the emerging "new reality" of the icon. Jacques Ellul asserts:

> Images are indispensable for the construction of the technological society. If we remained at the stage of verbal dialogue, inevitably we would be led to critical reflection. But images exclude criticism. The habit of living in this image-oriented world leads me to give up dialectical thought and criticism. It is so much easier to give up and let myself be carried along by the continually renewed wave of images. . . . Images are essential if I am to avoid seeing the day-to-day reality I live in. They glitter continuously around me, allowing me to live in a sort of image-oriented fantasy. . . . The word would only increase my anxiety and uncertainty. It would make me more

conscious of my emptiness, my impotence, and the insignificance of my situation. With images, however, everything unpleasant is erased and my drab existence decorated by their charm and sparkle.

Above all, I must not become aware of reality, so images create a substitute reality. . . . Artificial images, passing themselves off for truth, obliterate and erase the reality of my life and my society. (Ellul 1985:128, 208)

Neil Postman has offered a parallel, somewhat more accessible critique of the world of image:

There is no more disturbing consequence of the electronic and graphic revolution than this: that the world as given to us through television seems natural, not bizarre. For the loss of the sense of the strange is a sign of adjustment, and the extent to which we have adjusted is a measure of the extent to which we have changed. (Postman 1986:79-80)

To be unaware that a technology comes equipped with a program for social change, to maintain that technology is neutral, to make the assumption that technology is always a friend to culture is, at this late hour, stupidity plain and simple. . . . Without a vote. Without polemics. Without guerilla resistance. Here is ideology pure if not serene. Here is ideology without words, and all the more powerful for their absence. (Postman 1986:79-80, 157-58)

It is not a big move from the warning of Moses to the present image-dominated context. At that ancient boundary, Moses understood that the ethical stakes in a decision for Torah were very high. They continue to be very high. Choosing covenant with all its prerequisites, perplexity, and exposition was not easy then. Nor is it now.

REMEMBERING THE DECISIVE CONFRONTATION (4:44–5:33)

Israel has thus been summoned, at the boundary, to urgent decision making (1:1–4:43). The next section of text lines out the substance of the decision for obedience that Israel is to make. It consists of an introduction (4:44-49), an assertion of the contemporary pertinence of the covenant (5:1-5), a reiteration of the foundational commands of Sinai (5:6-21), and the legitimation of Moses as the single, approved mediator and interpreter of Torah (5:22-33). This unit may be regarded as the foundation from which the instructional program of Deuteronomy unfolds. It serves as introduction and reference point for the appeals of chapters 6–11.

Exegetical Analysis

4:44-49: The introduction to the address of Moses in 4:44-49 is a formal parallel to 1:1-5 and 29:2, the points at which the three large "addresses" of Moses are introduced. Thus the verses introduce the second of the three speeches of Moses that make up the book of Deuteronomy. Moses' second speech that extends through 29:1 (Heb. 28:69) accounts for the major material of the book of Deuteronomy and constitutes its essential teaching. The first and third speeches have been subsequently added. The location of the address is in agreement with that of 1:1-5, so that the tradition is consistent in addressing Israel "at the boundary" of decision making. The particular phrasing, "this is the Torah," suggests that the tradition now has in mind an identifiable corpus of commands. The notion of a *written* Torah may by this time be well advanced.

In addition to the mention of the Jordan as the boundary, it is likely that the detailed geographical data of these verses are intended to call unobtrusive attention to a number of theological realities that are readily signaled by geographical reference:

1. The mention of *Beth-peor* (v. 46; see 4:3) alludes to the pivotal narrative of Num 25:1-5. The mention functions as a reminder of the urgency of obedience and the grave risks that accompany waywardness from YHWH.

2. The reference to the *land of Sihon and Og* (vv. 46-47) recalls the mighty victories of YHWH and attests that this land in which Israel stands before the Jordan is already safe land, secured by YHWH's faithful power (1:16–2:11).

3. The tracing of the boundaries *east of the Jordan* (vv. 48-49) may more generally refer to the promise of land to the ancestors, thus suggesting that this powerful promise of YHWH is indeed in effect.

4. The final mention of *Pisgah* may be a reminder that in the tradition of Deuteronomy (see 3:2-7) Moses—and with him the entire faithless generation—cannot enter the new land (see 3:2-7).

If these references are more than geographical, then they alert the listening community to the deeply grounded hopes and the ominous dangers that surround them as they face a coming time of decision.

5:1-5: The speech begins with a summons to embrace in this moment of hearing the commandments given as the covenant was made at Sinai (5:1-5). The first word Moses speaks to Israel at the Jordan is "listen." The relationship YHWH now offers Israel is one of address and obedience. The one who speaks through the words of Moses is the one who commands. Israel who listens is cast in a role of singular, unqualified obedience. The "statutes and ordinances" that constitute "this Torah" (4:44) include not only the ten commands of 5:6-22, but also the extended exposition of chapters 12–25.

The brief, urgent appeal that introduces the Ten Commandments weaves together two sorts of affirmations. The words of Moses allude to what has *already happened* at Sinai (vv. 2, 4):

The LORD our God made a covenant with us at Horeb. . . . The LORD spoke with you face to face at the mountain, out of the fire.

The statements at the same time bring the later, contemporary listening community into the orbit of Sinai. The time and space between *this moment* at Sinai and *that moment* at Sinai are deftly overcome. The promises are direct, "with us, with you."

These verses, however, are qualified by the statements of verses 3 and 5. First, verse 3 shows the tradition dealing self-consciously with the problem of treating an ancient remembered event with all the contemporary immediacy it requires. It would be easy enough to conclude that the present (seventh-century?), belated generation of Israel is not under the compulsions of the meeting at Sinai. Moses, however, shows that this reservation has no merit. In fact, says he, the covenant is *here and now,* not *there and then.* It is made liturgically contemporary, so that every covenant ratification is as serious, laden, and dangerous as if it were the first. Such an eclipsing of time and space is only possible in liturgical time whereby one can ask, "Were you there?" The answer, characteristically, is that later generations of worshipers were indeed "there." So in Christian liturgy, the congregation is endlessly able to "be present" at Christmas, at Good Friday, at Easter. And certainly every new generation of the Jewish faith remembers and is "there" at the Exodus in the celebration of Passover. The words pile up in verse 3 to establish contemporary pertinence: "with us, we, these here, today, all of us, alive." *This* is the generation of covenant, the ones bound in covenant, situated in a distinctive identity, precluded from the optional worlds of idols, committed to this singular, all-demanding loyalty.

Second, verse 5 (in an anticipation of vv. 22-33) qualifies the face-to-face claim just reported. This qualification perhaps serves two purposes. It may, on the one hand, intend to enhance the authority and office of Moses, an enhancement crucial to the tradition of Deuteronomy and pursued later in this chapter. It may, on the other hand, hint at lack of faith on the part of Israel. Thus, at the very outset Israel has been timid and not able to enter fully into the risk that life with YHWH entails. Be that as it may, the point is a minor one, for the tradition moves directly to the great commands of Sinai.

5:6-33: Moses' address now arrives at the most elemental self-announcement of YHWH, words first uttered at Sinai. The Deuteronomic text, in the mouth of Moses, is not itself the primal utterance, but is a reiteration of Exod 20:1-17. In that primary context, the ten utterances of YHWH have been framed by theophany (Exod 19:16-25) and mediation (Exod 20:18-21). They are bracketed to show how peculiar and authoritative they are. At

Sinai this is all that YHWH said to Israel. Now in this reiteration at the Jordan, these same words of YHWH continue to carry distinctive force and authority.

The Ten Commandments, treated in Deuteronomy as a settled corpus, have received a succession of expositions, none greater than those of Luther and Calvin. (See also Childs 1985, 63-83; 1974, 385-469; Harrelson 1980; Philips 1970; Brueggemann 1994, 839-853.) They begin with the self-announcement of YHWH. This is the God who enacted the Exodus and who continues to enact exoduses (v. 6). The Exodus has been the ground of YHWH's claim upon Israel in 4:20; now it is the ground for YHWH's command of Israel. In the Exodus YHWH has displaced Pharaoh as Israel's rightful lord and master. As Pharaoh could (legitimately?) command Israel (Exod 5:10-11, 18), so now YHWH can legitimately command Israel (see Lev 25:42). The God who has liberated issues commands that intend to create a community that will practice an emancipatory ethic.

The commands of verses 7-11 articulate the rightful claim YHWH has upon Israel and the ways in which YHWH's character curbs familiarity with or presumption upon YHWH. Nowhere is the word "Holy" used of YHWH in these three commands, but it is a quality that stands behind them (Anderson 1999:37-38). YHWH is beyond Israel in majesty, power, authority, and dominion. Indeed YHWH is outside any of the conventional categories of religious affiliation. Israel is commanded to deal with YHWH differently, in order to reflect the decisive difference in YHWH's character. Israel's point of access to its God is through the defining event of the Exodus (v. 6). In that event YHWH has been decisively disclosed to Israel, disclosed as massively powerful, as deeply engaged for the slaves, as profoundly involved in socioeconomic matters, as completely unwilling to share power with Pharaoh. From the claims of that defining event, Israel learns of the new regime of this Exodus God. Thus in the Exodus, YHWH will "get glory" over Pharaoh and will not share it with Pharaoh (Exod 14:4, 17). Unlike Pharaoh or any other would-be sovereign, YHWH is irreversibly on the side of emancipation. A covenantal history governed by and reflective of YHWH's rule will be a history that overcomes oppression and exploitation in the interest of emancipatory justice.

Unlike any of the other gods available, this God claims undivided loyalty (v. 7). Deuteronomy 4:35, 39 articulates a more sweeping statement of monotheism, but that is not the claim made here. Here the claim is more concerned with a relationship that must be exclusive, that depends on willing, glad fidelity. It is impossible to trace any "development" in the "history of religion" to arrive at this no-nonsense claim of YHWH. While some other parts of the Old Testament may hint at differing judgments on this matter of monotheism, the tradition of Sinai is uncompromising. The negative prohibition on other gods is matched by the equally important, positive affirmation of 6:4-5. Israel must love and adhere *only* to YHWH. Thus the command is not an abstract statement of monotheism but the characterization of a covenantal relationship that is all-demanding and all-giving. This primary claim from Sinai comes to grand articulation in Isaiah 42:8; 45:21; 48:11.

Unlike the other gods available, this God refuses any religious form (vv. 8-10). Ways in which religious form is inimical to YHWH have already been considered (4:15-23). The exposition in 5:8-10 suggests that the prohibition against images is in order to safeguard the freedom of YHWH to be fully person, fully relational, fully involved in covenantal transactions. This is a God who is jealous enough to punish, faithful enough to show steadfast love, capable of extreme and surprising engagement with this God's partner. Any articulation of YHWH that detracts from that freedom of full covenant engagement is a prohibited attempt to tone down YHWH. The freedom of YHWH that this commandment asserts is not capricious. It is a covenantal freedom in which YHWH is completely capable of response to the obedience or disobedience of the covenant partner. YHWH is free to punish the disobedient, free to be faithful to the obedient. In Israel's exile, moreover, it became necessary to assert YHWH's freedom afresh, including freedom to move beyond old scores and old grudges, to respond promptly and willingly to new initiatives from Israel. A Jeremiah text congruent with the theology of Deuteronomy asserts:

At one moment I may declare concerning a nation or a kingdom, that I will pluck up and break down and destroy it, but if that nation, concerning which I have spoken, turns from its evil, I will change my mind about the disaster that I intended to bring on it. And at another moment I may declare concerning a nation or a kingdom that I will build and plant it, but if it does evil in my sight, not listening to my voice, then I will change my mind about the good that I had intended to do to it. (Jer 18:7-10)

It is precisely this divine freedom that makes possible YHWH's initiative of forgiveness in the sixth century (Jer 31:34; Ezek 18:31-32; Isa 40:2). Every effort to curb YHWH's capacity for newness is an attempt to make YHWH *like* something else. It is prohibited!

Unlike other gods available, this is not a god who lends God's name to any earthly "cause" (v. 11). Contrary to conventional interpretation, the third prohibition is not primarily about cursing or bad language. Rather it resists ideological employment of YHWH's power, authority, or reputation for any of a variety of causes—political, economic, moral, ecclesial. The avoidance of the "misuse" of YHWH's name suggests that YHWH is not "useful," has no utilitarian value, is always an "end" and never a "means." This God will be worshiped only for the sake of YHWH's own life, purpose, and way in the world. The wrong use of YHWH's name seeks to draw YHWH's power into more frivolous modes of life where human beings retain control. Thus instead of honoring YHWH, YHWH is put to use, so that the right relationship of God and the human partner is inverted.

It is in the commandment on sabbath that Deuteronomy departs most noticeably from Exod 20; for that reason the sabbath commandment in Deut 5 is the most decisive reflection of Deuteronomic conviction. Indeed, Patrick Miller has shown that this commandment stands at the center of the Decalogue in Deut 5, and provides a clue for the central vision of the Deuteronomic law (Miller 1985). Addressed to a new community at the boundary facing life-or-death decision, Deuteronomy is concerned that Israel should rechoose its own distinctive identity as the people of YHWH. While that peculiar identity in part depends upon *thinking* differently, it also requires visible *practices* and concrete *disciplines* that can be regularly undertaken and seen publicly by the young of the community and by non-Israelites (see 4:5-8). The Deuteronomic tradition in the sixth century accented sabbath as a visible, concrete attestation of difference.

The most important feature of this commandment when contrasted with the parallel in Exod 20:8-11 is that the grounding of the sabbath is no longer in creation but in the Exodus. On this day, Israel reenters the emancipatory world of the Exodus narrative, the one characteristically inhabited by YHWH (v. 6).

The commandment in verse 16 invites reflection upon the fullest, richest notion of "family values." It is unfortunate that in recent time "family values" have been reduced to the thinnest kind of moralism that pays no attention to the real issues of power and powerlessness. This commandment does not seem to be concerned with the need for young, dependent children to defer to their parents, for that is an inescapable reality as long as the children are young. Rather the commandment addresses children who have come into maturity and power, so that they are no longer dependent upon their parents, and are in a position to neglect or maltreat them. That is, the commandment apparently addresses contexts in which the conventional relationship of parental dominance and oversight of children has been nullified or reversed, and children are tempted to "belittle" or demean their parents.

Only the commands on sabbath (vv. 12-15) and parents (v. 16) are stated positively and not as a prohibition. This may suggest that the two commands may have a peculiar linkage to each other. If that is so, then perhaps the fifth commandment reflects parents who have by aging lost their productive capacity and therefore their social utility. When parents (or others) become older and are no longer "useful," it is easier for children and the larger society to disregard their needs and their dignity. If the circumstance in the command is that the parents have lost social productivity and so are made vulnerable, then it comes close to the sabbath command that affirms that life does not consist in productivity. Sabbath is the celebration of life beyond and outside productivity.

The terse series of four commands in verses 17-20, all connected by conjunctions to form one sentence, seeks to bring every zone of communal life under the rule of YHWH's governance. In each case, the prohibition curbs freedom of action that could be undertaken if the agent were autonomous. The point of each command is that there are no autonomous agents in the realm of YHWH's rule; each actor stands under YHWH's intent, and therefore must live responsibly in the presence of the neighbor. The One who issues these commands is the One who insists that autonomous freedom must be corrected and limited by the reality of the neighbor whose entitlements are guaranteed by YHWH.

1. In verse 17, the very life of the neighbor is held dear, protected, and guaranteed.

2. In verse 18, the dignity of the spouse is guaranteed by the prohibition against self-serving sexual satisfaction outside the marriage relationship. Whereas the original patriarchal casting of the ban permitted a married man to connect with an unmarried woman, a more developed interpretation of the command applies equally, prohibiting either partner in a marriage from any external alliance. The seriousness with which these matters were regarded is evidenced by the harsh provisions of 22:13-30.

3. In verse 19, the property of the neighbor is protected against violent or secret confiscation. It is plausible, with reference to Exod 21:16 and Deut 24:7, that an early form of this ban pertained to kidnapping: "Thou shalt not steal a man." Such theft was characteristically for the purpose of selling into slavery (Gnuse 1985, 5-9).

4. In verse 20, the prohibited offense expressly concerns the neighbor. This commandment recognizes that a viable, functioning society must have a reliable judiciary, so that members of the community have confidence in a fair hearing and settlement of claims (see 1:9-18) (Brueggemann 1997:2-9). When truth-telling is compromised, society will reduce to barbarism.

Recognizing that the neighbor's claim is central to each of these last five commands underscores their crucial importance.

Entertain for a moment the alternative of complete autonomy of "each against all." Without legal, moral, covenantal restraint, the life, family, and property of each are at risk. Such an environment of rapacious violence makes human community impossible, either in constant anxiety, or in the heavy imposition of the powerful over the powerless.

It has long been thought that "coveting" in the last commandment concerns an internal attitude of envy (v. 21). Marvin Chaney, however, by making primary appeal to Mic 2:1-4, has persuasively urged that the command concerns the practices of an acquisitive society in which the seizure of what belongs to a neighbor (a life, a spouse, any property) is fair game for the clever against the slow, for the strong against the weak (Chaney 1982). The prohibition thus addresses not simply attitude, but practices and policies that may be legalized by carefully arranged laws whereby the weak are made defenseless.

Paul reasoned that such coveting is equivalent to idolatry (Col 3:5). The worship of the true God leads to a due sense of self vis-à-vis neighbor. It is only an undue sense of self, linked to a false discernment of God, that can give mistaken warrant for usurpatious action against the neighbor. To see *coveting* as the neighborly enactment of *idolatry* discloses the close interface between the legitimating function of false religion and the falsely legitimated antineighborliness of acquisitiveness. The binding of the beginning (5:6) and the end (5:21) of the Decalogue permits one to see that the commands of YHWH mean to redefine both the legitimating *function of faith* and the legitimating *function of political economy*.

After the reiteration of the commands of Sinai, the speech of Moses at the river continues (vv. 22-33). For the most part, these verses are a retrospect, recalling the decisions at Sinai in Exod 20:18-21. In that Sinai encounter, it is remembered:

1. YHWH spoke to the entire assembly of Israel (v. 22a).
2. What YHWH spoke, YHWH gave to Moses in tablets (v. 22b).
3. Israel at Sinai is frightened by the direct address of YHWH

and bids Moses to mediate YHWH's command to them (vv. 23-27). Most notably, Israel promises to "hear and do" (v. 27), the same words of promise given reverse order in the oath of Exod 24:7 (see Exod 24:3).

4. YHWH accepts Moses' mediating functions and undertakes to give Moses "commandments, statutes and ordinances" for the land that are well beyond the ten words already given (vv. 28-31).

At the end of the chapter remembrance ceases and the text moves to direct, contemporary address. Moses exhorts the generation at the Jordan with a strong imperative; Torah observance is the condition for possessing the land (vv. 32-33). These latter two verses correspond to the imperative of 5:1-3 at the beginning of the unit. Together they bracket the reiteration of the Decalogue. Of special notice in this remembrance is the wistful comment of YHWH to Moses in verse 29, a wistfulness reflected in the covenantal indictment of Ps 81:13 (Heb. v. 14), "O that my people would listen to me." It is as though YHWH knows—knows already at Sinai—that Israel will not keep its vows and will not obey Torah. Thus even the buoyant imperative of chapter 5 recognizes that discussion of covenant possibilities takes place midst its continual violation. The tradition knows of the fracture that marks the exchange at the river.

Theological and Ethical Analysis

It should become evident in these reflections that the Ten Commandments are not simply ten rules related to specific attitudes and actions. They are that. Taken all together, however, they are a sketch of an alternative way of envisioning and living in the world. One addressed in the second person singular imperative in these commands is by this address resituated in a covenant horizon, that is, in a *connectedness* that changes everything. From the perspective of the world, the restraints of connectedness (to God and to neighbor) are not obvious. They require intentionality in the ordering of an alternative community that daily lives differently in the world. The commandments urge a life beyond social utility and productivity. The sabbath commandment serves as the foundation for asserting that the value of the neighbor is *intrinsic* not *utilitarian*.

• **The sabbath is to be an occasion of *distinctive memory* of the Exodus.** This memory of emancipation guards against the amnesia of the world of production that seeks to talk Israel out of its identity by vetoing its past.

• **The sabbath is a courageous *public act of identity*.** On this day Israelites act differently; they can be seen acting differently and they can see each other acting differently. The difference that disrupts the daily routines of life is immediately economic, but it is at the same time profoundly theological, for the "rest" that is enjoined is a rest that slaves never enjoy, a rest now available because YHWH was then and is always engaged in breaking the coercions of slavery. The sabbath is an act of free men and women whose freedom is ensured by YHWH. Jacob Neusner has suggested that sabbath is among the acts of "enchantment" whereby Israel engages in the imaginative act of being intentionally Jewish, thus dramatically distinguishing itself from all other communities (Neusner 1991, 85-99).

• **The sabbath is an *act of resistance*.** The key characteristic of the day is not worship but rest. It is work stoppage. And in that work stoppage, Israel attests that it does not belong to and is not defined by the production pressures and schedules and quotas of the world. As long ago as Egypt and as recently as Babylon, Israelites were pressured into the production necessities of the empire. Work stoppage is not only a great act of trust in YHWH, but it is a daring act of refusal. Israel refuses because to be defined by production (and consumption) entails the loss of the very freedom given in the Exodus. Thus Israel must dare to be different in the real world, even at some cost and risk, for the empire never takes such refusal easily.

• **The sabbath is an occasion for *alternative community*.** This is particularly evident in the final phrase of verse 14, your servant shall rest "as you." In the ordinary business of any community, there are important social distinctions related to power and privilege. Some rest while others work. The command intends that on this day of work stoppage, all such distinctions are momentarily but regularly disrupted. There is for the day communitarianism whereby slaves and masters have common identity and common possibility. The sabbath is the provisional overcoming of social distinctions when slaves participate with masters in a world guaranteed by the Great Emancipator, without any conventional demands of performance. As communitarian generosity extends in the community from the powerful to the powerless, so it also extends from the insider to the outsider. The injunction of 1:16 had already insisted that "aliens" be included in covenantal justice; the resident alien is invited to the work stoppage as well. One day out of the week aliens have no need to justify their presence in the community by productivity.

• **The sabbath is an inchoate** *earnest of environmental sanity.* A society that does not practice sabbath inevitably exploits and uses up "natural" resources on the unexamined assumption of usurpatious greed that more resources can always be found. The fact that the work stoppage pertains not only to all members of the human community (masters and slaves, insiders and outsiders) but also to nonhuman creatures (donkeys and livestock) indicates a recognition that the emancipatory impulse of YHWH extends to all of the community, a recognition that will eventuate in the rest of the land in Jubilee. (See Exod 10:26 on the inclusion of the nonhuman in emancipation.)

• **The sabbath is inescapably** *an act of hope.* It is a foretaste of the reorganization of the political economy so that production is kept subordinated to human well-being, in contrast to the practice of market ideology or state socialism that persons exist only for the sake of the economy (see Mark 2:27-28). This act of hope is indeed a visionary one in which the community is invited to dream of an ultimate alterative (see Heb 4:9-11). But beyond such visioning, the extension of rest from production may permit slaves, aliens, and all sorts of disadvantaged underlings to arrive at a different sense of self that may in turn produce restlessness, resistance, and finally revolutionary refusal. Erskine Clarke has considered the way in which the Christian tradition of baptism has the power to create free men and women of slaves, even though those who baptized hoped in part for something other (Clarke 1979). The liberating power in Christian baptism stems in large part from the Exodus tradition. Thus the command to "rest" sets in motion a rich interpretive trajectory, and a visionary alternative of social relationships that may generate concrete, revolutionary change. While such futures no doubt run beyond the awarenesses of this text, they surely do not run beyond the memory of Exodus and the daring interpretive transformation of the commandment accomplished by Deuteronomy.

The commandment to honor one's aging parents is closely related to the sabbath. It, too, insists that human worth cannot be assessed in terms of economic productivity. Parents who may be belittled because they are no longer productive are indeed special candidates for sabbath, endlessly at rest, sabbath-enacting members of the community. As the sabbath command sweepingly celebrates *life beyond productivity,* the command that follows may be a subordinate, derivative concern that provides a case study in work stoppage and in the ways in which society is to treat *those no longer productive.* If that is so, then the command is not just about "family values," but it is an imperative about social relationships not grounded in utility.

Deuteronomy and the entire covenantal tradition thus envision a total renovation of social relationships that are intrinsically valuable, and that are to be safeguarded by the community without respect to utility. It is commonly noticed that this command has no counterpart about how parents are to treat children (on which, see especially Eph 6:1-4). If, however, the command is a general statement about social relationships beyond productivity, then it implies a vision of an alternative community in which children are also honored before they have reached any capacity for "productivity." That same vision of the future is articulated in Mal 4:5-6, the final verses of the Christian ordering of the Old Testament:

Lo, I will send you the prophet Elijah before the great and terrible day of the LORD comes. He will *turn the hearts of parents* to their children and *the hearts of children* to their parents, so that I will not come and strike the land with a curse. (emphasis added)

Elijah is a harbinger of the coming world of God's rule. As Elijah intervened decisively on behalf of the poor and disadvantaged in his lifetime, so the prophetic tradition anticipates that Elijah will return with more decisive intervention in time to come. And when Elijah comes, he will cause a great "turning," a great healing and reconciliation of all that has been alienated. The oracle seems to assume a deep alienation of parents and children, perhaps an alienation that is inevitable and inescapable where power and utility are at work. (Indeed, the alienation reflected here may also be reflected in the commandment, and, in chapter 6, between parents who remember and children who forget.) In the coming age, it need not be so and it will not be so.

The vision of Elijah's coming, moreover, is utilized in the angelic oracle of Luke concerning the coming of John:

"With the spirit and power of Elijah he will go before him, to turn the hearts of parents to their children, and the disobedient to the wisdom of the righteous, to make ready a people prepared for the Lord." (Luke 1:17)

The angel quotes from the oracle of Malachi, but then extends the parent-children image into a larger transformation of the "disobedient" to the "righteous." The purpose is to "make ready a people prepared for the Lord," to create social relationships hospitable to and habitable by YHWH. It may be that the dangerous social renovation about which Mary sings in Luke 1:51-53 and the radical social transformations that Jesus subsequently enacts in the Gospel of Luke derive from this visionary commandment. It is important not to lose the particularity of the commandment that concerns real people in real social relationships, but at the same time to see that the commandment initiates a visionary trajectory of social relationships of fidelity and respect not shaped by the pressures and values of the "productive" world. Perhaps such reconciled relationships are exactly the outcome of a sabbath vision of a community that refuses and breaks with the vicious cycles of a production-oriented society (Dawn 1989).

The sabbath rest and the honoring of parents commandments urge a life beyond social utility and productiveness. It is possible to suggest that an *unrestrained commitment to productivity* has its counterpart in *unrestrained violence and exploitation* in which there is no fabric of respect or restraint. Thus the entire series of commandments, from sabbath rest through the prohibition of false witness, proposes a radically different perspective in which the neighborhood and not the unbridled self is the unit of social meaning. The adjudication of individual and community entitlements is of course continuously problematic; here there is a heavy tilt toward a neighborly ethic in which members of the community must yield to claims that lie beyond the self.

Restraint on utility (vv. 12-16) and *restraint on violence and exploitation* (vv. 17-20) converge in the final prohibition against coveting (v. 21).

The reiteration of the Sinai commands at the Jordan means that this (and each) generation in Israel is being summoned—yet again—to redecide about the kinds of connectedness that make human life viable. It is often noticed that these prohibitions contain no threats or sanctions (though v. 16 is a notable exception). It is clear that the unstated threat of disobedience—as unthinkable as is disobedience in this address—is death. These commands constitute "a way of life" (see Deut 30:15; Matt 7:13-14). The death that disobedience produces, Deuteronomy knows well, does not come by the vengeful intervention of YHWH. It comes, rather, by the slow collapse of common viability, until these prohibited practices destroy the fabric of community and make life unlivable.

These commandments are a demanding condition of a viable community life. Moses knows that "there is no free lunch." A genuinely human life is expensive. At the turn of the century in the United States, it takes little imagination to see the connection between the self-serving extravagance of the consumer economy in an unfettered market economy and the rapid erosion of public institutions, to see that a mode of life committed solely to unrestrained productivity and acquisitiveness is indeed a recipe for death. The recovery of an ethical vision at the Jordan was urgent in this tradition; so a recovery of vision in our environment of anti-covenant is urgent. Such a recovery will not happen by the mere assertion of old codes. It will only happen by carefully rethinking the costs and requirements of a sustainable community. When such a reconsideration is seriously undertaken, it will eventually come to the reiteration of Moses, for Moses has uttered in Israel the simplest, most urgent conditions for life. No amount of cleverness, technology, or arrogance can finally circumvent these terms of well-being.

It is of course a truism that Jesus did not abolish the commandments, but came to "complete" them. Thus in the Sermon on the Mount, the "new teaching" of Jesus affirms the old commandments and characteristically makes them more radical (Matt 5:17-48). Jesus aims to generate a "contrast society" that embraces the commands in their greatest radicality. It becomes clear in Jesus' exposition of the commandments that they cannot be understood as simple moralisms or as a series of virtues to be embraced, but are rather a practical revisioning of how life may be lived in a world where YHWH governs (see Mark 10:17-22).

Obedience to the requirements of the holy God entails a divestment of the treasures of self for the neighborly rule of God. Such a narrative exposition as Mark offers shows that the demand of Moses at the Jordan is urgent and costly.

The most important interpretive issue in this chapter is the recognition that the "statutes and ordinances" announced in chapters 12–25 are quite distinct from the Decalogue (vv. 1, 31-33). These statutes and ordinances have not been heard by Israel at Sinai, but are given only to Moses. They will be announced for the first time in Deut 12–25, for the first time even though Moses has long since received them at Sinai.

Two additional interpretive issues surfaced in Deut 4:44–5:33. First, the entire narrative account is designed to accent and celebrate *the distinctive authority of Moses* (Brueggemann

1997:578-87). He is the one who was "standing between" Israel and YHWH even for the Ten Commandments. He is the sole authorized interpreter before whom Israel has no alternative. It is not a great leap to see that the figure of Moses becomes the reference point that leads to canonical authority.

Second, it is important to reflect on the relation between the ten words and the statutes and ordinances. The latter are clearly secondary, but they are also quite indispensable. The Ten Commandments are *completely non-negotiable* for Israel. Of course! But they are *endlessly negotiated,* that is, disputatiously interpreted to determine, occasion after occasion, that the command means this rather than that (Brueggemann 1991; Childs 1974:437). The Decalogue itself is open to specific interpretation that it receives in the ongoing work of the Mosaic office. As Moses has substantiated the *non-negotiability* of the ten utterances ("do not add or subtract"), so Moses presides over their *negotiability.* Deuteronomy is the primal exhibit that Israel is a community of ongoing interpretation, so that Israel is always reconsidering the precise claim of Torah commands. Indeed the book of Deuteronomy evidences interpretive freedom and imagination of a dynamic sort, because Torah is an ongoing, lively engagement between YHWH's will and concrete circumstance wherein Israel must always again embrace its identity and vocation as YHWH's people.

The ingenuity of the Deuteronomic tradition in its capacity to link the *Decalogue* to subsequent, derivative *"statutes and ordinances"* through the person of Moses is an important interpretive principle (Levinson 1997). The connection between the two affirms at the same time (a) that the primary authority of the Decalogue is undoubted and (b) that subsequent interpretation of a more specific kind that is germane to concrete circumstance is an urgent and always unfinished task. This means that as absolute as the Decalogue is, more must always be said. Within Judaism and Christianity, it is clear that the expository task is always to be continued—in rabbinic interpretation and in continuing ecclesial reflection. Any "strict constructionism" that seeks to stop ongoing interpretation is in spirit and in substance alien to the very process undertaken in the tradition of Deuteronomy. The commands of YHWH are not understood as flat, self-evident "principles," but are serious and normative guides whereby Israel and the church seek faithful obedience when "new occasions teach new duties."

This dynamic principle, moreover, while thoroughly biblical, is not confined to the Bible and its internal interpretive practice. It is fair to say that this same sense of ongoing interpretation has become a staple of Western democratic jurisprudence. Thus Samuel Levine shows the way in which the U.S. Supreme Court finds in constitutional law: "the identification of unenumerated principles through reference to textually enumerated principles" (Levine 1998:512). As a case in point, Levine cites the governing opinion of Justice Powell in a 1977 rule, *Moore v. City of East Cleveland*. The court ruled against an ordinance concerning housing arrangements of a woman and her two grandchildren on the basis of the Fourteenth Amendment. Powell wrote for the court:

> The full scope of liberty guaranteed by the Due Process Clause cannot be found in or limited by the precise terms of the specific guarantees elsewhere provided in the Constitution. Thus "liberty" is not a series of isolated points picked out in terms of the taking of property; the freedom of speech, press, and religion. . . . It is a rational continuum, which broadly speaking, includes a freedom from all substantial arbitrary imposition and purposeless restraints. (Levine 1998:515)

Thus the enumerated provisions of the Fourteenth Amendment lead to unenumerated guarantees. In Deuteronomy, the statutes and ordinances of Moses, to be articulated in chapters 12–25, are not enumerated in the Decalogue of Sinai, but are found there by ongoing interpretation.

The reader of Deuteronomy may appreciate and pay attention to this remarkable freedom and dynamic that permits the God of Sinai to sustain a remarkable vision of life in the world pertinent to many different circumstances and conditions. At the same time, we may recognize that this subtle and bold theory of interpretation is precisely the foundation of jurisprudence that keeps law pertinent to lived reality in contemporary society. Such a dynamic process, already signaled in the remarkable words of verse 3, precludes any "strict constructionism" and legitimates the crucial, bold, ongoing work of "making law." In commenting on verse 17, Philip Berrigan offers an example of interpretation that goes well beyond "strict constructionism"; in the midst of his protests against nuclear weapons and their immense potential for killing, he has said:

> Everything connected with the reign of God begins with the commandment, "Thou shalt not kill."... Everything in Christian life is based on this foundation against killing. Nothing is going to happen until we stop killing one another. That's the first step toward loving our enemies, which is the summit of the Gospel. The bottom line is to stop killing one another and prevent others from killing one another. (Dear 1995:32-33)

Sharing the same conviction, his brother Daniel has written:

> I would like to say as simply as I know how, to other Christians, that I'm convinced that in our lifetime we have no contribution to make to one another or to the world at large except a modest and consistent No to death. Our churches can go tomorrow; our schools could have been closed yesterday; our institutions ground under by the next wave of tanks of the next phalanx of violence. And what will remain of Christianity except that we have said audibly and consistently and patiently over our lifetime: "We are not allowed to kill. We are not allowed to be complicit in killing. We are not allowed to commit the crime of silence before these things." (Dear 1995:43-44)

THE THREAT OF AMNESIA (6:1-25)

After the reiteration of the Decalogue (5:6-21) and the confirmation of Moses as the sole legitimate interpreter of the Decalogue (5:22-33), chapter 6 begins a series of homiletical appeals that prepare for the annunciation of statutes and ordinances in chapters 12–25. Chapters 6–11 are the richest instructional, homiletical, and theological materials in the book of Deuteronomy, for they articulate the historical memories and motivations that frame and give context to the commandments to follow.

Chapter 6 includes a pivotal covenant command to Israel (vv. 1-9), a warning against forgetful disobedience (vv. 10-19), and a model for instruction of the young (vv. 20-24).

Exegetical Analysis

6:1-9: The pivotal covenant command of verses 1-9 may be divided into two rhetorical elements, an introduction (vv. 1-3) and the actual imperative (vv. 4-9). The introduction in verses 1-3 contains the characteristic rhetoric of Deuteronomy as *imperative* and *consequence*. Verse 1 equates "the commandment" with the "statutes and ordinances" to follow. It does so by the absence of a connecting conjunction before "statutes" as reflected in the NRSV, so that "statutes and ordinances" stand in apposition to "the commandment," and are offered as an equivalent. The force of this grammar is to enhance the authority of what is to follow, daring to suggest that the statutes and ordinances are, in this utterance, on a par with the commands of chapter 5. The obedience required in verse 1 has as its outcome in verse 2 "so that" the children may learn to fear and obey. That is, obedience is the way to teach obedience. The imperative of verse 3 that anticipates the more famous parallel in verse 4 yields a second consequence ("so that") of durability in the land. This speech intends to ensure covenantal obedience across the generations, as the nonnegotiable condition of keeping the land. The tradition knows that if the specifications of covenantal command are not obeyed, the land will revert to its anti-covenantal condition of exploitation, and Israel, as a social experiment in the world, will evaporate before the forces of greed and anxiety. The quality of life in the land is completely connected to and dependent upon the quality of Israel's covenant with YHWH.

The pivotal covenantal command of this chapter—indeed, of the entire tradition of Deuteronomy—is the utterance of Moses in verses 4-5, to be implemented according to verses 6-7. It is impossible to overstate the importance of this particular summons, on which see the expositions of Patrick D. Miller (1984) and S. Dean McBride (1973). These two verses are recited daily by faithful Jews, thus termed by some "the Jewish creed," and are reckoned in the teaching of Jesus to be "the first commandment" (Mark 12:29-30). The address is to "Israel," the one covenanted people of YHWH. The verses not only assume the existence of such a community of faith, but convene an assembly that, in this address, is always being formed, re-identified, and reconstituted as the Israel of God, for Israel becomes Israel through hearing. The imperative "hear" is fundamental to a covenantal understanding of this people of God. In listening, Israel is summoned, commanded, and assured by the One with authority who takes an initiative and imposes upon Israel a will, purpose, and identity other than any it might have taken for itself. The imperative brings Israel into a defining relationship, whereby this people now lives completely in the sphere of YHWH's will and purpose.

As the substance of this address Israel hears that YHWH is fully the God of Israel. YHWH, the one who makes and keeps promises, the one who has delivered from slavery, is the reference point that characterizes the life of Israel. The precise translation of the lead sentence is disputed (McBride 1973:291-92). The key phrase may be rendered as "YHWH is one," in order to stress the *unity* of YHWH who cannot be divided or parceled out; or it may be translated "YHWH alone," in order to accent YHWH's demand for *exclusive, uncompromising loyalty* from Israel. McBride is correct that the latter translation, "YHWH alone," is existentially more poignant in its direct requirement for a full, unreserved commitment to YHWH. McBride, moreover, has usefully shown that the factoring out of "heart, mind, soul" as distinctive spheres of commitment or psychological elements is not very helpful, even though it may permit a nice homiletical outline. Rather the effect of the triad is cumulative, "to accent the superlative degree of total commitment to YHWH" (McBride 1973:304).

This "superlative degree of total commitment" is expressed through the word "love," a peculiar contribution of Deuteronomy to the characterization of the YHWH-Israel relationship. In light of "set his heart" *(ḥāšaq)* in 7:7, it is clear that the term has affective dimensions. Nonetheless, here "love" refers to the kind of practical fidelity that a lesser party in a formal relationship must enact toward a greater party in order to demonstrate and implement vows of loyalty already made (Moran 1963). One must not romanticize the Deuteronomic use of the term "love," as though it were primarily a "feeling" or even an aptitude. It concerns, rather, practical acts of obedience in every sphere of daily life, acts that Moses will soon line out. When the terms "hear, love, only" are taken all together, it is appropriate to see that this positive imperative is commensurate with the uncompromising prohibitions of the first two commandments in 5:6-10. Nothing less is commanded than that Israel will be totally, exclusively, without reservation devoted to the purposes of YHWH in the world.

The claim of total loyalty is one mark that makes the God of Israel incomparable, that makes Israel problematic in a world that wants to "go along and get along," and that makes the book of Deuteronomy pivotal for the most serious claims of biblical faith. The costliness of the demand of exclusive loyalty is perhaps most savagely exemplified in the Old Testament in the theological revolution fostered by Elijah and Elisha in the ninth century; that religious revolution can be seen as a harbinger of the Deuteronomic vision of faith. In Elijah's great "contest" at Mt. Carmel, the prophet puts the question before his community:

"How long will you go limping with two different opinions? If the LORD is God, follow him; but if Baal, then follow him." (1 Kgs 18:21)

In the end, the community assents to Elijah's vigorous demand:

"The LORD indeed is God; the LORD indeed is God." (1 Kgs 18:39)

The tradition has in view an intergenerational community of those who live out a radical vision of covenant. The command to hear is to be kept "in your heart," that is, at the center of one's sense of self. And if kept so focally, then it will be effectively transmitted to the children. Deuteronomy always has its eyes on the children, on the coming generation (see v. 2). For that reason, the command is followed in verses 6-9 by a series of imperatives: "recite, bind, fix, write" (see Prov 6:20-22). The core claim of YHWH is to be everywhere available to Israel, audible and visible. Moses proposes "saturation education" so that a child's imaginative horizon is completely pervaded by signs and reminders of this imperative. In the Jewish tradition, this imperative has issued in signs on the body and at the door. In the Christian tradition, such saturation narrative has conventionally taken many forms, notably mottoes that are stitched and hung on the wall. In the early practices of education in colonial America, the McGuffey reader in all of its teaching and exercises voiced a certain advocacy that was, in tone and intent, close to the religious exclusivism and discipline of Deuteronomy.

The instruction of verse 7 has a close parallel in Judg 5:10, in which the community is enjoined to celebrate the deliverances of YHWH:

> "Tell of it, you who ride on white donkeys,
> you who sit on rich carpets
> and you who walk by the way."

The verbs, "ride, sit, walk," paralleled in our verse by "at home-away, lie down-rise up," mean "everywhere, all the time."

6:10-19: The imperative to radical, exclusive obedience (vv. 1-9) leads to a weighty warning about disobedience (vv. 10-19). The address of Moses takes place at the Jordan; Israel is still in the wilderness where life-support systems are tenuous. But Moses looks across the Jordan as do his listeners. There he sees a future context for Israel that is ripe for disobedience, for the good land of promise is in every way a contrast to the present wilderness (vv. 10-12). The coming land, the one promised since Genesis, has on offer everything a displaced people might want for well-being and security: cities, houses, cisterns, vineyards, groves, all the signs of blessedness and measures of prosperity. The cities are "great and good," the houses are full, everything is in abundance. All these props for well-being, moreover, are pure gift. Israel did nothing to achieve them, did not build, did not fill, did not hew, did not plant. Everything is given, everything is the gift of YHWH who gives in abundance. All the prosperity and fruitfulness of the new agricultural economy will cause desperate, land-hungry Israel to gorge itself without restraint.

It is only in verse 12 that one arrives at the main verb of the sentence. Everything before has been a temporal, dependent clause. But now the imperative: "take care." Pay attention! Moses knows that *satiation* produces *amnesia,* and amnesia is the great threat to a community whose defining relationship is grounded in a concrete, nameable memory. Satiation banishes the past and obliterates the future. Everything is reduced to an endless present tense, rather like the absence of clocks in the casinos of Las Vegas. No one any longer knows what time it is, and no one can any longer recall a time other than this time that appears, with gorging, to be without beginning and without end. In a state of satiation, Moses anticipates, Israel will lust for the gift but be uninterested in the giver. Israel will be tempted to forget the Exodus as the defining disclosure of this God, will forget the slavery and the wondrous act of deliverance from slavery. YHWH will no longer be remembered or known as the God of transformation; the distinctiveness of YHWH will evaporate into a religious plethora of the gods of stability and equilibrium.

The speech of Moses senses the grave risk to Israel. In verses 13-15, Moses puts the deep decision of the Jordan again before this new generation, the *either/or* about which Deuteronomy cares the most. One option before the listening community is YHWH. As the people of YHWH, Israel is to fear, serve, and swear by YHWH. In Hebrew, the normal word order of the sentence is inverted so that the emphasis falls upon YHWH: *YHWH* you will fear; *him* you will serve, *his name* you will swear by.

The alternative is "the other gods." They are unnamed, because Moses has no interest in them and will not give them the credit of name and identity. There are scores of them, and they are indistinguishable from each other. *Unlike YHWH* these other gods have never made or kept a promise. *Unlike YHWH,* they have never emancipated slaves. *Unlike YHWH,* they have never issued any uncompromising commands. To "follow" such gods, to walk after them in liturgical expression, is to walk away from YHWH and to depart from what must have been YHWH's festive processions that gave public support to YHWH and public exhibit of Israel's loyalty.

The other gods are real options, and Israel is always tempted by them. Except, says Moses, those gods are not really an option for Israel. The reason is that YHWH is jealous and will not countenance Israel's departure from exclusive covenant fidelity. Thus Israel has a choice, but it is not a choosable choice. Before Israel chooses, Israel has already chosen, and YHWH will permit no reneging. The threat to Israel is like a Catch-22, so that other gods that seem choosable are a mirage that can produce only death.

The warning of Moses would seem to reach its climactic point with verse 15. After that, however, the speech moves to cite historical precedent by appeal to the narrative of Exod 17:1-7. The term "test" is the root for the place name "Massah," so that the narrative turns on the testing of YHWH. In that ancient memory, Israel had disputed with YHWH over a need for water. In the end, the protest of Israel resulted in water produced by the wondrous action of Moses. The narrative does not identify what it is that constitutes "testing." The narrative may suggest that in their anxiety over thirst, Israel had refused to submit itself to YHWH's care, had panicked and forced YHWH to act. It is evident that the "testing" in Exod 17:1-7 is not commensurate with the envisioned crisis of our text. The text of Exod 17 is a desperate response to *extreme need;* the present warning is a response in *complete complacency.* What is shared in the two cases is that Israel does not submit willingly or wholly to YHWH, being one time disputatious, the other time seeking alternatives to YHWH.

The brief citation of verse 16, however, barely interrupts the more expected rhetoric of verses 17-19. Israel is summoned back to obedience. The alternative to the threat of amnesia is the intentional embrace of YHWH and YHWH's commandments, thus an acknowledgment of the giver as well as the gift, an obedient acknowledgment of the giver that defeats amnesia. The outcome of such renewed obedience, governed by "so that" (in parallel to v. 2), is that the land may be kept and Israel may dwell in well-being. The warning issued by Moses is a recognition that the very prosperity promised and given by YHWH is an occasion for amnesia; that amnesia, moreover, produces alienation from YHWH and consequently forfeiture of YHWH's good gifts.

6:20-25: The text returns to a focus on the children (vv. 20-24; see vv. 2, 7-9). Already in verse 2 it was affirmed that the obedience of the parents is done "so that" the children will fear and obey YHWH. That is, lived faith itself is a form of nurture, perhaps the most telling form of nurture. Or said with verse 20, lived faith is a way of evoking questions on the part of children, in order that instruction may be given to children at the point of their asking. The tradition has no doubt that lived faith will evoke such wonder in an observant child. The evoked question, however, is for the sake of the answer. The answer given here, as observed long ago by Gerhard von Rad, is a stylized recital of the standard, most elemental narrative memory of Israel (vv. 21-24) (von Rad 1966:3-8). The recital includes three remembered elements of the past plus a contemporary appeal. The remembered events are:

1. *The Exodus* (vv. 21-23a). The most prominent feature here is the capacity in recital to situate the present generation in the ancient event: "*We* were slaves . . ."
2. *The gift of the land* (v. 23b). This motif is rooted in the Genesis promises, and is a central concern of Deuteronomy.
3. *The utterance of commandments* (v. 24). Though the event of Sinai is not specified, the verse clearly alludes to that mountain of commandment.

Along with the fundamental attestation of YHWH's committed power in the Exodus event, the recital to the children joins together the two primal concerns of Deuteronomy, the gift of *land* and the condition of *commandment*. The final phrasing of verse 24, "to keep us alive, as is now the case," echoes 5:3 and forms an *inclusio* with that statement that preceded the presentation of the Decalogue. The point is to insist that the commandment pertains to the present generation and to the generation of the children who make inquiry.

The word order of final appeal is inverted in the NRSV. In Hebrew the sentence begins, "Righteousness will be to us . . ." The statement assumes that the land can only be held by those who qualify as practitioners of YHWH's Torah, and so the children must learn from early on, that the wealth and abundance of the land is not a flat, irreversible given, but depends upon attentiveness to Torah.

Theological and Ethical Analysis

In the later ministry of Jesus, much informed by the traditions of Deuteronomy, the costly summons to discipleship is of the same demanding absolute quality, though the practice of Jesus is without the savage implication of the earlier prophetic revolution (Mark 8:34-35; 10:21, 28-30). The same command to "love Jesus" issues in the same uncompromising demand of obedience (see John 21:15-19). Even the final narrative exchange with Peter in the Fourth Gospel ends with the same terse requirement, "follow me" (John 21:19).

Reflection upon Moses' demand invites the following thoughts:

1. It is a defining characteristic and peculiar claim of biblical faith—rooted in the "uniqueness" of YHWH—that individual lives and the common life of the community are healthy when they are about one loyalty. Thus Søren Kierkegaard in his uncompromising demand can affirm that "Purity of Heart is to will one thing." This core tradition of biblical faith will have no patience with the notion of a "Protean" personality that is encouraged in a fragmented, pluralistic society, because it believes that such incessant adaptability is in fact fickleness that cannot result in personal or communal well-being (see

Lifton 1993). That is, singular response to the jealous God is not simply an archaic witness to a cosmic crankiness, but it is a judgment about what is possible in human life and on what basis.

2. The demand of singular loyalty to the all-defining, all-governing God is an expectation never fully attained. The liturgic tradition of the church knows that such "perfect obedience" is never attained, even though it continues to be the primal imperative of the life of faith. It is possible that such an awareness of "falling short" might lead to despair and self-hatred. In the Christian context, the full liturgical tradition that enjoins such singular loyalty, however, is marked at the same time by the readiness of this God to forgive and invite again to loyalty, as in Deut 6, the jealous God becomes the merciful God. Those who do not attain (on which see Phil 3:12) are invited always again to the joyous task of singular loyalty: "But grow in grace and knowledge of our Lord and Savior Jesus Christ" (2 Pet 3:18).

3. While it is self-evident that none attains such singular loyalty, there is in the very rhetoric of such loyalty a seductive invitation to imagine that one may "arrive." A misperceived sense of self at the least may produce self-righteousness (on which see the example of Luke 18:11-12). Such self-confidence may be only offensive and not destructive. But such a sense of self or of community may lead to a more virulent danger, namely, an assault on all "lesser faith." While there is a reference point for such self-confidence in the violent aspects of Elisha's prophetic revolution (see 1 Kgs 20:42), the history of the Christian church is strewn with examples of those who occupy and monopolize singular loyalty in ways that have produced judgment and violence upon others, for example, the Crusades, the Inquisition, witch-hunts, and a variety of excommunications. What is forgotten in such destructive presumption is that even in such would-be attainments, it is still YHWH who speaks and Israel who is addressed. Israel is always receiver and never initiator, always subordinate and never in charge, always responsive, never primary.

Thus the command to exclusive loyalty commensurate with YHWH's singularity is fraught with temptations to both *despair* and *pride*. Either of these, however, distorts what is intended by the God who commands a singular life of glad obedience.

The warning issued in this text does not seem remote from the circumstance of the faithful in a society as affluent and secure as in the United States. Ours is an economy of abundance that lives by an ideology of satiation. The seemingly limitless capacity of the consumer economy—supported (as I write this) by a market that keeps growing, kept in place by a military establishment without parallel in the history of the world—leads to a common, thoughtless assumption that it has always been this way and will always be this way—"world without end." In such an economic extravagance, it is nearly impossible to remember anything important, to remember the kind of discipline that was required for the founding of the democracy, to remember the circumstances out of which European and Asian immigrants came at great risk, the suffering African captives endured, and the endless process of courage and compassion that lies beyond the present "peace and prosperity."

Of course none today would "test" the God of the dominant theological tradition. Indeed none would ever bother to do so. The "testimony" that is unwittingly practiced is rather the broad readiness to try alternative ways in the world that include nothing of covenantal accountability or the disciplines of covenantal neighborliness. The great question in this plethora of consumerist options is whether such an indulgent way in the world can be sustained without grounding in the holy demand of covenanting. Deut 6 is quick to answer, "No, it cannot be sustained." But then, a part of the problem is that satiated amnesia is slow even to notice the warning. Characteristically, the ones addressed in amnesia are slow to discern that it is they who are being addressed at all.

This chapter has at its beginning (vv. 1-9) and at its end (vv. 20-25) appeals to the children to remember. These two appeals to memory frame a warning not to forget (vv. 10-19). The issue of remembering/forgetting pertains both to the *concreteness of command* and to the *narrative lore* that energizes the commands. That

91

is, the next generation must be fully embedded in the "life-world" of covenant. That embeddedness, moreover, takes place only by constant, intentional verbal reiteration (vv. 7-9, 20-25) plus the parents' vigorous obedience (vv. 1-2). The teaching community is in a life-or-death struggle for the heart, commitment, and imagination of the younger generation. Michael Fishbane pays particular attention to the pronouns in the question of verse 20 and in the answer of verses 21-25 (Fishbane 1979:79-83). The child asks about what the Lord *your* God has commanded *you*. Fishbane sees these as distancing usages, suggesting that the child is alienated from the parents' claim. The parent, in response, seeks to overcome the distance by using the inclusive pronoun "us":

> Deut. 6:20-25 discloses a tension between two generations' memories, sets of experiences, and commitments. It questions the ability of the fathers to transmit their laws and faith to their sons, who see these as alien and do not feel the same responsibility concerning them. . . . That the fathers would want a continuity through their sons of their special relationship with God is understandable. But what was subjective and immediate to them is seen as objective and mediate to their sons. . . . The teaching of the fathers in Deuteronomy 6:20-25 is an attempt to involve their sons in the covenant community of the future, and undoubtedly reflects the sociological reality of the settlement in Canaan. The attempt by fathers to transform their uninvolved sons from "*dis*temporaries" to "*con*temporaries, i.e., true-life sharers, is an issue of supreme and recurrent significance in the Bible. (Fishbane 1979:81-82)

Thus it is the younger generation, the one completely blessed in the land, that must "take care that you do not forget" (v. 12).

The particular reference to Fishbane indicates the ways in which the anxieties of Deut 6 are pertinent to the contemporary community of faith. There is no doubt that the Enlightenment explicitly intended to defeat the traditional memory of the church, to considerable effect. That long-standing danger, moreover, is more recently intensified with the host of postmodern cultural realities and forces that work against intergenerational embrace of a remembered past that may energize a present-tense obligation. It is certain that many of the young in the community of faith are *dis*temporaries who scarcely have the categories available through which to become *con*temporaries. Both the lived practices and the intentional verbalizations of the parental generation are thin and in general lack conviction.

This text asserts that the community is at risk when the younger generation is alienated. The text does not, however, settle for despair, but proposes the intentional reassertion of the memory as a source for a radically different future. Israel has always known that the claiming of the next generation is no automatic process but requires great intentionality. Assmann has suggested that a culture that is inattentive to its memories trades its tradition and culture to remember something else (Assmann 1992:68). In Deuteronomy, the "something else" was "Canaanite religion" in its many forms. In Western culture at the beginning of the twenty-first century, the likelihood is that the "something else" is an ideology of consumerism rooted in anxiety and expressed as greed susceptible to brutality. It is no wonder that the teaching tradition of Deuteronomy exhibited a deep sense of urgency in its strategy of saturation as it struggled for the glad assent of its own young.

THE WONDER AND RIGOR OF BEING CHOSEN (7:1-26)

Chapter 7, a continuing address of Moses, fervently asserts the distinctiveness of Israel that is to be affirmed and appreciated in the context of the other nations. Given the accent on the children in chapter 6, the anxiety of this chapter is that the next generation will fail to recognize and cherish Israel's distinctiveness that is rooted in YHWH's love and embraced in Israel's obedience. The intention of the chapter is to take deliberate steps so that the coming generation will choose covenant with YHWH. The chapter pivots on the affirmation of verses 6-15. That affirmation is bracketed in verses 1-5 and verses 16-26 with a harsh negation of other nations, other cultures, and other religious options that constitute a threat to Israel's distinctiveness. All three sections of the chapter are concerned for the single issue of Israel's distinctiveness, but take it up in variously negative and positive tones.

Exegetical Analysis

7:1-5: The articulation of Israel's distinctiveness begins with the elimination of seductive alternatives (vv. 1-5). The land of promise is a land filled with seductions, that is, the religious alternatives of those who now occupy the land, whose religious symbolism, though non-Yahwistic and false, has been adequate for them. Indeed, in 4:19, all kinds of religious symbolizations are "allotted" to the nations that are not permitted to Israel. And now Israel comes face-to-face with those symbolizations that will seduce and distort its peculiar identity as the people of YHWH.

By any critical judgment, this statement poses complex problems. The text is commonly dated not earlier than the eighth or seventh century. But the seven peoples named in verse 1 have long since disappeared, and so constitute no threat for Israel. Thus the list of seven nations is an archaic slogan that represents, in context, any alien culture with its religious temptations for Israel. Those alternative religions already recognized in chapter 4 will lead Israel into alien forms of imagination that will in turn erode the covenant. When the covenant with YHWH is eroded or compromised the very survival of the community is placed in jeopardy.

The recommended strategy for dealing with an image-saturated culture is stated in two very different ways. First, "you must utterly destroy" (*herem*, v. 2). The term, stated with an emphatic verbal form, is a technical term derived from an ancient practice of wholesale obliteration of an enemy as an act of theological obedience. The brutalizing tone of the rhetoric surely is not commensurate with the felt threat that an alien culture may constitute for a religiously self-conscious community. The commanded destruction of verse 1, moreover, concerns not the destruction of images but the destruction of peoples. By any stretch, the modern reader is sure to find this language deeply offensive and problematic.

The most recent, careful assessment of the notion of *herem* is by Philip Stern (1991). Stern proposes that:

1. The extreme force of the injunction to destroy is a negative *counterpart to the first commandment*, "Only YHWH." That is,

because YHWH is a jealous God and will tolerate no rival, every such practice and every such practitioner is subject to destruction as an act of obedience to the command of YHWH.

2. The threat of the other religious options is perceived not simply as political and cultural, but as *mythic*. That is, alternative religious practice has the potential to bring deep disorder into the community. The elimination of such a religious option therefore is to overcome the danger of *chaos* and so to assure the good order of society intended by YHWH as creator.

3. Because the seven nations are long gone, the rhetoric in this text is now to be understood *symbolically and not literally;* Israel has long since given up its readiness to undertake such barbaric actions.

Whether Stern's third judgment, something of historical speculation, is correct or not, the first two points make sound theological sense. The rhetoric reflects activity "brought about by the most elemental circumstance of a people's struggle for life and land" (Stern 1991:217).

The second proposed strategy is not the destruction of the peoples, but the destruction of their systems of religious symbolization (v. 5). While the rhetoric is as violent, it is now action committed against religious objects and not against persons. Nonetheless, the force of the entire paragraph is brutalizing, in the recognition that the "children," the ones who must "take care that you do not forget" (6:12), will promptly find their faith placed in deep jeopardy. It seems clear that the tradition does not have excessive confidence in the appeal of its own claims to its children.

7:1-6: The violent action urged and legitimated in verses 1-5 is placed alongside the positive affirmation of verses 6-15. The thesis sentence of verse 6 contains two affirmations that are decisive for the theology of Deuteronomy. First, Israel is a people "holy to YHWH." The term "holy" here means separated for and belonging to. The language re-enforces the notion of contamination through contact with other religious symbols that would compromise Israel's singular adherence to YHWH. Thus "holiness" is the positive counterpoint to *herem,* the latter undertaken in order to assure the former. The term "holy," moreover, is a relational term; Israel has no intrinsic religious specialness, but is holy to (reserved for) YHWH and must be singularly devoted to YHWH. This affirmation is reinforced by the second phrase, "chosen . . . to be his people, his treasured possession." The language parallels that of 4:20; it asserts that while YHWH is ruler of all nations and has many peoples over whom to preside, Israel is YHWH's intimate personal property upon which YHWH especially dotes. Israel enjoys a special status with YHWH, the ruler of all the earth, and must take care to maintain that relationship. Thus verse 6 suggests a personal motivation of *exceptionalism* that both requires and justifies the harshness of verses 1-5.

7:7-11: In what follows, the text reflects upon the bases out of which YHWH chooses Israel (vv. 7-11). Israel might have thought that it was especially chosen because Israel is large and impressive; but that is not so. Israel is "fewest," and so no claim in that regard can be made. (See the parallel statement in 9:6*a*.) No, the reason for the special status of Israel is not to be found in Israel, but in YHWH. YHWH "set his heart" (*ḥāšaq*) on Israel. The verb bespeaks a strong emotional attachment that runs beyond any reasonable, explicable act. YHWH made a leap of love in committing to Israel. YHWH's inscrutable act is (a) rooted in YHWH's own love—willingness to enter into a sustained and abiding covenant commitment, and (b) based on the ancient oath to the family of Abraham in the book of Genesis. Thus YHWH's treatment of Israel is rooted in commitments that stretch back behind the present generation and indeed back behind the entire scenario of Moses— the commitments to Israel that have been operative since the time of Abraham and Sarah. That ancient oath of fidelity is remembered as the elemental motivation for the Exodus and for the coming gift of land. Israel is rooted in commitments that YHWH remembers and honors, even when Israel itself is given to amnesia. YHWH does not forget!

The affirmation of YHWH's *free act of love* is in Deuteronomy characteristically matched by the *urging of obedience,* here stated in verse 11. The two-sided relationship of *love* and *required obedience* may be logically problematic to Christians, but it is not a difficulty for Deuteronomic theology, for this two-sided reality has its rootage in YHWH's own life. In language that closely parallels the pivotal text of Exod 34:6-7, Moses affirms (a) YHWH is the God who is faithful, keeps covenant and steadfast love to faithful covenant partners, and (b) YHWH is the God who punishes the disobedient promptly and harshly (see Brueggemann 1997:215-24).

While the rootage of YHWH's free act of commitment to Israel in Genesis promises is crucial in understanding Israel's peculiar status, Israel in its contemporary setting should not count excessively on such an initiatory act. In the present moment, according to Deuteronomy, the covenant is a bilateral one between partners who are bound together in mutual obligations that carry deep sanctions. There will be no problem for the obedient: "therefore . . ." (v. 11). The disobedient, however, cannot count on ancestral love, but must reckon with their own destruction. The relationship is grounded in free grace, but it operates according to symmetrical expectations in which there is no easy, assured forgiveness.

7:12-15: This bilateral, symmetrical relationship is explored positively in verses 12-15. The paragraph is governed by "if" *('qv).* This condition of obedience is an echo of the Mosaic "if" of Exod 19:5, the premise of the Sinai covenant. Everything depends upon obedience. The text enjoins obedience and the promise that follows assumes obedience. In response to full, glad obedience, YHWH will keep the covenant fidelity promised to the ancestors. In light of verse 8, the ancestors here may be the Genesis community, but they might also refer to the generation of Sinai. Either way, YHWH will love, bless, and multiply, that is, guarantee complete well-being. As it characteristically is, the promise here is quite material and reflects the hoped-for prosperity of an agrarian community. Animals and fields will produce in abundance, the best hope of a farming community.

The unstated affirmation is that Israel does not need to seek agricultural well-being from the gods of the land, for YHWH is completely capable of being a "fertility god" (Harrelson 1969). Because of YHWH's full fidelity toward this people "holy to YHWH," Israel will experience none of the setbacks of troubled agriculture—sterility, barrenness, disease. All the language here has to do with material success, prosperity, abundance, fertility. The ancestors of Genesis were endlessly vexed about the birth of an heir. Now fruitfulness will function on every front. Israel becomes the carrier of the best promises of the creator God. According to 4:32-34 there has never been anything like Israel before in all creation. Indeed, this is the new creation, all the goodness of creation is now given as intended, and Israel is its recipient. Insofar as this text appeals to creation themes to antici- pate "new creation," the hope for the new land is that it will indeed be "The Kingdom of God," a realm fully embodying the rule of YHWH.

The premise of such a full working creation is covenantal obe- dience. It is important that the positive "if" of obedience is not matched here by a negative "if not." The threat is held in abeyance, even if signaled in verse 10, because the text here makes an unqualified affirmation of YHWH's goodness to Israel.

7:16-26: The chapter is completed in verses 16-26 by a harsh dismissal of other peoples, a dismissal that matches the opening lines of verses 1-5. Israel is commanded to "have no pity" (v. 16), "have no dread" (v. 21), "blot out" (v. 24). These peoples and their religious symbolizations deeply threaten Israel, because they will talk Israel out of the obedience that is the prerequisite to its prosperity in the land of promise (v. 17).

Israel may be intimidated by peoples more numerous than it is (v. 17; see v. 7). The antidote to such intimidation is the memory of the Exodus (vv. 18-19). YHWH continues to be capable of other Exodus-like acts. The great empire of Egypt was no match for YHWH. These lesser peoples in the land are no serious chal- lenge to YHWH. Verse 20 suggests that if YHWH's devices with Egypt are not sufficient in the present circumstance of threat,

YHWH has other strategies available as well, though the exact meaning of verse 20 is not clear.

The summons to "no dread" in verse 21 is a characteristic invitation to trust YHWH in times of risk, for YHWH is perfectly adequate and willing to defend Israel (see 1:29). All that is required for well-being is confidence in YHWH. But of course that is what Israel characteristically finds too demanding.

After the sweeping assurances of verses 18-24, Moses issues a final warning about images (vv. 25-26), thus returning to the accent of verse 5. The images of the other peoples are a huge threat to Israel. Verse 25 suggests that what may be coveted is the power of the icon, power that permits social control through appeal to an available divine power; alternatively it may be simply the "gold and silver" that evoke the lust of Israel, without reference to the religious potency of the image. Perhaps a distinction cannot be made between the two, for both—precious metal and religious icon—drive Israel away from the simplicities of the Yahwistic covenant. (See the narrative of disaster in Josh 7, especially 7:21. "Coveting" is wanting something that lies outside the range of permissible covenantal attractions.) The final verses of Deut 7 employ some of the most abrasive language in the entire tradition:

"abhorrent thing" = abomination,
"utterly detest"—an emphatic verbal form,
"abhor"—the same term as "abhorrent thing," here also an emphatic form
"destruction"—finally, again *herem*.

This cluster of terms states in the strongest language imaginable that Israel is to stay clear of that which will destroy Israel. Israel, as a theological-social experiment in the world, can be eliminated from the world. This need not signify that every living Israelite would be killed, but may perhaps mean living as a covenantal community with an intentional social ethic rooted in holiness may become impossible if there are not those who can withstand the pressures and seductions of the surrounding society.

Theological and Ethical Analysis

This chapter contains one of the most magnificent affirmations of YHWH's intense and intimate covenantal love for Israel, rooting that relationship in nothing other than YHWH's readiness to commit to Israel (vv. 6-15). That affirmation, however, is bracketed by theological mandates that are sure to evoke deep awkwardness for any sensitive theological exposition (vv. 1-5, 16-26).

With verses 6-11 at its center this chapter envisions Israel to be a radically distinctive community that is totally and singularly committed to Torah obedience, without any cultural accommodation. The text knows how urgent and how deeply problematic such a mandate is for a community that must live in the real world that is pervaded with compelling alternative ways of faith. The distinctiveness of this community, moreover, is not in the establishment of doctrine, but in actual, concrete practice in the world.

Such a mandate for the community of faith calls to mind all "communities under discipline"—among Jews the Orthodox, among Christians such "sects" as the Amish or the "Peace Churches." Those who choose, against such "sectarian" self-consciousness, to "live faith in the world" are inclined to view such self-conscious communities as odd, embarrassing, and perhaps pathetic. If, however, one thinks of "contrast communities" as those under a different obedience that concerns every aspect of life, then it is impossible to dismiss such disciplines without being aware of how compromised other forms of faith may become (Willimon and Hauerwas 1989). In any case Deuteronomy offers one articulation of the urgency of distinctiveness that is rooted in YHWH's generosity and that lives by demanding obedience. The text invites reconsideration of the disciplines that belong to a community of serious covenant.

The rhetoric in verses 1-5, 16-26 (and most especially v. 26) suggests the massive if elemental anxiety evoked when a community worries about the loss of its children to the faith. It may be that every generation worries about such a loss, when the children are drawn in new directions and old forms of faith no longer seem credible to them. It is perhaps the experience of every immigrant community when the second and third generations grow away from old patterns and habits of faith. There are many who discern that established culture in the West and with it its church culture face a time of sharp transition and discontinuity, a prosect that makes church communities candidates for deep anxiety. This chapter may provide a way to think about such anxiety, for in our time as in that time, what may be afoot is not simply rejection of certain "forms" of faith, but a nullification of the most basic assumptions of faith about life in the world.

Anxiety causes human communities, including religious communities, to do strange, brutalizing things. Anxiety characteristically makes a community defensive toward any outsider, and reductionist toward any "other" who is unlike "us" (Douglas 1970). The practice of *herem* may be understood mythically (with Stern) as the purgation of the threat of chaos, and the implementation of the first commandment in all its fierceness, then explained historically as an anachronism. Given all of that, *herem* or any lesser form of such exclusionary brutality toward the "other" is a recipe for and justification of violence that is nearly beyond utterance . . . and all in the name of the holy God. This text and the others that entertain a memory of *herem* invite critical reflection upon the ways in which *absolute faith claims* bring with them incipient *violence* (Schwartz 1997). However the rhetoric may be explained, it is loaded with extreme visions of ferocity, all justified as a response to the love of God. Absolute certitude requires the elimination of the "other," whose very existence is always an awkward note of protest against absoluteness.

The issue is problematic whenever faith is practiced in a community that is not completely homogeneous. The contemporary reality of religious "pluralism" tells against any ferocious absolutism. The Deuteronomic strand of the Old Testament is of little help in that regard. It does represent a warning against faith communities that constantly accommodate cultural claims and have little sense of any peculiar identity or ethic. Whether this tradition with its harshness is a resource or a temptation may well depend on whether the interpreting community faces primarily a crisis of

excessive exclusiveness or a crisis of *excessive accommodation.*
Both questions must remain in the purview of a serious community of faith, but Deuteronomic faces only one of these crises.

Finally it is worthwhile returning to the ways in which "alien
images" vex the tradition of Deuteronomy. Every Reform movement from Gideon (Judg 6:28-32) and Josiah (2 Kgs 23:4-20) to
the sixteenth-century Reformation and Cromwell's revolutionary
movement has felt compelled to destroy religious symbols that
detract from faith and that legitimize unacceptable forms of
power. The destruction, moreover, is accomplished with a violence
legitimated by theological passion.

This text has a peculiar point of contact with the current "com-
munications revolution" sweeping the Western world, with particular reference to children's access to the Internet. There is no
doubt that the Internet, with its accompanying ideology of unrestrained freedom, now gives children exposure in the most graphic possible ways to degrading images concerning sex, violence, and
every other form of distorted and cheapened human interaction.
These icons, moreover, are exceedingly well financed in a direct
challenge to traditional and long-standing notions of what constitutes viable human community. The shrill attacks currently being
made upon "the media" and "Hollywood" evidence the profound
anxiety that is widely felt in our culture, matched by a deep sense
of helplessness.

One does not need to be a right-wing fanatic or an extremist
reliant upon a mantra like "family values" in order to see that the
new iconography is a sustained threat to the values of humanness
that are rooted in the conventional neighborly virtues of honesty,
dignity, respect, justice, and compassion. This iconography, moreover, is available to children who lack any sustained point of reference or critical capacity to sort out what is to be taken seriously and what is to be dismissed as distorting absurdity. The alien
quality of the images now available everywhere evokes anxious,
nearly hysterical rhetoric and a kind of sectarian propensity to
create "safe places"—Christian schools for example—in which
the young can be nurtured according to a symbol system that witnesses to human qualities of another kind.

There is a remarkable parallel between our current crisis and this ancient text. The current crisis may help modern readers to understand the felt urgency in the text. It takes no great imagination to conjure a parent in that ancient community using the extreme rejectionist rhetoric of verses 25-26 in order to warn against "bringing into the house" such alien symbols. It is not clear that current zealots have understood ideologically what is at stake concerning the contemporary programmatic destruction of a humane social fabric, but the felt threat is sufficient to see the point. In addition to a ban on such icons, Deuteronomy sponsors nurturing children by saturating them with narrative that tells a powerful alternative to the narrative implied in the seductive icons (6:6-9, 20-24). Such a community under threat never knows whether its efforts with the children will succeed. In Deuteronomy, it surely is not for want of trying.

FAITH AS ALTERNATIVE TO COMPLACENCY AS ALTERNATIVE TO DEPRIVATION (8:1-20)

This chapter, a continuing speech of Moses, has important affinities with chapter 6. For that reason, one may assume here, as in chapter 6, that the text is anxious about the next generation of children (see 6:2, 7-9, 20-24), who may in their new security forget the defining narrative of rescue and the God who dominates that defining narrative. The present chapter begins with a restatement of the core assumption of Deuteronomy (v. 1). It then juxtaposes two circumstances of faith that constitute the central drama of the chapter (vv. 2-5, 6-10). The long concluding paragraph of the chapter moves from the scenario of verses 6-10 to issue a stern warning about the consequences of forgetting (vv. 11-20). Thus the chapter is dominated by the *threat of forgetting* and the *urgency of remembering*.

Exegetical Analysis

8:1-6: The chapter opens, yet again, with a bid for obedience to the entire command of Moses, that is, the whole corpus of statutes and ordinances soon to be promulgated (v. 1). The accent on "all" of the commandment suggests that of the many specific and detailed commands to be enunciated in what follows, not one is negotiable or secondary; every part of the corpus is a life-or-death issue, perhaps on the assumption that if a community reluctant to obey begins to pick, choose, and rank commandments, very soon the submissiveness of obedience will collapse in an exercise of assertive autonomy.

The "so that" that provides the hinge of the thesis verse is the same as that used in 6:21. Obedience has consequences, as does disobedience. The linkage between *obedience* and *consequence* is definitional to all Torah teaching and particularly to the traditions of Deuteronomy (Koch 1983). The two are connected in Yahwism by the conviction that it is YHWH who presides over the process of covenant sanctions. But to the extent that Deuteronomy is informed by wisdom teaching, there is also a pragmatic, common-sense awareness that certain acts produce certain consequences in a quasi-"automatic" way, that is, "automatic" given YHWH's governance and purposes (Weinfeld 1972).

The consequence anticipated in verse 1 (in contrast to that of vv. 19-20) is entirely positive. To "go in and occupy" the land here does not refer simply to an initial entry, but refers to long-term retention and enjoyment of the land in a peaceable, prosperous state. The purpose of the imperative is that Israel "live and increase" over the long haul; to prosper so that family, property, livestock, and all the measures of agricultural wealth can grow. It is surely important that the phrase "live and multiply" echoes the initial blessing pronounced over human and nonhuman creation (Gen 1:22, 28). This is "creation theology"; Deuteronomy anticipates that a land rightly ordered by Torah will become fruitful, blessed by the *shalom* anticipated already in the doxologies of creation.

8:7-10: The verses that follow explicate the decision to which Israel is summoned. The explication proceeds by placing in juxtaposition two scenarios of Israel's life with YHWH. The force of the argument depends upon the juxtaposition between *the remembered scenario of wilderness* (vv. 2-5) and the *anticipated* *scenario of the good land* (vv. 6-10). In the first scenario Israel is addressed by an initial "remember," an imperative that is important to the community threatened by amnesia. Thus even the imperative asserts that there was a time other than this time. The community, moreover, will learn something important about *this time* by remembering *another time.*

The "other time" so crucial for the present generation seems remote. But it is not. That time—narrated in Exod 16–18; Num 10–36; Deut 1–3—is immediately germane to the present. The "sojourn tradition" is all about the difficult learning that Israel is totally dependent upon YHWH. The testing of Israel took forty years. The process was twofold. First, Israel was humbled and tested. Israel was reduced to extreme vulnerability and total dependence by being placed in a circumstance where none of its own resources was adequate. It had not been able to carry with it enough bread for the journey. The humbling is to permit Israel to recognize that it was not self-sufficient, could not manage its own way, and therefore could not pretend that it was in charge of its own life. The wilderness memory is one of vulnerable dependence, the shattering of all illusions of adequacy. The series of verbs that accomplished this awareness—"humble, test, know"—culminates in verse 3 with "caused you to be hungry."

The second step was that in the wilderness of hunger, "manna" is given when Israel no longer had any bread of its own. The memory appeals to the narrative of Exod 16:14-15. In contrast to the "bread of affliction" supplied by Pharoah, the gift of manna was bread they had never seen, could not explain, and were to never possess. The creator God is fully and readily capable of transforming wilderness into a place of wondrous sufficiency. After Israel learned of *its own dreadful inadequacy,* it promptly learned of *YHWH's generous adequacy.* This is the creator God who can turn chaos into creation, and inadequacy into superabundance. The generous capacity of YHWH is more than commensurate with the needful vulnerability of Israel. The interface of *generosity and vulnerability* as a mark of this relationship is a durable learning from wilderness.

The learning extracted in this speech of Moses from that

ancient drama of vulnerability and generosity is that "bread" is not sufficient for life, but life is in "the word from YHWH's own mouth" (v. 3). That contrast of *bread* and *word* is open to a variety of readings, including a warning against materialism that will not yield life without the word of the gospel. If, however, we permit the gospel narrative to illuminate our text (see Matt 4:4; Luke 4:4), then perhaps the contrast is not "material/spiritual." Rather "bread" may be understood as "autonomous bread," the produce of one's own life whereby one secures one's own existence (on which see Luke 12:18-19). By contrast, "every word that comes from the mouth of the Lord" may refer to the *decree* of the sovereign who wills and declares that bread shall be given, but given from God's own storehouse of food. That is, what proceeds from YHWH's own mouth is a word of decree that produces bread as gift. Thus the contrast is between two kinds of bread, *self-generated bread* that produces autonomy and *gift-bread* that invites gratitude and reliance upon YHWH.

What Israel learned in this moment of free bread is that YHWH is reliable and generous; Israel will be cared for and safe in every circumstance. The adequacy of YHWH evidenced in the bread is re-enforced by verse 4. Forty years of trekking is a long time! In that time, one may rightly expect clothes to become tattered and feet to become sore. But it did not happen, because the wilderness is not what it seemed to be. It seemed to be a resourceless, "anti-life" place. It was, however, a place of safety, and well-being, because it was a place over which YHWH presides. Moses' speech now makes an appeal on the basis of the astonishing memory of generous sustenance (vv. 5-6). The relationship between *Torah-giver* and *people of obedience* is not an adversarial relationship in which Israel is coerced into obedience. It is rather a relationship between a *caring parent* and a *grateful child* (see Exod 4:22; Hos 11:1). The term "discipline" *(yāsar)* does not bespeak harshness, but rather attentive nurture and guidance in order to protect the child from injury. The imagery of parent-child seeks to put the Mosaic summons to obedience on a different basis. There is an affinity between the two parties in which trustful gratitude is appropriate and natural.

The imagery is paralleled in Ps 103:13-14, though in different words:

> As a father has compassion for his children,
>   so the LORD has compassion for those who fear him.
> For he knows how we were made;
>   he remembers that we are dust.

The parent knows of the vulnerability of the child and of the child's limited resources. The parent, moreover, wills good and gives good gifts to the child (see Matt 7:9-11). For that reason, the imperatives to "keep, walk, and fear" in verse 6 are an appeal for a response in kind, obedience to Torah which is glad gratitude to the parent, whose knowledge and goodwill are demonstrated by the gift of bread. The wilderness that could have been a profound trauma for Israel is here presented as a place of deep caring and well-being.

The speech of Moses now moves to a second, quite different scenario of Israel in a place with YHWH (vv. 7-10). Israel's different response to YHWH is anticipated, as the new generation waits at the boundary of the Jordan to enter the land. The characterization of the land in these verses sounds like the hyperbolic imagination of those long without land who anticipate in the most overstated ways the idyllic quality of the new situation. (It is the same hyperbolic imagination in Christian tradition that imagines "the next world" in the most wondrous way.) After all, as the tradition tells us, Israel has been waiting for this moment of land occupation at least since the Exodus or even since Abraham and Sarah.

The characterization of the land—different from that of 6:10-11, but with the same rhetorical intent—is framed in verses 7 and 10 with the phrase "good land," on which see Exod 3:8. Between these two markers, the term "land" is used five times. This land offers everything of abundance and prosperity not available in the wilderness about which such a disadvantaged community might dream. After the arid territory, where Israel depended upon water from rock (Exod 17:1-7), this will be a land of abundant water (see v. 7; Ps 104:10-12). The rhetoric of water—streams,

springs, deeps—speaks an abundance of water, water everywhere, ample, overwhelming! A result of such water is luxuriant
growth, vegetation, and crops in superabundance (v. 8). And
now, again, bread (v. 9)! This is not bread for which Israel must
wait upon a miracle. This is bread that is at hand and in hand, a
regular supply. When Israel crosses the Jordan, Joshua will immediately observe that in the land Israel need not wait for manna
(Josh 5:12).

The bread—the outcome of wheat that is on time, the result of
ample water—will be more than enough. Israel will be sated and
without anxiety about food. This reference to bread supports the
suggestion that the issue in verse 3 is not bread versus word, but
it is a different kind of bread, a bread not possessed by Israel but
given by YHWH. The promise is about bread. There will be so
much bread that Israel in the land of abundance will "not lack."
The term is the same as the familiar phrase of Ps 23:1. YHWH
gives amply and Israel has no unmet desire. Beyond the produce
of the land, moreover, Israel also knows about "mineral rights."
There will be enough iron and copper for wealth and stability.
Israel will have the resources to be a formidable power backed by
a growth economy!

This anticipated land is the fulfillment of a dream for Israel.
More than that, it is the fruition of the lyric of creation: all will
"be fruitful" and Israel will be the glad recipient and beneficiary
of the abundance willed from the beginning (Gen 1:22). The culmination of the anticipation is that Israel will *eat,* a contrast to the
hunger of verse 3: no more hunger! Israel will be fully *satiated.*
Indeed eating and satiation are not all. The third verb of verse 10
is that Israel will *bless YHWH.* Israel will know and acknowledge
that it is the creator God who has given all this, who has kept
promises, who must be praised and magnified. The expectation of
Moses is that the anticipated place of well-being will evoke in
Israel unguarded, unrestrained gladness in which it holds nothing
back, but cedes itself willingly to the faithful God out of whose
decree has come the abundant life.

Moses has sketched two contrasting scenes, one of remembered
wilderness scarcity, the other of anticipated *abundant land* that is

anticipated. The two scenes are so different. And yet, in the imagination of Moses and in the purview of YHWH, *wilderness* and *good land* are exactly the same. Both are presided over by the faithful God, both are arenas where life is amply guaranteed, both are wonders designed to evoke trust in and gratitude to YHWH. The point of it all is that in both circumstances, in every circumstance, YHWH gives what is needed and Israel responds in glad obedience.

Everything is the same in the two circumstances; except that Moses and the tradition are too discerning to be sanguine about the parallel. The anxiety behind this speech of Moses is that the two circumstances and the two great acts of generosity by YHWH will not produce the same glad response of obedient gratitude. The tradition knows better than that. Gifts given to the vulnerable do indeed evoke gratitude. The crisis reflected in the text—and in Israel's lived reality in the land—is that gifts given in abundance to the satiated do not finally eventuate in trusting gratitude but in complacent self-congratulations. A gift kept long enough begins to seem like a possession. A gift kept long enough becomes separated in the memory of the recipient from the giver, so that the giver is forgotten.

8:11-20: Thus read covenantally, wilderness and good land are parallel and should evoke the same glad obedience. In reality, however, *complacency* conjures a different future from that evoked by *vulnerability.* Therefore, this speech that begins by anticipating obedience (vv. 1, 5-6), ends with a harsh, warning against disobedience (vv. 11-20). The cautionary "take care" of verse 11 is the same term as in verse 1, "diligently observe." Complacency breeds amnesia (v. 11). Amnesia in turn leads to autonomy and the negation of obedience. The rhetoric of verse 12 begins as in verse 10, "eat and are sated." But strikingly, the third term "bless YHWH" has dropped out. Reference to the giver of the gift has been scuttled. The rhetorical pattern of verses 12-13 echoes 6:10-11:

full stomachs, fine houses,
multiplied flocks and herds, multiplied silver and gold,
multiplied, multiplied, multiplied!!!

Now, instead of "bless YHWH" as the third term of response, it is "exalt yourself" (v. 14). Self-congratulation is more likely when there is abundance, and the name of the giver is no longer current.

There is high irony in the dire expectations of this warning from Moses. It is the very gifts of YHWH that will cause the forgetting of YHWH. The YHWH who will be forgotten is the YHWH that the tradition endlessly remembers and teaches. The YHWH remembered, in a reference back to the scenario of verses 2-5, is the God of Exodus emancipation, the God of wilderness protection and guidance. The God to be remembered—and now forgotten—is the one who protected Israel from the threat of snakes and scorpions (see Ps 91:11-13), who gave water from the rock (Exod 17:1-7), and who gave strange bread in the wilderness (Exod 16:15). Again one finds the terms from verse 2, "humble and test," but to the end to do "good" (v. 16). The speech reiterates the narrative memory of vulnerability and dependence from verses 2-4.

In the very reiteration of that memory, however, the speaker knows that the memory is in jeopardy. Gifts without givers become property and occasions for self-enhancement. Thus it is anticipated that the very Israel who has been incapable of doing anything to sustain itself will soon imagine that its own power— and not the limitless power of YHWH—has given this circumstance of satiation.

The expected illusion grounded in amnesia leads, finally, to a most severe warning. Following after other gods instead of YHWH—the gods of production and consumption, the gods of illusion who come without Torah imperatives—will lead to death. Israel has before it the evidence of the failed peoples that it displaced, displaced at YHWH's behest (see 9:5). And now Israel, so recently celebrated as YHWH's special people (7:6-10), is to be classified not as special, but like all the others, failed and destroyed. And all because Israel did not *listen,* did not acknowledge its contingent status; by refusing to listen, Israel imagined it was not addressed but was autonomous. Autonomy produces death, because the self-sufficient think they live without limit, without accountability. That illusion in the long run is not sustainable.

Theological and Ethical Analysis

The argument of this speech is simple: obedience makes public life possible; autonomy leads to ruin. This simple, straightforward insistence is shrewdly articulated by a reentry into ancient memory that permits a juxtaposition of then and now. Such a juxtaposition that champions the truth of *what was* against the illusion of *what is,* is congruent with every parental generation that worries about the children:

1. Immigrant communities who have, through great hardship, come to the United States are anguished when a later generation no longer remembers the hardship and the risks of emigration, and only sees what is present now, minus the risks of the past that have made the present circumstance possible.

2. Parents of the "depression era" whose livelihood and savings were so hard-won have anxiety about children who have no memory of "hard times," but who live carelessly on credit without imagining that there are limits and costs.

3. Parents in minority communities who can remember the dangers of the civil rights movement and the high costs paid for a modicum of equality grow anxious when the young do not remember, and live in an affluent indifference, unconcerned about the needs or entitlements of those left behind.

4. In the culture of the United States there is the rank indifference of the affluent young who swim in a bottomless ocean of goods, entertainment, and indulgence, all with amnesia.

Indeed one could imagine Moses with his uncompromising "take heed" speaking to any of these self-congratulatory situations. The tradition knows that in the land of affluence one finally depends upon gifts as much as did the mothers and fathers in an earlier environment of vulnerability.

It is important to notice in passing that this "creation theology" articulated in Torah categories is not simply the stringent harping of an ancient theological tradition. Rather the "wisdom" of this tradition has belatedly been reiterated in the contemporary environmental movement and in the most discerning advocates of wise land management and land usage. Wendell Berry (1981, 1993), for example, has shown repeatedly that land that is cared for and managed covenantally is inexhaustible in its productive capacity. Conversely, land that is used exploitatively (that is, disobediently), as though it is simply a usable commodity from which to extract gain, is eventually exhausted and incapable of productivity. Exploited land becomes land under curse. Isaiah 5:8-10 is a lyrical expression of land handled acquisitively (disobediently) that eventually will be cursed. All of this is implicit in the initial imperative of verse 1 of the present chapter. The land is a gift of YHWH's promise, but it is a promise from Genesis that is securely defined by Torah. Of course one might conclude about this chapter or about any cautionary lesson from it that it is only the voice of cranky parental displeasure that functions as a killjoy of present self-affirmation and exuberance. Of course one could!

• Except that Israel's lived life that culminated in the land loss of 587 BCE stands as a vindication for the Mosaic scenario of "perishing."

• Except that in the twentieth century the autonomous, self-congratulatory regimes of apartheid in South Africa and the Soviet Union abruptly and almost inexplicably perished. These dramatic acts of perishing bear witness—for those who read discerningly through Torah—that there are not enough tanks or dogs or computers to fend off the inexorable patient, not always visible claims of Torah.

• Except that in Western culture in general and the United States in particular, there is growing evidence that the autonomy, economically termed "privatization" with the forfeiture of what is "public" is leading to violence and the thinning of the quality of human life. Reading through this Torah utterance, one can see how complacency breeds amnesia and amnesia sponsors self-sufficiency while humanity perishes in an illusion. The text may give one pause even in such a belated context as ours. For Moses and the Deuteronomists, the reality given in the text is more than a meditative pause. It is an occasion for repentance, for a new decision. The choice is so stark: Listen or die!

The stern warning of verses 11-20 has moved rapidly past the caring parental figure presented in verses 4-5. In those earlier verses, the Parent was an attentive giver (see 1:31). But the God of Israel readily appears in more than one role. One may imagine, given the alienation anticipated by Moses in our chapter, that the mood of the erstwhile parent changes:

    1. This could be a parent committed to the child (Hos 11:1-4), but so appalled by the child's sin as to be ready to abandon the child (vv. 5-7), then finally and with pats unable to punish (vv. 8-9).
    2. This could be a parent who had hoped "You would call me 'My Father'," and now is stunned in rejection (Jer 3:19-20).
    3. This could be mother Rachel weeping, refusing to be comforted because the beloved child has perished (Jer 31:15; see Matt 2:17-18).
    4. Or it could be the one who comes in the flesh to weep, because the people did not recognize "the things that make for peace" (Luke 19:41).

There could be such painful, saving pathos from this parent who disciplines the beloved child (Heschel 1962:221-278). All of that, however, comes later in the context-evoking imagination of Israel. Here there is only severe warning and a powerful bit of remembering. It is never known ahead of time if those who forget can reengage the memory in time. That is, of course, Moses' hope, his insistence, and his rhetorical strategy.

ISRAEL RECONSTITUTED BY PRAYER AND GENEROSITY (9:1–10:11)

This extended speech engages in a long retrospective reflection on Israel's sorry relationship with YHWH, in order to make a point to the present generation being addressed. That retrospective appears to be framed by imperatives in 9:1 and 10:11 that enjoin *obedient* ("hear") *entry* ("get up, go") to the land of promise. The bracketing imperatives of obedient entry as a present appeal contrast completely with the retrospective of recalcitrant disobedience. The retrospective, moreover, is shaped to contrast *the failure of Israel* in the past and the decisive *work of Moses* in giving a future with YHWH to this people that deserved no future at all.

9:1-14: The initial imperative of 9:1 appeals to the central theological claim of Deuteronomy. To "hear" means to submit the entire life of Israel to YHWH in glad dependence and willing obedience. It is only glad dependence and willing obedience that constitute the necessary condition for land entry. Thus the imperative bespeaks trust, confidence, and obedient attentiveness to YHWH as the sole condition for success in the land, without any reference to wealth, power, or arms (see Josh 1:6-9).

The retrospective to support the imperative begins immediately in verse 2. As it ponders this new land entry, Israel is invited to recall the ancient "giants," Anakim, who had appeared to be formidable, but in fact had been readily defeated by YHWH (see 1:10, 21). In this presentation, the speech of Moses treats the Anakim as a current problem, and does not acknowledge that this is a reference to the past. It is clear nonetheless that appeal is made to an older tradition, on which see also 2:10-21. YHWH is already known in Israel as one capable against any adversary. In 4:24, YHWH is portrayed as a "devouring fire" who will destroy recalcitrant Israel. Here, however, YHWH as "devouring fire" will turn destructiveness toward the "strong and tall people," enemies of Israel, who now occupy the land (v. 3). Israel needs do nothing to secure the land, except listen! YHWH will do all else. The land will be the completely free gift of YHWH to Israel.

That of course raises a crucial question in Israel concerning the motivation for YHWH's risky generosity to Israel. The question implied in verse 4, "why?" is a parallel to 7:7. In both cases, Israel sought to explain its special status and circumstance in terms of some virtue or claim of its own. In 7:7, the proposed explanation is that Israel is "more numerous," but it is an explanation quickly rejected. Here the proposed explanation is that Israel is "righteous," also an explanation promptly rejected. In verses 4-5, the narrative is not really interested in Israel's professed righteousness and does not refute the claim, only insisting that YHWH has other motivations. The reason for Israel's reception of the land is that the occupying peoples have been "wicked." It is as though Israel receives the land by default, as the people not declared to be "wicked," as are all the others.

This explanation for the elimination and expulsion of other peoples from the land is remarkable, for it suggests that in a non-negotiable way—a way not known to them—the other nations are also accountable to YHWH and have failed to be responsive to YHWH. This peculiar condemnation is not pursued, but it raises important issues about YHWH's relationship with other nations (see also positively 2:1-23), and eventually raises issues of "natural law," that is, the will of God known in creation outside Israel's Torah (Barton 1979). In these particular verses the explanation treats Israel as YHWH's afterthought (an important afterthought, to be sure), related to the Genesis promises of the land.

The statement of verses 4-5 takes no trouble to deny Israel's righteousness, but only declares it to be irrelevant to the case. That of course leaves open the thought that Israel may indeed be righteous, even if here such righteousness does not count for anything. That interpretation of verses 4-5 is quickly vetoed in verses 6-13, verses framed in verses 6 and 13 by the assertion that Israel is a "stubborn people." The phrase means "stiff-necked," that is, not easily led, not readily submissive, not obedient. The phrase "stubborn people" is thus the antithesis of "righteous." The latter term, a major accent of Israel's covenantal theology, is a juridical term meaning "innocent" as "wicked" is to be understood as "guilty." The ground for the verdict of "guilty" and not "innocent" concerns a lived, practiced communal life that is or is not congruent with YHWH's own character, will, and purpose. While Israel's imagined "innocence" is surely irrelevant to the question at hand in verses 4-5, in verse 6 it is declared to be an illusion.

Thus Israel's good fortune in receiving the land because the other nations are "guilty" does not substantiate Israel's claim of innocence. The text does not pursue the relative gravity of the "wickedness" of the others and the "stubbornness" of Israel, for it is an issue that does not relate to the major point here.

Before the point of accent in this speech, however, verses 6-14 are offered in evidence that Israel has been rebellious against YHWH since its very inception. The entire history of Israel, already beginning at Sinai, has been a refusal of glad dependence and willing obedience. (The tone of these verses is not unlike Ps 106 that casts the entire tradition of Israel as a tradition of rebellion against YHWH.)

The stubbornness of Israel has predictably and legitimately evoked the wrath of YHWH. The sum of this argument is given in verse 7, "from the day you came out of the land of Egypt until you came to this place" (see Jer 3:25). The wilderness is first named as an arena for rebelliousness (v. 7). It is, however, Sinai that receives top billing as a place of disobedience, with particular reference to the narrative of Exod 32. The event of Exod 32 is defining for Israel. The narrative, moreover, is deeply ironic, for Sinai as *the place of covenant* becomes *the place of rebellion*. Verses 8-13 retell the story line of Exod 32 in careful detail. It is Moses' absence while he is on the mountain plus YHWH's lack of an image that evoke the crisis of the golden calf. The felt need Israel has for an image is in sharp contrast to the imageless character of YHWH as affirmed in the second commandment (5:8-10; see 4:15-20). This defining mark of YHWH is disregarded at Sinai, in the absence of Moses, by the leadership of Aaron who generates an "image." (There are all sorts of interesting religious questions related to this remembered narrative, e.g., the particular significance of the calf and the special role of Aaron in representing a strand of priestly history. None of that, however, is germane to the present text and the point being made about Israel's stubbornness.) Israel refused to accept YHWH on YHWH's own terms and distorted YHWH to make YHWH more compatible to its own needs. It is the distortion of YHWH that is at issue in Aaron's act. Beyond that distortion, moreover, is the mistaken notion that

Israel holds initiative over YHWH and can have YHWH on its own terms.

The response of YHWH to Israel's elemental disobedience is simple and, for Israel, devastating. This people designed for a peculiar life with YHWH has so offended YHWH that YHWH is ready to "blot out" Israel, to terminate the bold experiment that was Israel (v. 14). This simple, logical end to a failed covenantal experiment seems the most plausible outcome of Israel's stubbornness; and so the tradition wants us to suppose. There is, however, a single mitigating factor that turns out to be decisive, that averts the termination of Israel.

That mitigating factor is Moses, the one authorized to be a mediator (5:22-33), who now makes the continuation of Israel possible. As Moses tells it in this speech, even YHWH recognizes that Moses is a check on God's disposal of Israel. Thus in verse 14, alluding to Exod 32:10, YHWH asks Moses to "ease up, relax," in order that YHWH may be free to act in the vigorously negative way toward Israel that is YHWH's determined intention. It is as though YHWH is not free to destroy Israel as long as Moses is vigilantly present. That is, Moses' presence is a decisive check upon YHWH's predisposition. It is Moses who saves Israel from the legitimate wrath of YHWH.

9:14-24: Thus the *rebellion of Israel* and the *wrath of YHWH* are reconfigured by the decisive and courageous *role of Moses*. In verses 14-21, the speech of Moses focuses on the role of Moses as the one who makes the future of Israel possible. Again there is a detailed retelling of Exod 32. While Moses has checked YHWH's wrath in verse 14, by verse 16 Moses has now seen the "corruption" that YHWH had already seen. Now Moses shares YHWH's dismay over the disobedience of Israel. The role of Moses from this point on does nothing at all to soften the rash condemnation of Israel. If anything, that condemnation is intensified by the dramatic act of smashing the tablets of Torah, thereby witnessing that the covenant of Sinai is terminated and Israel's life with YHWH is over.

The report on the action of Moses continues in verse 18. Moses is not finished when he has expressed his wrath commensurate with the wrath of YHWH and when he has smashed the tablets in a gesture of termination. This surely is the marvel of this narrative: Moses *fasts* and Moses *prays* (see Mark 9:29). He positions himself as mediator between this people that deserves termination and this God bent on termination. Moses does not know the outcome of his intercession; he is "afraid" of what YHWH may do to Israel, afraid even as he prays. The intercessory prayer of Moses is no pleasant psychological transaction, no soft meditation on possible futures for Israel. It is rather a life-or-death engagement with YHWH, to see whether YHWH can be turned, whether the God of wrath who is "devouring fire" can be turned to mercy and forgiveness (see 4:29-31). Moses puts himself at risk, and is able to report to Israel in its jeopardy, "but YHWH listened to me."

Just as "righteousness" and "wickedness" are juridical terms so this "intercession" of Moses is a juridical act. Moses files a petition with the judge to see if he can provide the judge reason for ruling on behalf of Israel in face of overwhelming evidence. It is YHWH's readiness to listen to Moses that makes a future for Israel possible. The obliteration of the calf (v. 21) and the destruction of the tablets (v. 17) together indicate that nothing old will be brought to the new resolve for covenant. This movement of prayer and answer is a null point in the relationship of YHWH and Israel. If there is to be anything between these two parties, it will perforce be given now, all new, without appeal to the false assurances of the old calf, without appeal to the old offer of covenant tablets—all new.

The themes of *recalcitrance* and *intercession* are woven together in verses 22-29 in a way that exposits the crisis of Exod 32. In verses 22-24, the speech of Moses returns to the general thesis of verse 7: "You provoked the LORD your God to wrath in the wilderness." Four cases of provocation are cited:

1. Taberah. In Num 11:1-3, Israel complained against YHWH, an act that greatly irritated YHWH, for the complaint is here reckoned as an act of faithlessness. In response, YHWH's fire burned out parts of the camp. The place name *Taberah* is derived from the Hebrew term "burn" *(bā^car)*. The brief episode suggests extreme recalcitrance and alienation.

2. Massah. This narrative episode in Exod 17:1-7 (see also Num 20:1-13), already cited in 6:16, again suggests that complaints against YHWH are reckoned to be acts of unfaith, bespeaking Israel's unwillingness to trust. The outcome of this complaint, however, is spectacularly different from that of Num 11:1-3. In the account in Numbers, the complaint evoked destruction from YHWH, while at Massah the complaint evoked miraculous water by the action of Moses.

3. Kibrothhattaavah. This place name, derived from the narrative of Num 11:31-35, is "Graves of Craving." The narrative concerns YHWH's gift of quail and Israel's eager collection of the quail. The narrative is laconic and explains nothing; it seems to suggest that Israel's overeager desire for meat evoked the deadly wrath of YHWH, so that the graves of the dead are caused by craving. The craving in turn suggests that Israel, in its self-serving restlessness, was unwilling to rely upon the gift of YHWH that made such craving both unnecessary and inappropriate.

4. Kadesh-Barnea. Deuteronomy 1:19-32 has already stressed that Israel at the oasis was fearful and lacking in trust in YHWH, and thereby refused YHWH's authorization to take the land.

The four references together are a highly selective reading from the wilderness memory of Israel. Based upon these citations, the present text draws the conclusion: You have not *trusted;* you have not *listened.* The first of these terms echoes the judgment of 1:32 and the second picks up the central imperative of Deuteronomy as in 6:4. In sum, Israel has refused the life that YHWH would give it. In the logic of this tradition, Israel merits rejection and destruction. The entire memory of Israel, as given here, leads inexorably to this conclusion.

9:25-29: This inescapable conclusion is overridden only by the countertheme of Moses' intervention (9:25-29). Moses' self-characterization appeals to the intercessory tradition of Exod 32:11-13 and Num 14:13-19. It is this prayer in Exod 32 that stemmed YHWH's resolve to terminate Israel. The prayer as given us in Deuteronomy 9 is a clear, carefully structured theological statement in four parts:

1. Verse 26 is the petition in which Moses vigorously addresses YHWH in an imperative and seeks to reverse the divine resolve.

2. Verse 27 willingly acknowledges that Israel is a "stubborn people." Thus Moses admits that YHWH's wrath is fully merited and does not dispute the legitimacy of YHWH's resolve to destroy. That acknowledgment, however, is to serve the petitionary appeal to the promise to the ancestors. Moses intends that the promise should override the stubbornness, an override that is Israel's only chance.

3. Moses offers to YHWH a motivation in addition to the ancient promise (v. 28). He appeals to YHWH's concern for YHWH's own reputation, an appeal that makes powerful sense in a "shame society." YHWH does not want to be shamed in the eyes of the watching nations (on which see also Ezek 36:22-33). In the earlier text of Exod 32:12, the presumed Egyptian construal of YHWH's proposed judgment against Israel is that YHWH had an evil intent in the first place, that is, YHWH is not *faithful*. This petition, however, offers a different verdict by the watching nations, more in line with Num 14:16, "not able," that is, YHWH is not *powerful*. Either verdict, not *faithful* or not *powerful*, would be an unbearable scandal to YHWH. Here the appeal concerns the power of YHWH.

4. Finally, after an appeal to a public, external motivation, Moses appeals to a more intimate matter that is internal to the covenantal relationship of YHWH with Israel and has nothing to do with the watching nations. Thus Israel is YHWH's special *inheritance*, most treasured, most intimate, personal possession, not to be lightly cast off. The rhetoric is somewhat different, but the sense of the argument recalls the powerful verb of 7:7 and 10:15, "set his heart." YHWH has an emotional attach-

ment to Israel, like a peasant may have to a particular plot of land (see 1 Kgs 21 on Naboth's inheritance). The inheritance cannot be sloughed off lightly, for its loss personally diminishes the owner. It is as though YHWH, in a fit of rage, had forgotten YHWH's own deep personal commitment, of which Moses must now issue a reminder.

The intercessory activity of Moses is an act of daring, already evident in Exod 32 and Num 14. If YHWH is an absolute ruler, then it ill-behooves any member of the divine court to intervene, to talk the absolute ruler out of an intended act of rage. Such an intervention might extend the rage to the intervener. Moses intervenes nonetheless. He sets his own appeal to YHWH in verses 14-21, 25-29 against the undisputed data of verses 6-13, 22-24. According to that data, YHWH's resolve to terminate Israel is legitimate. It is by going behind such *public data* to the *internal life of covenant* and to the most *intimate affections* of YHWH that Moses makes appeal.

10:1-11: There is no doubt that chapter 10 continues this narrative. It is worth noticing that at the end of chapter 9 the outcome of Moses' intervention is still undisclosed. It is not yet clear if YHWH's legitimate wrath can be curbed, whether the data of provocation and rebellion on the part of Israel can be overcome. It is this dangerous moment of not knowing to which this rhetoric wants to bring the listening community. In this moment, now, at the Jordan, Israel has no claim upon YHWH and no right to expect anything from YHWH. The lack of trust and obedience on the part of Israel has placed Israel in a situation of acute vulnerability before its God. All that tells against this risk is the authority, courage, and insistence of Moses.

There is a pause between chapters 9 and 10, a pause so that the reader may notice that the two narratives are arranged in point and counterpoint. Chapter 9 is all risk, threat, and danger. In 10:1-11, however, that is past with only an allusion to it in verse 10. Now all is new. It is evident in 10:1-5 that Moses' petition to YHWH in 9:25-29 has been answered affirmatively. There is, however, no explicit acknowledgment of such divine affirmation as has been offered in Exod 34:10 and Num 14:20. Instead Deuteronomy simply tells of YHWH's next act, as YHWH moves on to newness on the basis of Moses' petition. It is unmistakable, but not articulated, that Moses' prayer has made possible a new vista for YHWH's covenant with Israel.

In a tone of administrative decisiveness YHWH proceeds with the renewal of covenant and the making of new tablets of the commandments for the ark. By the conclusion of verse 5, the renewal is complete; the covenant begins again; all is in place. YHWH, in the act of renewal, expresses no doubt, no rage, no allusion to the past. It is as though YHWH's implied response to Moses' prayer has abruptly and completely put all of that away forever. This passage raises three matters that may reflect a development whereby the intensity of a relationship moves toward institutionalization.

1. The tablets contain "the ten words." As recognized in chapter 5, the Decalogue is now a fixed corpus that constitutes the primary requirements of the covenant. Whatever may be the prehistory of the Decalogue, Israel has it in complete form.

2. The commandments are now assigned a place in the ark. This connection suggests some stable institutional form of Torah. The text nicely and with closure observes, "They are there." Everyone knew where they were. One need not make any historical judgment about the Decalogue in the ark, except to notice that in Deut 31:9 the tablets are linked to the ark and in 1 Kgs 8:9, the ark contains the tablets as a part of the temple arrangement. This connection of tablets and ark may reflect nothing more than a deliberate interpretive convergence of several traditions, designed to show that the Decalogue is available—and doable (see 30:11-14).

3. These are "the same words." The new tablets reiterate the old tablets. The disruption of broken covenant has not altered the bases of covenant. This hermeneutical judgment is important if the "new covenant" is offered after the disruption of 587 BCE (In Jer 31:31-34 the Torah commandments are not different in the new covenant, but are only received differently, "written

on your heart." Moreover, the announcement of the new covenant culminates with YHWH's readiness to forget and forgive. The movement from chapter 9 to chapter 10 evidences YHWH doing just that. In the enactment of new covenant in chapter 10, YHWH gives no hint of remembering anything from chapter 9, but is ready to move on. Thus it could be that the fissure between these two chapters is closely paralleled to the announcement of Jer 31:31-34.) The new offer of YHWH to the generation addressed at the Jordan—presumably exiles— is the same offer as at Sinai. It is the sameness of Torah that permitted Moses to declare:

Not with our ancestors did the LORD make this covenant, but with us, who are all of us here alive today. (5:3)

In 10:6-9, the presentation of Moses again appeals to the wilderness tradition, with reference to Num 33:31-39. The sequence of the text—Beeroth-Bene-jaakan-Moserah-Gudgodah-Jotbathah—parallels the itinerary in Numbers with a variation in the sequence and with Gudgodah in the Deuteronomic text reckoned as an equivalent for Horhaggidgad in the Numbers text. The variations are not important for our purposes. It is plausible that this material is reported in order to acknowledge the transmission of the priesthood from Aaron to Eleazar, perhaps to create an opening for the recognition of the house of Levi in verse 8 (on which see Exod 32:25-29). In any case, in this portion of the sojourn tradition, there is none of the recalcitrance or abrasion seen in 9:6-13. This sojourn is of a people in the new covenant of willing obedience. Moreover, in Num 33:50-56, the tradition brings Moses and Israel to the Plains of Moab, exactly the purported setting of Deuteronomy. Thus the citation of this tradition from Numbers helps to situate the interpretive work of Deuteronomy in what may pass for an older tradition.

The culmination of this note on sojourn in verses 8-9 legitimates the tribe of Levi as "set apart" for ministry. This small notice is exceedingly important for Deuteronomy. On the one hand, it looks back to the culmination of the narrative of the golden calf where the Levites are seen to be the faithful adherents to

Moses (against the vagaries of Aaron). Thus the brief reference to Aaron, Eleazar, and Levi may reflect an old and deep tension concerning different priestly communities. On the other hand, scholarship in general regards the tribe of Levi as the successor of Moses, the proper Torah teacher concerning the traditions of covenant, and perhaps the continuing community that generated the tradition of Deuteronomy (see 33:8-11). The notice that Levi has no "allotment" in the land may be an attestation that the priestly house of Levi is without vested interest, honest and trustworthy, in contrast to other priestly orders that are "on the make." Gerhard von Rad has gone so far as to suggest that the phrase "YHWH is my portion" is the quintessential claim of the house of Levi that has no portion of land but has "the better part" of intimacy with YHWH (von Rad 1966:243-66). In any case, it is likely that the entire unit of verses 6-9 with its brief itinerary and a report on Aaron, Eleazar, and Levi is not a mere historical note, but stakes an important interpretive claim about the ongoing authority of Moses through the Levites, a tradition in continuing tension with rival interpretive claims.

The concluding note of verses 10-11 skillfully draws together (a) the Sinai experience of Moses' effective intercession, (b) the reiteration of the land promise of Genesis, and (c) the goal of the land under Mosaic leadership. The tone of these verses suggests that all is in readiness. The recalcitrance of Israel and the wrath of YHWH have been put behind through the good work of Moses. The convergence of all of these traditions, however, only creates a context for the decisive utterance of Moses concerning the ultimate disposition of YHWH toward Israel, an astonishing utterance only now sounded: "The LORD was unwilling to destroy you" (v. 10)! This is the ground of Israel's future and the hope of Israel as it arrives at the land. The verdict is terse and decisive. Had it been elaborated on, Moses might have claimed to have converted YHWH to the cause of Israel. Had Moses commented on the verdict, he might have said that YHWH's anger, even withdrawn, was legitimate. But none of that is stated. The text reports only what needed to be said, that YHWH would not destroy. On this stark truth hangs Israel's future.

Theological and Ethical Analysis

This text yields a powerful invitation and warning to Israel. Five accents may be suggested:

1. The structure of the text itself evidences a dramatic model for biblical faith:

broken covenant	→	*intercession*	→	*new covenant*
9:6-24	→	9:15-21, 25-29	→	10:1-11

The speech of Moses engages in a reminiscence. The memory provides a model for present and future faith and places Moses at the pivot point between what is old and failed and what is new and hope-filled.

This structure closely parallels the movement of Exod 32–34 that traces Israel's life with YHWH through brokenness, Mosaic mediation, and renewed covenant:

32: broken	→	33: mediation	→	34: newness

2. This explication in Deuteronomy, however, is not focused upon that ancient memory, but upon the defining crisis of 587 BCE and the deportation. Thus the parallel might be stated as follows:

Broken covenant: The long, failed history of Israel (9:24)	Intercession: The activity of the Deuteronomists, the Levites (9:15-21, 10:8-10)	New covenant: The offer of homecoming based on YHWH's generosity (10:10)

By such parallelism, the present generation replicates the old memory in its own time and circumstance, replicates *brokenness, negotiation,* and *newness.* In the replication, everything turns upon mediation and YHWH's "unwillingness" to destroy, unwillingness to permit the deportation to be the termination of Israel.

This pattern of brokenness-mediation-new covenant, rooted in Mosaic memory and replicated in the exile, becomes a defining paradigm through which Israel discerns all of its life and its world as a drama of brokenness and forgiveness, totally dependent upon YHWH's "unwillingness" (Brueggemann 1997, 552-64). It is clear in any reading that Israel—including the generation at the Jordan—has no claim upon the future. It received an unmerited future only by the readiness of YHWH to make new covenant with the people of the failed covenant. Under this large rubric, the following points emerge.

3. Israel has a chance for the future only as it remembers; it has no chance for the future while it engages in amnesia. The remembering for which Israel has responsibility is two-sided. In 6:10-15; 8:7-11, Israel is enjoined to remember *YHWH's goodness and generosity.* It is to recall that all of its life of abundance and well-being is a gift from YHWH. In chapter 9, however, Israel is to remember its *own recalcitrant autonomy.* That memory is framed by reference to the wilderness (vv. 7, 22-24) that names the occasions of disobedience. At its center, moreover, is the Sinai disobedience in the "image" Israel cast for itself (vv. 8-13). This memory is so overwhelming that it requires the general verdict: "You rebelled . . . neither trusting him nor obeying him" (v. 23). It is telling that the wilderness is cited for both accents. In 8:4, the wilderness is a place of providential care and protection, in chapter 10 it is a place of disobedience.

This two-sided accent concerning YHWH's fidelity and Israel's infidelity is made to assert to Israel that its future is completely in YHWH's generous hand. The two-sided accent is nicely explicated in the two long psalms, 105 and 106. The first of the two is a recital of YHWH's overwhelming wonders that give life. The second is a sustained acknowledgment that Israel has characteristically refused YHWH's generosity and has been incapable of gratitude. The conclusions of the two psalms (Pss 105:43-45; 106:47) express the twin responses of faith that sum up covenantal faith.

4. It is impossible to overstate the importance of Moses in this presentation of Israel's life and faith. It is Moses who makes possible a future for Israel where none was on offer. We have

seen in 5:22-33 that Moses is the normative *teacher and interpreter* of the covenant of Sinai. Here Moses is the powerful and single *intercessor and mediator* who at great risk (see 9:19) enters into the zone of YHWH's anger on behalf of Israel and turns that anger to a new "unwillingness to destroy." The twin functions of *interpreter* (to bring Israel to obedience in covenant) and *intercessor* (to bring YHWH to a new inclination toward Israel), are both important; here the emphasis is upon Moses' intercessory role that moves YHWH to a new inclination toward recalcitrant Israel. That YHWH is "unwilling to destroy" is because of the work of Moses. The prayer of Moses is an effective intervention with YHWH whereby a new future is created for covenant where there was none.

If "righteous" and "wicked" in 9:4-6 are juridical categories, then Moses' intercession may be more than simply religious activity; it may be viewed as intervention in court before the judge in order to give the judge reason to rule positively toward this disobedient "guilty" people. The outcome of YHWH's "unwillingness" is evidence that Moses' intervention with the judge is effective. Israel's future is wholly different because Israel is "prayed for."

Two extrapolations from this dramatic turn are available in Christian tradition. First, in Christian tradition Jesus is the one who intercedes on behalf of the church and on behalf of the world. Both church and world are dealt with differently by the Father because of the role of the Son. Specifically John 17 provides evidence that *the church is being prayed for,* and therefore it has a future from God that it could not have on its own terms. Second, when Moses' intercession is understood juridically, the way is open to see connections to the entire argument of Paul in Romans and Galatians concerning "justification" (that is, acquittal) by grace, even though the world or the individual person is neither trusting nor obedient (as in 9:23).

5. The vocabulary of *righteousness and wickedness* in verses 4-6, in the Christian trajectory of Reformation teaching, invites attention to the way in which this "stubborn people" is sum-

moned to new covenant. In verse 4, Israel opines that both its own righteousness and the wickedness of the nations have made the gift of the land to Israel possible. The response of verse 5 dismisses Israel's righteousness (innocence) as a factor in YHWH's generosity. Israel receives nothing from YHWH for its righteousness, because it is not innocent but rather stubborn and guilty. Thus the hopeless status of Israel and the risky intervention of Moses are the antecedents to YHWH's new readiness for new covenant. The dramatic development of the text is quite different in nuance from conventional Reformation renderings, but the plot is the same (see Rom 3:21-26).

In context the plot development of intercession by Moses and generosity by YHWH opens a future not otherwise available to sixth-century Israel. The memory of failure, the effectiveness of intercession, and the gift of newness resituate Israel. This reconstrual mattered decisively to Israel at the Jordan, even as it matters decisively to the faithful community whenever it is declared. The text itself, when well said and well heard, is a generative power to resituate the faithful in the generous, future-creating "unwillingness" of YHWH.

IMITATIONS OF A CARING GOD (10:12-22)

This unit articulates one of the loveliest, most powerful, most freighted summations of covenantal theology offered in the book of Deuteronomy. It makes a bid for Israel's most serious and most willing obedience to YHWH, with the central motivation being who YHWH is and what YHWH has done. The initial "so now" (paralleled in 4:1) appeals for obedience on the basis of what has gone before in the great drama of 9:1–10:11. If we connect this rhetorical particle to verses 10-11, then the basis for the current appeal is that (a) YHWH is "unwilling to destroy," that is, continues faithfully in covenant with Israel, and (b) YHWH bids Israel to occupy the land of promise. It is clear that the appeal in Deuteronomy to occupy the land is primarily neither geographical nor military, but pertains solely to embrace of Torah. This unit, linked to verses 10-11, is a *summons* to be fully the Torah people of YHWH, supported by a series of *motivations*.

Exegetical Analysis

The unit begins with a rhetorical question. The question has the same cadences as the more familiar one in Mic 6:8, except that the address here is not "Adam" as in Micah, but specifically "Israel." The question concerns YHWH's intention for Israel. Verses 12-13 give answer to the question in characteristic Deuteronomic rhetoric: *fear* YHWH, *walk* in YHWH's ways (commands), *love* YHWH, *serve* YHWH fully. These four verbs, together with some other variations, refer to a complete commitment to YHWH without reserve, a readiness to be fully identified with and by YHWH and to enact that identity by an intentional and distinctive way in the world. That is, YHWH requires of Israel all of its life, nothing more, nothing less.

The rhetoric of this unit consists in a series of imperatives supported by a corresponding series of quite expansive motivations that are designed to give Israel reason and impetus for glad obedience. The first cluster of imperatives in verses 12-13 is supported by the motivational statement of verses 14-15. These latter two verses easily and without awkwardness articulate one of the most remarkable claims in covenantal theology. Verse 14 makes a cosmic claim for YHWH that is balanced in verse 15 with the particularity of Israel. The God with whom Israel has to do is the creator of heaven and earth; everything, everywhere, all peoples are subject to YHWH's governance.

That claim, however, in no way detracts from the specific Israelite affirmation of verse 15. The governing verb, "set his heart," is reiterated from 7:7. It indicates that YHWH has had a special emotional passion for Israel out of which YHWH has made peculiar commitments to Israel that YHWH has made to no other people. This affirmation of "election" in no way diminishes the assertion of verse 14. The concrete commitment to Israel, rather, is offered as a reason for which Israel should assent to the requirements of verses 12-13.

The next imperative in this passage is "circumcise," with its negative counterpart, "do not be stubborn" (v. 16). The positive imperative appeals to what must have been the long-standing practice of circumcision as a way to signify membership in the covenant with YHWH (see Gen 17:10-14, 23-26; Josh 5:1-9). In this text, as in Lev 26:41; Deut 30:6; Jer 4:4; and Ezek 44:9, the ritual practice of circumcision is transformed into a metaphor for intense loyalty to YHWH. It may be that the cutting away of the foreskin serves to make the organ more sensitive and responsive. Thus to "circumcise the heart" may be to make the heart "the organ of commitment," more sensitive and responsive to YHWH. The point is that Israel is to discipline itself to a more intentional obedience; this requirement is underscored by the negative imperative against "stubbornness," an allusion to 9:6, 13, 27. In stubbornness, Israel is not at all sensitive to the requirements of YHWH. Thus while the metaphors are mixed, the two images of "circumcise the heart" and "stiff-necked" form extreme opposites concerning Israel's disposition toward YHWH.

This imperative is reinforced by the lyrical motivation of verses 17-18, introduced by the characteristic "for" (= "because"). The reason Israel should be intentionally responsive to YHWH is because of who YHWH is. The neat tension of verses 17-18 corresponds to the tension in verses 14-15. As YHWH is creator of heaven and earth in verse 14, so YHWH in verse 17a presides over all the gods, all lords, all powers of every kind. It is likely that the language of "lord of lords" envisions a "divine council" of all gods who are here presented in a vision of common worship and common obedience to the high God who exercises dominion over them. The rhetoric concerns a vast throne-room filled with all manner of exotic and formidable powers (see 1 Kgs 22:19; Isa 6:1-8), but all gladly submissive to YHWH.

That same High God is seen in verses 17b-18, however, to be a God concretely and effectively involved in the affairs of the earth as advocate and protector of the vulnerable; this latter specificity corresponds to the "election claim" of verse 15. As YHWH "set his heart" on Israel, so YHWH cares about the specificities of justice and the victims of injustice. This is a God who cannot be bribed by the wealthy and powerful but who attends to the needs and wishes of orphans and strangers, who cares about the concrete implementation of justice that has to do with the elemental requirements of food and clothing. The commitment of YHWH to justice in verses 17b-18 is commensurate to the divine commitment to Israel in verse 15, for Israel is the primary recipient of YHWH's transformative justice that thus becomes a staple of covenantal ethics. The summons to sensitive, intentional obedience in verse 16 is grounded in the dazzling affirmation that the High God of heaven is completely engaged in the lowly, earthly work of justice (see Ps 146:5-9 for a parallel claim). Israel is permitted no escapist religion but is drawn into the exigencies of earthly justice, where YHWH's own sovereignty has been most fully engaged.

The third imperative in verse 19 picks up the term "love" from verse 15. What was YHWH's initiatory commitment to Israel is now to become Israel's derivative commitment to the stranger. Israel's attachment to YHWH is to be enacted as an attachment to the vulnerable in society (see 1 John 4:19-20). Covenant with YHWH always pushes one outside safe religion to the work of human community (see Isa 58:6-9). In 1:16, the tradition had already insisted that the "resident alien" (the same Hebrew term, *ger*) should be treated like the Israelite. Israel is not permitted to become a homogeneous, ethnic community turned in on itself, but is mandated, as a part of its most elemental responsibility, to reach beyond itself to those who do not quite belong, who are unlike Israel, but who are committed to life in a community of obedience.

The motivation for this ethical requirement in verse 19b, again introduced by "for" (="because"), is that Israel's own point of origin was as needy, vulnerable outsiders in Egypt. We are accustomed to think of Israelites as slaves. It is important, however, to remember that their status as slaves was an economic development from the vulnerable status as aliens and outsiders, because unprotected sojourners are almost certain to become economic slaves. The summons here is to protect strangers economically, precisely so that they do not end up as slaves, as did Israel. Israel's own Exodus memory is that YHWH—the one who executes justice for the vulnerable—came among them in Egypt and gave them a new life that they could not secure for themselves. Israel's distinctive covenantal work, in response, is the economic practice of hospitality and justice that will prevent other vulnerable outsiders from sliding into the wretchedness of slavery through indebtedness.

The final command of verse 20 is a cluster of imperatives that echo verses 12-13. Again, as in verses 12-13, there are four verbs, here a slight variation from the preceding: "fear, serve, cleave to, swear by." The sum of the four verbs is the same as the four verbs in verses 12-13, namely, total, unreserved commitment to YHWH in obedience. The rhetoric is here intensified by the inversion of normal word order so that in each case the object of the verb comes first:

> YHWH your God,
> him,
> to him,
> in his name.

The verbs summon Israel, but the rhetoric is kept focused upon YHWH.

The final set of imperatives is supported by a rather general doxology in verses 21-22 that functions as a final motivation. The reason for accepting these imperatives as definitional for the life of Israel is that YHWH is "your praise," that is, the one in whom you may properly boast (see Jer 9:23-24 [Heb. vv. 22-23]). YHWH is the one whom Israel brags about. Indeed, Israel has nothing else to gloat about, nothing else interesting to talk about or to sing about. Thus YHWH and YHWH's deeds are the overwhelming reality of Israel's life; this is the One whom Israel will gladly fear, serve, cleave to, and swear by. In this lyrical conclusion, Israel can think of no miracle of YHWH as overwhelming and convincing as what it has seen in its own life (v. 22). Israel was a nobody, an unnoticed little tribal community at the brink of extinction (see Gen 46:8-27, and in Christian extrapolation 1 Pet 2:9-10). The community is so small that its members can all be named! That little community "became a great nation, mighty and populous" as the fulfillment of the promises of Genesis, "as the stars in heaven" (see Gen 15:5). Israel's life provides all the data needed to substantiate the imperatives, if only Israel will remember its own life and reflect on the One who transformed its life, the one who will be obeyed.

This remarkable text is a rhetorical whole:

Four summary imperatives (vv. 12-13)
A motivation cosmic and concrete (vv. 14-15)
A particular mandate (v. 16)
A motivation cosmic and concrete (vv. 17-18)
A particular mandate (v. 19a)
A particular motivation (v. 19b)
Four summary imperatives (v. 20)
A motivation rooted in Israel's own life (vv. 21-22)

The rhythm of *imperative* and *motivation* bids for a present-tense embrace of identity congruent with the "so now" of verse 12. The power of the motivations keeps the imperatives from being coercive impositions. The motivations intend to dazzle Israel so that Israel will gladly and eagerly undertake the obedience that belongs properly to its life and identity with YHWH.

Theological and Ethical Analysis

The pattern of *imperative* and *motivation* may, in Christian extrapolation, be an important resource for the reformation of the church. It seems fair to say that the church in the U.S. (and perhaps more generally in the West) has become so domesticated, so much part of "the American system" (or its counterparts) that its distinctiveness is nearly forfeited. With the loss of distinctiveness comes the failure of energy and imagination for missional obedience. The recovery of self-conscious communal identity is to be found not primarily in the imperatives, but in the collage of miracles that constitute the life of the community of faith that has become, all too often, either jaded in familiarity or dismissed as incredible in a technological society. The core ecclesial tradition of the New Testament is an insistence that the church, like Israel its model and forebear, is a gift of YHWH's inexplicable love and grace. The tale of the book of Acts is an account of the ways in which this little community became a great assembly. It is, moreover, no stretch to see that it is precisely its practice of a missional ethic—to execute justice, provide food and clothing, love the stranger—that has been the occasion for its growth to be as "numerous as the stars" (Stark 1996). That is, the *missional imperative* and the *wonder of growth* are inseparable, just as articulated here by Moses.

When this appeal for missional self-consciousness in response to YHWH's miracles is set in relation to 9:1–10:11, it is clear that this community of failed covenant—failed through mistrust and disobedience (9:23)—is now the very community YHWH is "unwilling to destroy" (10:10). The judgment of 9:23 and the assurance of 10:10 together make the imperatives of Deut 10:12-22 an invitation to embrace again identity as YHWH's special people. By such an ecclesial recovery, the community is offered newness that cannot be a casual hobby. The series of imperatives makes unmistakably clear that the new chance for Israel is an invitation that means business. Such a recovery of identity entails the resituating of self-awareness and imagination in this repository of miracles whereby an unnoticed little community has been made formidable in the world, taken up into the purposes of the creator of heaven and earth who presides over all as God of gods. Israel now is in a position to be linked to this awesome Agency to whom there is, for Israel, no real alternative.

A LAND WATCHED OVER (11:1-32)

This chapter concludes the extended homiletical introduction to the "statutes and ordinances" that was begun in chapter 5. The themes of this chapter are by now mostly familiar, but they are given particular nuance in the articulation of this chapter. The primary focus of this chapter that seems to be comprised of short, distinct rhetorical units (vv. 1-7, 8-12, 13-17, 18-21, 22-25, 26-29) is *the land* that Israel is about to enter. Focus on the land, however, permits a variety of particular accents, most especially that the wonder of the good land is intimately linked to YHWH, and therefore the rigorous condition of Torah obedience that comes with the land.

Exegetical Analysis

11:1-7: The first verse announces the insistence of the chapter, namely, obedience as the price of the new land. The accent on obedience is underscored by the fourfold identification of YHWH's command, "charge, decrees, ordinances, and commands." Any one or two of these terms could have been sufficient to identify the following corpus, but together the four terms indicate both the urgency and the comprehensiveness of what Israel will now hear. The verb "keep," however, is preceded by the main clause, "You shall love the LORD your God." In 7:8 and 10:15, it has been asserted that YHWH has loved Israel; now Israel is enjoined to respond in kind to YHWH's initiative. It is now conventional, following William Moran (Moran 1963), to notice that the term "love" likely means to swear and enact obedient loyalty in a formal way. That is, it is a term referring to formal oaths made and kept. That meaning of the term need not, however, preclude an affective dimension that is present in the formal relationship with YHWH here commended to Israel. An affective inclination toward YHWH on Israel's part is commensurate with YHWH's own readiness to "set his heart" on Israel (7:7; 10:15). Both the formal and affective aspects of the imperative summon Israel to commit completely to this relationship. The characteristic maneuver of Deuteronomy, made in this verse, is to connect the expansive term "love" to the concreteness of practical obedience in daily life.

Verses 2-7 constitute a motivational clause to support the double imperative of verse 1. The tradition of Deuteronomy is insistent that only an active memory can sustain the imperative of verse 1. The normative memory given here one more time concerns the Exodus (vv. 2-4) as the primary exemplar of YHWH's great power and YHWH's deep commitment to Israel. But reference to the Exodus is not memory of a past event. It directly concerns the present generation: "It is you! . . . Your eyes have seen." This generation must decide for the God of the Exodus.

The concluding element of this memory as motivation is a reference to the wilderness (vv. 5-6). In 8:2-5 the wilderness is a place of sustenance. In 11:5-6, by contrast, the wilderness is a place of rebellion and consequently a venue of wholesale, violent death. The reference to the sons of Eliab is from Num 16, a report on a rebellious challenge to the leadership and authority of Moses that brings death to the rebels (Num 16:31-33). The point of that narrative is that Mosaic authority is absolute and dare not be challenged. The memory is designed to give gravity to the imperatives of verse 1. Thus the memory concerns *you* in the wonders of the Exodus and in the risks of wilderness, all converging in the interest of present tense adherence to the requirements of YHWH as given by *Moses*.

11:8-12: If verses 1-7 voice the demand of YHWH connected to the land ("the stick"), then verses 8-12 constitute "the carrot" of attractiveness. The command still comes first (v. 8), but it is followed by a double "so that" *(lĕmaʿan)* in verses 8-9. Obedience is instrumental in securing the land. Then entire characterization of the land in verses 9-12 is a forward-looking motivation for the imperative of verse 8a. The motivation consists of three elements:

1. A characteristic description of the rich abundance of the land that flows with "milk and honey" (see Exod 3:8). The tradition knows that the land will make prosperity a certainty.

2. A contrast with the land of Egypt. The tradition also knows that the land of Egypt is a thin land that depends completely upon the Nile for its vitality. The slave-memory, moreover, is able to recall that connecting the waters of the Nile with the arid land is hard work. The image of "irrigation by foot" presumably refers to irrigation pumps that depended upon the endless expenditure of slave energy to operate, pumping by foot. Without such slave power, the waters of the Nile had no chance to make the arid land fertile. Abundance in Egypt took immense human energy. Thus Egypt becomes a metaphor for survival that is endlessly exhausting and, from a slave perspective, futile.

By contrast, this land of promise teems with water and therefore with life. This land receives the water needed for abundant life, not by slave power but by the generous guarantees of the creator God; life in this land is a gift, not the result of endless slave labor (see 6:10-11; 8:7-10).

3. The wonders of the land are constituted by the normal workings of creation—regular, reliable, generous. The tradition knows, however, that such guaranteed life-giving productiveness is not the operation of autonomous "nature." It is rather the outcome of a generous, attentive decree of the creator who guarantees the gifts of life appropriate to every season (Gen 8:22; Ps 145:15-16). This characterization of the land turns on the nice phrase of verse 12, "the eyes of the LORD your God are always on it." The "eye of YHWH" constitutes YHWH's protective, generative action, that is, the commitment of the whole self of YHWH to willing life and good. In Deut 32:10 Israel is said to be "the apple of YHWH's eye," the one on whom YHWH dotes. In 1 Kgs 8:29, moreover, the eyes of YHWH are attentively on the temple in Jerusalem day and night. YHWH's very look can evoke well-being. (See Job 7:17-20 on the negative power of YHWH's eye.)

11:13-21: Thus far the chapter has issued two massive imperatives (vv. 1, 8) supported by a motivation of memory (vv. 2-7) and a motivation of anticipation (vv. 9-12). Now, in verses 13-17, the rhetoric returns to the "so that" of verses 8-9. The free gift of the new land so wondrously characterized in verses 9-12 is not an automatic given. It is, inescapably, a consequence of obedience. This is made unmistakably clear through the "if-then" structure of verses 13-17, a trademark rhetorical feature of the Deuteronomic tradition. The linkage of *land* and *obedience* that causes the good land to be "iffy," that is, conditional, is lined out clearly in the double "if-then" of this passage.

First comes the positive "if-then" (vv. 13-15). The "if" of obedience is stated in familiar cadences bespeaking total commitment: two standard verbs ("love, serve") plus the formula from 6:4. The "then," the consequence of obedience, is abundant rain in every season that will cause the land to produce everything needed, everything of which it is capable. The abundance is made explicit through three phrases. First, "grain, wine, oil" is a common triad to signal a rich, productive economy (Hos 2:8, 22). Second, an agrarian economy depends on the pasture land for cattle (see Pss 50:10, 104:14). Third, the rhetoric of satiation is reiterated from 6:11. All of this together yields "a land that the LORD your God looks after" (v. 12). The promised land is in every way a contrast to the wearisome slave land of Egypt in which no gifts are given.

Then follows the negative "if-then" that is clear, even though the "if" is only implicit (vv. 16-17). The negative, implied "if" of verse 16 concerns the nullification of the *shema*[c] of 6:4, the compromise of covenantal identity by embracing other gods who seem better at giving rain while making lesser demands.

The negative "then" of such infidelity is that there will come a drought; YHWH, the benevolent creator and guarantor of rain, will withhold rain, and Israel will cease to be economically viable in the land. It is not a "given" of "nature" that rain comes, but rain is in the gift of the creator (see Job 38:25-30). Indeed in the great curse recitals of Lev 26:19-20 and Deut 28:23-24 rain is given or withheld by YHWH as befits covenant response from Israel (see Amos 4:7-8; Ps 107:35-38). Short of Torah obedience, the supple land of promise can be reduced to a desert, worse than Egypt because this land has no Nile.

Because of the urgency of obedience, verses 18-21 return to the educational accent of 6:4-9. The goal is to *internalize* passionate covenantal conviction among the young; but such internalization this teaching tradition knows, depends upon *externalization* so that the passionate conviction of covenant is palpably available to the children (Berger and Luckmann 1967). Thus the mandate to produce signs, emblems, conversations, doorposts, and gates that are marked in an external process aims at internalization.

11:22-25: The "if-then" of verses 13-17 is reiterated in positive form in verses 22-25, without a negative counterpart. The "if" of obedience is given in the verbs, "love, walk, cleave," all to support the main verb, "surely keep," with an infinitive absolute. The positive "then" is expansive (vv. 23-25). The "then" is offered in the language of conquest. Israel will successfully displace the older population of the land, will completely intimidate its enemies, and will claim the land to the broadest imaginable borders. For the most part, Deuteronomy envisions a rather modest twelve-tribe settlement in the land. But here the tradition appeals to the vision of "Greater Israel" that is more readily connected to the Abrahamic promise (Gen 15:18-21) or to the empire of Solomon (1 Kgs 3:21).

This combination of demand and promise culminates in verses 26-29 with a summons to decision. Indeed, the powerful appeals of chapters 5–11 and the entire book of Deuteronomy seek to bring Israel to "a verdict," a decision to be the Torah people of YHWH.

Theological and Ethical Analysis

The line of argument here and throughout these great chapters 5–11 is not difficult to follow. But the intense, even hyperbolic rhetoric of persuasiveness suggests that the *either/or* of covenant was not so obviously compelling as the tradition itself insists. The extremity of appeal surely indicates that many in Israel were not readily persuaded by the demands of covenant and found other options for faith credible. The tradition of Deuteronomy is a self-conscious, mature statement of advocacy for how faith is to be understood and practiced that does not purport to reflect histori-cal fact but means to summon a later Israel to a more radical, single-minded practice. Viewed not as reportage but as advocacy, Deuteronomy suggests that the most serious covenant faith Israel could imagine revolved around *exclusive loyalty to YHWH* and derivatively *attentiveness to the neighbor.* These commitments (love God, love neighbor) bespeak a certain pattern of social rela-tionships that curb autonomy and acquisitiveness. This choice of religious commitment and affection has immediate derivative importance for social practice.

There is no easy or obvious extrapolation of that uncompro-mising, urgent decision from that ancient community at the Jordan to our time and place. Nevertheless it takes no great imag-ination to see that the same *either/or* is still before the faithful community. The exponential growth of technology into the electronic age creates a social-political-economic environment in which huge wealth, protected by equally huge military investments, invites the thought that a no-surprise, no-threat future on one's own terms might be possible.

It takes no special discernment to see that such autonomous acquisitive power, which has as its counterpart privatization and the loss of a public horizon, threatens the fabric of the larger human community. It is possible to decide to "go for broke" in self-sufficiency, no matter the cost to the neighborhood. Or it is possible to curb and redirect such self-focus in the interest of covenantal institutions, policies, and practices. There are inescapable contemporary signs that the neglect of the human infrastructure brings huge costs that the community of the many pays while the gains of the few go unchecked. For those committed to the covenantal option, as readers of Deuteronomy are likely to be, it is reasonable to think that such unfettered self-securing means, soon or late, forfeiture of a viable humanness in brutality, anxiety, loneliness, and despair.

One can indeed factor out the conviction that *disobedience* leads to the *demise of creation*. Consider the case of agribusiness with its huge combines of money and power, with preferential treatment by the government; land unloved but treated only commercially will finally refuse to produce (see Isa 5:8-10). Uncurbed greed may sooner or later destroy the rain forests of South America and thereby alter in significant ways the climatic conditions of the whole planet. The neglect of the urban infrastructure in the anxious escape to the suburbs produces zones of high crime, poverty, and social unrest that can scarcely be contained by more prisons. There is growing awareness that the destruction of the earth is accomplished slowly by the input of chemicals in the interest of "better living" and the periodic devastation wrought through wars that leave the environment unusable for generations. To be sure, there is no exact, one-to-one correlation between the summons of Deuteronomy and the decisions characteristically made in a technological society. But the Bible does not worry about exact correlations in any case. It works rather by hint, by trace, and by impression. What the hints, traces, and impressions of Deuteronomy might be saying to a technological, self-preoccupied society is that self-promotion that is not curbed by the dread of the holy, and self-sufficiency that is not impinged upon by the presence of the neighbor constitute a path to destruction. The destruction in the book of Deuteronomy is only occasionally presented as a direct intervention of YHWH. It is more often a consequence that comes without an expressed Agent (as in Hos 4:1-3).

The concern for teaching the faith and marking it visibly (vv. 18-21) is to produce a Torah community that is immune to the seductions of other offers of security so that they hold no allure for the young. That indeed is the educational burden of every self-conscious community of passionate conviction. Its work is to hold its young and to protect the young from seductions that will distort faithful habits. In an earlier day, the seductions in Western culture that were perceived by the religious community included tobacco and movies. Now, most visibly, the seductions that matter include drugs and alcohol. But underneath such evident issues, the fundamental temptation is the ideology of autonomy enacted through money-sex-power, the great triad of self-possession.

THE STATUTES AND THE ORDINANCES (12–25)

With the conclusion of the powerful, persuasive rhetoric of chapters 5–11 summoning Israel to obedience, the speech of Moses shifts to articulate the "statutes and ordinances" to which Israel must adhere in the land. In 5:22-33 subtle hermeneutical maneuvers attach this subsequent layer of command to the Decalogue and invest it with all of the authority of the Mosaic mediator. This material that follows is diverse and variegated, and probably has a complex history of origin, development, and transmission. In the final form of the text, it is offered, despite its evident diversity, as a single, unified teaching, all of which bears the urgency of Mosaic imperative. Israel must heed all of it!

The purpose of the corpus that follows is to bring every aspect of the public life of Israel under the aegis of the God of Sinai. Because that God is in every way incomparable, Israel's appropriate response of faithful obedience is to enact a different social practice that is commensurate and congruent with the character and will of YHWH as articulated by Moses. Israel's peculiar public obedience is "a practice of YHWH," who is made visible and palpable in the public policies and daily actions of Israel.

There is a long scholarly debate concerning the shape and arrangement of this extended corpus of "statutes and ordinances." On the one hand, many scholars believe that the collection is almost completely random; particular commandments must be taken, each on its own terms. On the other hand, there are scholarly proposals, already with John Calvin, suggesting that this corpus is intentionally arranged in correspondence to the Ten Commandments of 5:6-21, so that in sequence each part of the corpus correlates with and more or less exposits a command of Sinai (Kaufman 1978-79; Olson 1994:62-125).

The correlation of commandments with statutes and ordinances cannot be pressed too far. At the very least, in any case, such suggested correlations may have an important heuristic value in our discernment of what is at issue in any particular Mosaic imperative.

On Right Worship (12:1-32 [Heb. 12:1–13:1])

The initial imperative of the corpus of statutes and ordinances is an insistence on Israel's right worship of YHWH as the first venue in which Israel's loyalty toward YHWH is to be enacted. Significantly, the corpus of imperatives opts to begin with this emphasis on worship. The Mosaic tradition understands that right symbolization—right public imagination—is defining for everything else in the life of the faithful community. The focus of Israel's worship will determine the quality of its life. It will be important at the outset of this chapter to recognize this shrewd appreciation of worship that has a deep grip upon imagination.

Chapter 12 has an introduction (v. 1) and is framed by what was likely a conclusion in verse 28, and now with a second conclusion in verse 32 (Heb. 13:1). Between introduction and conclusion are four units (vv. 2-7, 8-12, 13-19, 20-27), each of which takes up another aspect of the importance of the "public performance" of Israel's undivided loyalty to YHWH.

Exegetical Analysis

12:2-7: In verses 2-7, Moses articulates three accents that will recur in this exposition of right public performance.

Israel must resist the worship practices of the culture it will find already in the land of promise (vv. 2-4). These alternative practices are a seductive threat to Israel. If they are embraced at all, they will talk Israel out of YHWH and out of a covenantal vision of social reality. Indeed, the danger is so great that resistance requires destruction of anti-covenantal images, with the verb for "demolish" in the absolute infinitive, and emphatic construction. The wording of this negative imperative recites a list of despised cult objects—altar, pillars, sacred poles, idols—in order to be comprehensive. It is likely that the tradition has no interest in the particulars of "pagan" cult objects and perhaps no specific knowledge of them either. They are treated *en masse,* all of them together as a threat to Israel. The list of despised objects is matched by a series of verbs of violence, a rhetorical strategy to underscore the urgency of resistance to the threat and temptation.

The positive counterpart to such negatives is that Israel shall engage in its own distinctive ritual performances (vv. 3-6). This speaker prefers enumerated lists, so that the catalogue of sacrifices in verse 6 corresponds to the negative list of verse 3, and includes in the repertoire of Israel every thinkable sacrificial act. What is important about the latter, and what will be important in the intentional performances of these sacrifices, is that they are all *to YHWH.* Every one of them, in performance, will demonstrate the *sovereignty* of YHWH over the land and the undivided *fidelity* of Israel, a fidelity that resists any other performance of faith.

The radical decision made negatively in verses 1-3 and positively in verses 5-6 *culminates in joy* that is the hallmark of a community gladly situated in YHWH's generous care (v. 7). This joy, moreover, is this-worldly and material. It is a festival in which Israel exhibits and enjoys the blessings of the creator God. Right worship as joyous eating is not only a faithful enactment of the goodness of creation. It is also an act of hope, a foretaste of the common abundance when there will be more than enough for all.

In Christian extrapolation, this act of joyous eating in the Eucharist is an earnest of "the Heavenly Banquet."

12:8-12: The text remembers that the address is at the Jordan, with the land in prospect (vv. 8-12). The same accents are found here as in verses 2-7, right worship with manifold offerings to YHWH and joy unlimited. This unit of text sounds three distinctive notes.

1. The text makes a differentiation between now at the Jordan and time to come in the land. The time to come in the land will be a time of "rest," that is, security, peace, and safety free of every threat (see Josh 21:43-45). The coming land, the primal expectation of Deuteronomy, gives the tradition a thread into the future that opens the way for eschatological hope. The well-ordered, safe, good land where YHWH's will is done is what the Bible comes to mean by "the kingdom of God."

2. As often noticed, Deuteronomic tradition insists that in worship, YHWH is not completely committed to being present to Israel, but YHWH's name is given in the place of worship. Such a theological stratagem wants to guard against an excessive perception that God is given over to God's people. The presence of the name is an assertion that YHWH's full sovereignty still remains beyond the control and administration of Israel (see 1 Kgs 8:27-30).

3. The mention of the Levites is characteristic in Deuteronomy (see 10:8-9). Their particular acknowledgment here is a recognition that Israelite joy in worship is never apart from the gifts and demands of the Torah, for the Levites are above all Torah teachers and interpreters (see 33:8-11). Thus Israel's public worship is distinctive on all counts—in complete safety ("rest"), without autonomy, with transcendence preserved, and with Torah sensitivities kept honed. Nobody could confuse such an Israelite public performance with the other cultural options that Israel must resist.

12:13-19: "The place" for the public performance of YHWH is a very different sort of place (vv. 13-19). The accent on place means that Moses envisions a "free zone" for Israelite practice whereby the distinctiveness of Israel may be fully on display, without any cultural accommodation.

The tradition of Deuteronomy is life-affirming (v. 15). Israel can kill, eat, and enjoy what "you desire," or, more literally, its "life's desire." That permit envisions not only abundance and prosperity but also self-indulgence. The blessings of the creator God give much and Israel is to enjoy much. It is especially poignant to take this permit of "life's desire" in tension with "right in your own eyes" that is prohibited in verse 8. The difference is that it is defined in the context of YHWH's blessing, so that "life's desire" is shaped in Yahwistic fashion. That permit for "life's desire," moreover, is carefully related to the claims of YHWH in two ways. First, the blood of the meat must be poured out and not eaten, a tacit acknowledgment that Israel presides over its own life only penultimately, for the gift of life is finally held by YHWH and is not given over to Israel. Second, the tithe of everything (notice again the comprehensive list) is an acknowledgment of YHWH's ownership of all, for the tithe is as rent paid by the tenant to the landowner.

Given that crucial acknowledgment in verses 16-17, the "life desire" in verse 15 is to be enjoyed in an inclusive communal celebration, counting the Levites among those enveloped in the joy of eating. The tithe reserved as an acknowledgment of YHWH's sovereignty over the land is also given over to Israelite joy. This "owner" is not greedy or parsimonious, and wants nothing for self. Thus Israel may enjoy the 90 percent of produce at home and the 10 percent "at the place"; Israel may enjoy 100 percent of the produce of YHWH's blessing in YHWH's land. The public performance of the 10 percent elsewhere, at the place, on YHWH's specified turf, however, is an unmistakable acknowledgment that Israel's abundant life is not self-made or self-sufficient.

12:20-28: It is likely that the statement of the requirements of worship in verses 13-19 envision a small agrarian community. Verses 20-27 seem to suggest an important adjustment in requirements if the land is enlarged, so that some Israelites live far from "the place." If that is the purpose of this paragraph, then it exhibits the kind of interpretive dynamic we considered in 5:22-32.

The adjustment made here is in the context of affirming Israel's heart's desire (vv. 20-21). These verses seem to suggest that Israel, far removed from "the place," is permitted to eat and enjoy at home. The tradition is generous and does not intend that the Yahwistic requirement should be a hardship. In worship Israel is only required to commit an overt act that makes it clear that it lives by an expectation other than its own.

The provisional conclusion of verse 28 may at one time have served as the conclusion to this long chapter. In any case, the verse echoes the pivotal expectation of verse 25. Israel is not autonomous, but must act by "YHWH's eyes," a guide that places the life of Israel in a very different context.

12:29-32: The final unit of this chapter (vv. 29-32) is peculiarly intense, and may have been added after the conclusion of verse 28 in order to underscore and accent the deep *either/or* of right worship. This textual statement is alert to the power and subtlety of religious alternatives, for they will continue to seduce even after they have been destroyed. The rhetoric of "imitation" calls to mind the yearning to be like the nations that swirled around the question of monarchy in 1 Sam 8:5, 20, and that came to fruition in the reign of Solomon. Indeed for the tradition of Deuteronomy, Solomon is the great case study in compromise and entrapment that lead to exile (1 Kgs 11:5-7). The term *abomination* comes easily to the lips of the Deuteronomists when contemplating Solomon. It is the same abomination ("abhorrent thing") warned about in verse 1. This final polemic cites only one specific example of an abhorrence to YHWH: child sacrifice. Such a practice, taken here to be grossly anti-covenantal, is a failure to recognize that life belongs to YHWH and not to Israel, and cannot be disposed of in such a brutalizing way. Likely the text here cites the "worst case scenario" of departure from the rigors of covenantal discipline, but the worst case is only an example of the deep temptations in culture that may draw Israel outside the range of legitimate Torah options.

Theological and Ethical Analysis

The community of faith that sustains a distinctive sense of itself is always under pressure to distort and accommodate. For that reason it must be intentional about the maintenance of right worship that is the public performance of its distinctiveness. "Right worship" is worship that is congruent with the God who is worshiped, so that the proper ordering of worship is derived from a prior conviction about who God is. While the entire tradition of Deuteronomy is germane to the question of right worship, in this chapter several clues are clear:

1. Right worship is *life-affirming,* open to one's "life desires," but not catering to every "appetite" (v. 8).

2. Right worship is under *the discipline of offering and sacrifice,* requiring the bringing of serious, costly, intentional gifts that bespeak acknowledgment of YHWH's sovereignty.

3. Right worship is an enactment of *communal joy,* a celebration possible because of confidence in YHWH, a joy that is public and available from YHWH in every circumstance. Such worship is affirmation in every circumstance, but when necessary it can also be circumstance denying.

4. Right worship is *profoundly material;* it is an act of bodily enjoyment through eating the good gifts of the blessed land.

5. Right worship includes the Levites, and therefore it is consciously permeated by *the narrative memories and current demands of Torah.*

While right worship is characterized from the center out, that is, from the character of YHWH, it is equally important to recognize the polemical character of this chapter to see that the right worship of Israel is in conflict with available alternative liturgies. In contemporary thought about right worship, it is important to pay attention not only to the decisive internal points of reference in the truth of God but also to the rival liturgies that seduce and threaten the integrity of the community of faith.

In this text, the alternatives include "other gods" (v. 31) and "your own desires" (v. 8). These two reference points, along with the third alternative of YHWH, might make useful appeal to Paul Tillich's triad of *autonomy, heteronomy, and theonomy,* though Tillich's articulation is in rhetoric very different from the intense passion of Deuteronomy:

> The words "autonomy," "heteronomy," and "theonomy" answer the question of the *nomos* or the law of life in three different ways: Autonomy asserts that man as the bearer of universal reason is the source and measure of culture and religion—that he is his own law. Heteronomy asserts that man, being unable to act according to universal reason, must be subjected to a law, strange and superior to him. Theonomy asserts that the superior law is, at the same time, the innermost law of man himself, rooted in the divine ground which is man's own ground: the law of life transcends man, although it is, at the same time, his own. (Tillich 1951:63)

By autonomy Tillich refers to the illusion that one may be the center of one's own life. This corresponds in Deut 12 to all that is "right in one's own eyes" (v. 8). There is no doubt that such self-indulgence is a huge temptation in contemporary Christian worship in the United States, wherein worship is reduced to therapeutic self-help and self-enhancement, characteristically offered in emotive romanticism without any notion of covenantal requirement or rigor. Such a romantic-therapeutic distortion of worship is powerfully attractive, precisely because it can be made to appear in terms of covenantal affirmation, but with the absence of any "Holy Other" in the transaction.

By "heteronomy" Tillich refers to the power of ideology whereby some lesser loyalty occupies center stage and is affirmed in uncritical fashion as the truth of faith. While every society has its own ideological temptations to "other gods," it is clear that in the worship of the church in the dominant United States culture, the primal seductive ideology is that of market capitalism mixed with a celebration of national military power. All of that, of course, is couched in the language of piety and altruistic goodwill, on the general assumption that this ideology is a true and nonnegotiable articulation of the gospel.

"Theonomy" offers a sharp contrast to the *autonomy* of therapeutic self-realization and the *heteronomy* of market ideology. Tillich formulates "theonomy" as "the God beyond God" who eludes all categories of domestication and management. While the tradition of Deuteronomy, with its class consciousness, its ethnic propensity, and its patriarchal prism of perception, engages in some aspects of heteronomy, at its best, the thinking of Deuteronomy concerns a God who has no form and who will not be reduced to any domesticated pattern. It is to that God—in rejection of other gods and in curbing of one's own desires—that Israel brings its offerings and responds in joyous, inclusive eating. The savage rhetoric of Deuteronomy against both autonomy and heteronomy is indeed an insistence upon this God who is beyond all gods.

Beware of Seductions! (13:1-18 [Heb. 13:2-19])

At the Jordan Moses reluctantly lays down for Israel an urgent, costly, nonnegotiable *either/or*. Israel must choose YHWH *or not*. Israel must choose to be the people of YHWH *or not*. And in these choices, Israel will choose to live well in the land of promise *or not*. The simple, comprehensive either/or that pervades the teaching of Deuteronomy is, in this chapter, starkly stated in three parallel scenarios.

The chapter consists of three episodes, verses 1-5; verses 6-11; and verses 12-18. Each episode follows a repeated pattern in four elements:

1. A seductive invitation to an alternative;
2. An insistence upon YHWH;
3. The harsh disposal of the seducer; and
4. A concluding formula concerning the outcome of resistance to the seduction.

Exegetical Analysis

The first episode concerns a would-be religious authority who claims to have access to religious vision or knowledge (vv. 1-5). The labels "prophet" and "dreamer" are not used with any precision, but refer to those who assert special religious authority. The invitation to "follow after other gods" is of course a bid for religious loyalty, but may concretely refer to participation in a liturgical procession. Israel is given a summary prohibition against seductions that lead away from YHWH.

In verses 3*b*-4, the radical covenantal alternative of YHWH is stated more fully than anywhere else in Deuteronomy. First in verse 3*b*, the chance to "love" with heart and soul reiterates with two elements the familiar triad from 6:4. In verse 4, the text sounds the series of imperatives that we have already seen in 10:12-13. Only here the series consists in six parallel verbs: follow, fear, keep, obey, serve, hold fast; this is the most complete list of such verbs anywhere. The normal word order is inverted so that in each case the accent falls on the object of the verb, that is, YHWH. In substance, nothing new is asserted by the rhetoric in verses 3-4. Its intensity, however, is noteworthy, for the speaker wants to overwhelm the alternative offer of a god "you have not known."

The seducers of Israel must be eliminated as an intolerable challenge to the identity of the community. The term rendered "treason" combines political betrayal, a violation of a public commitment, with deception. In characteristic fashion, the speaker in 13:5 manages in the same sentence to condemn the perpetrators who will drive Israel away from YHWH and to witness one more time to the God of the Exodus whom Israel knows and is to obey, thus voicing the powerful *either/or* of covenant.

The concluding formula, "purge the evil," is a harsh formula of excommunication (v. 5). This community committed to radical obedience cannot have in its midst advocates of an alternative. Thus the maintenance of singular loyalty to YHWH depends upon and justifies harsh treatment of such seductive advocates.

13:6-11: The second scenario is developed in quite parallel fashion, though with interesting rhetorical variation (vv. 6-11). Here the perpetrator is not a professional religionist as in the first case, but someone close to an Israelite, a member of the household. The rhetoric is at pains to indicate that the seducer may be among one's most treasured companions. Thus the seducer may be not only your wife, but "the wife of your bosom." It may be not only one of your friends, but your friend who is "like your own life." Even such trusted, treasured people may be a threat because they may "entice in secret." The verb is the same used in 2 Sam 24:1, and with reference to the insidious distortion of Jezebel in 1 Kgs 21:25. The text wants Israel to imagine a secret advocacy done in private, which is perhaps on the face of it convincing because of its intimate source.

The threat of distortion of Yahwism, however, is the same in the second case as in the first, even if it is the work of an "insider." No matter how persuasive or intimate, the alternative is still "other gods." Here the verb is "serve" and not "follow" as in verse 2, but the verb "serve" can also refer either to liturgic activity or more broad-based loyalty. The case is the same—abandonment of singular obedience to YHWH.

For that reason the punishment is the same, though the rhetoric of violence is even more exaggerated here than in the first case (vv. 8-10). The negative of verse 8 is stated in five terse verbs, a pattern hardly discernible in English translation:

do not yield;
do not listen;
do not pity;
do not have compassion;
do not shield.

The repetition and intensity of the mandate are commensurate with the list of potential candidates in verse 6. That is, the harshness of punishment correlates with the ones with whom one is most intimately connected. One may especially want to "have pity" on the wife of one's bosom, or "have compassion" on a friend who is like your own life.

But no! The theological threat of the seduction overrides all normal social and familial inclinations. The text is ruthless. The one who is "secretly enticed" must lead the public execution, must take the initiative and throw the first stone, only then to be ratified by public participation in the execution. The verb *kill*, moreover, is in an emphatic form. Covenantal distortion is seen in this text as massively dangerous, and one must be vigilant to it in any circumstance, even in one's most trusting relationships.

The Yahwistic alternative is given in almost formulaic cadences (v. 10). Whatever other god is worshiped—unknown, near or far—that god will not be an Exodus deliverer, because there is only one such deliverer, the God who commands from Sinai.

The concluding sentence of verse 11 differs from that of verse 5. In verse 5, the purgation of false teaching maintains the purity of the community. Here the purgation, even of one's intimates, sounds like it has a cautionary, pedagogical purpose: Kill, to warn others off, so that the next wife or next friend will be on notice. The harshness of the teaching is unrelieved, and for this reader is nearly unbearable.

13:12-18: In the third case, the details are different with the same plot line (vv. 12-18). In case one, the threat was a professional. In case two, the culprit is an intimate. Now, in the third case, the threat is "scoundrels," "sons of worthlessness" who go about urging religious alternative. Such nomenclature is meant to conjure up social losers and outcasts who warrant no respect and who themselves have no respect for the norms and mores of the community. These are the social misfits who always rock the boat for no good reason, and who knowingly offend and gladly disrupt everything settled. At the same time, however, one must recognize that such a labeling is given always by the social establishment that uses such labels for social control and social marginalization. The usage here might suggest that these advocates of "other gods" are not themselves serious but are only fed up with the intolerable piety and rectitude of "true believers." In any case, the seduction in these verses, as in the other scenarios, is "other gods."

The disposal of such distorters of truth and justice will be severe but according to due process. In the first two cases, the seduction has concerned "you"; that is, the one bringing the charge has firsthand experience of the matter. In this third case, the seduction from Yahwism is a report from elsewhere, that is, an unsubstantiated charge. The zealous party of Yahwists at work here is not to act on rumor, but must make a careful judicial determination of the facts of the case. If the charges are not proved, the case of course dissolves.

But if proved—and now the text appeals to the most extreme rhetoric, the kind not seen since 7:25-26:

Indictment: It is an "abhorrent thing," an abomination, an unbearable obscenity to YHWH.

Sentence: "Utterly destroy" *(herem)*.

The community must take extreme measures in order to eliminate such irreverent, unrespectful advocacy that is a threat to the entire community of YHWH.

The presentation of indictment and sentence is simple and straightforward. But because the "abomination" is such a threat and "utter destruction" is so urgent, the statute is at pains about its implementation (vv. 16-17a). The entire town that has been led astray shall be burned in a dramatic public act and left as a ruin and as a warning. All the contents of the city, moreover, shall be destroyed. Everything in such an aberrant town that followed after other gods is contaminated, every sheep and cow, every dog and cat, every plate and pot, every toy and tool, everything! The text calls to mind the costly miscalculation of Saul in his struggle with the Amalekites: a rescue of booty seemed permissible but is condemned by Samuel in a devastating way (1 Sam 15). This text permits no such miscalculation.

The conclusion of the burning, killing, and annihilation is a considerable variant from the concluding statements of verses 5 and 11 that were negative (vv. 17b-18). This concluding statement is introduced by "so that" *(lĕmaᶜan)*, and anticipates YHWH's glad response to the harsh purgation. The public act of annihilation will give evidence to YHWH and to any who observe that this Yahwistic community is serious and undeterred in its singular loyalty to YHWH. Notice that proper obedience is to adhere to what counts in the "sight of the LORD" (more literally, in "YHWH's eyes"; see 12:25). That is, Israel must eschew autonomy.

A consequence of such convincing attestation to loyalty is that YHWH will have compassion on Israel, and in compassion will bless and multiply Israel, keeping old promises and causing "peace and prosperity." The text moves from violent execution to divine compassion without missing a beat, and apparently without any sense of irony. Compassion for true-blue *insiders* depends upon violent elimination of all *outsiders,* all "others" who refuse to conform and who thereby threaten the integrity and well-being of the community of insiders.

Theological and Ethical Analysis

The three sources of seduction that are here identified merit consideration.

1. *Prophets* and *dreamers* may refer to religious professionals, people who have skill, knowledge, and expertise to commend them. In contrast to the Deuteronomic norm "YHWH alone," there were religious teachers and proponents who perhaps were ready to compromise covenantal loyalty with an accommodation that may to them have appeared as innocuous, but was seen by Deuteronomy as a life-or-death sellout.

2. *Intimates* in family and community suggests that internal to the life of the community, among those most trusted and valued, another less rigorous, less focused loyalty was advocated, on which perhaps see Job 2:9-10. This may suggest that within "the household of faith" lives the deepest threat to faith.

3. *Scoundrels* may refer to those who are not inside and who have no credentials, but who believe they know a less costly way of living that may have nothing to do with the claims of covenant.

Contemporary equivalents to these sorts of alternatives might include:

1. Religionists who regard the faith tradition of Israel as narrow, harsh, and exclusivist.

2. Compromisers inside the body of believers who lack any firm vision of faith as a genuine alternative to cultural norms.

3. Outsiders without any sensitivity to faith. In the present context, perhaps one might find a parallel in the scandalous offers of macho money, sex, and violence in dominant ideology that has as its counterpoint romantic offers of beauty—beautiful home and gardens, beautiful cosmetics, beautiful cars, and so forth.

Further reflection upon the seductions and compromises present in the contemporary community of faith suggests on all fronts what is offered as alternative is a "Theology of Glory" that imagines a triumphal gospel of worldly security, success, and peace, a way of construing reality that is remote from any "Theology of the Cross" with its costs and invitations to suffering for the sake of the world. To embrace a Theology of Glory, a triumphalism that is visible in the world, is to banish the cost and joy of discipleship that are present in Israel's covenant and in the church's summons to obedience.

Having acknowledged the seriousness of this critique of seduction and compromise and distortion of faith, it is necessary to observe that the tone and force of this chapter is that of an ideological movement that "takes no prisoners." Granted that exclusive loyalty requires vigilance and granted that compromise in small things may lead down a road to abandonment of faith, the rhetoric of this chapter betrays a vigilante mentality of deeply anxious exclusivism:

1. The assault on intimates conjures that worst use of "party discipline" that rewards informers who squeal on intimate family conversation.

2. The pedagogical justification for execution sounds not unlike the practice of "neckties" during the social revolution against apartheid in South Africa, whereby compromisers and informers in the movement were publicly exhibited with a burning tire around the neck as a cautionary "lesson" to others.

3. The readiness to burn a village sounds too much like the anticommunist passion of the United States in Vietnam, a justification for "burning villages" in order to save them.

The chapter focuses upon the dilemma of exclusive loyalty, a dilemma known in religious communities of high *discipline*, in party *ideology* and *exclusivism* in every *sectarian* mind-set that must fend off "the other" in order to maintain a sense of community in obedience. The dilemma is that in the practice of such vigilance and discipline, the community engages in brutalizing actions that give the lie to its own best sense of itself. In any event, these three cases exhibit a community that believes that the maintenance of loyalty to YHWH is worth the effort and that such loyalty is deeply under threat. Church readers of this text might conclude that a large measure of accommodation is preferable to even a small amount of brutalizing vigilance. Deuteronomy of course is unpersuaded by such a judgment, unpersuaded but not self-critical about its own urgings.

Holy Identity, Holy Practices (14:1-21)

Deuteronomy is engaged in a deep dispute over the identity of the community of Israel that is derived from its religious loyalty and that is exhibited in its "public performance." The present chapter is a series of *prohibitions and permits*, punctuated by *primal theological affirmations*.

Exegetical Analysis

The most poignant element of this text is the way in which the most sweeping and intentional theological claims for Israel are readily and without awkwardness connected to quite specific disciplines of community identity. The chapter includes three programmatic statements that are characteristic of Deuteronomy. First, in verse 1: "You are children of the LORD your God." The statement is terse and without elaboration. The word order, moreover, is inverted to accent the status of Israel as sons and daughters. The use of familial imagery bespeaks an intimate sense of belonging with and belonging for YHWH and has a strong, derivative development in the tradition (see Hos 11:1-9; Isa 1:2; 63:16; 64:8; Jer 3:19-20; Matt 2:15; Gal 4:4-7). The status as "children" implies for Israel a sense of belonging that includes both rigorous expectation for Israel's conduct and sure protection.

The second statement of theological identity is in verse 2. The term "holy" in reference to Israel attests to no intrinsic quality of Israel but to an exclusive relationship to YHWH to which Israel must attend at all costs. The second, more interesting term, "treasured possession," refers to that part of larger economic holdings that are especially prized. Used with reference to YHWH, the term acknowledges that YHWH governs many peoples. But of all the available peoples to whom YHWH might be especially attached, Israel is the one on which YHWH has settled affection, intimacy, and special privilege. The term is a most important one for Israel's sense of specialness (see Exod 19:5; Deut 7:6; 26:18; Ps 135:4; Mal 3:17).

The third statement in verse 21 reiterates the claim of the second statement in verse 2. All three statements articulate Israel's special status in relationship to YHWH, a status that betokens special blessing and protection, but that also implies special responsibility. All three statements are unqualified indicatives. Israel's status as "offspring," "holy people," "treasured possession" is not an outcome of obedience but a premise for obedience, a premise established by YHWH's inexplicable initiative of the relationship, on which see 7:6-7.

These three statements sandwich a series of quite specific prohibitions which, taken point by point are difficult and elusive:

You must not lacerate yourselves (v. 1)
You must not shave your forelocks for the dead (v. 1).
You must not eat any abhorrent thing (abomination) (v. 3).
You must not eat anything that dies of itself (v. 21).
You must not boil a kid in its mother's milk (v. 21).

These quite specific prohibitions, making a series of five, are given tersely, except for the long exposition of the third one. The text explicates neither the significance of these practices nor why they are linked to the great theological claims that are voiced in their midst. Scholarship, moreover, has been noticeably unsuccessful in interpreting these prohibitions. The best suggestions have been that (a) these stipulations concern hygiene, (b) they are counter-

Canaanite, not to be done because Canaanites do them, (c) they are a defensive response to a situation of communal threat, or (d) they are disciplines to be enacted for the sake of identity, without any substantive significance, but performed only for the discipline of the act. It is plausible that each of these scholarly proposals has an element of truth in it.

Mary Douglas has initiated a new trajectory of biblical interpretation that has since then been much adopted and much refined. She insists (a) that these prohibitions are not nonsensical but do have identifiable significance and (b) that the prohibitions cannot be understood one at a time, but must be interpreted as an intentional, programmatic unity:

> Any interpretation will fail which takes the do-nots of the Old Testament in piecemeal fashion. The only sound approach is to forget hygiene, aesthetics, morals, and instinctive repulsion, even to forget the Canaanites and the Zoroastrian magi, and start with the text. Since each of these injunctions is prefaced by a command to be holy, so that must be explained by that command. There must be contrariness between holiness and alienation which will make over-all sense of all the particular restrictions. (Douglas 1970:66)

Douglas suggests that the prohibitions are rules for separating clean and unclean, sacred and profane, in order not to mix or confuse what is properly distinct, for mixing and confusing in even the most elemental matters is to invite destructive chaos:

> We can conclude that holiness is exemplified by completeness. Holiness requires that individuals shall conform to the class to which they belong. And holiness requires that different classes of things shall not be confused. Holiness means keeping distinct categories of creation. (Douglas 1970:53)

The prohibitions, which seem odd or distasteful, in fact are designed to preserve order that is continually under threat, and thereby to enhance the well-being and proper order of creation and so glorify the creator. The "holy people" of Israel is to conduct its daily life as a way of maintaining the good order of creation willed by the creator. The violation of these prohibitions amounts to mixing and thereby polluting the good order, thus entering the zone of death.

The boldness and importance of this text consists in the confident connection of *theological affirmation* and specific *daily discipline*. The holiness of Israel is a generous gift of YHWH; it is, however, exemplified in Israel's willingness to live in a particular way, guarding its life from uncleanness and pollution that will threaten not only its own existence but will endanger the coherent fabric of the entire creation.

In Christian extrapolation from this identity of God's holy people, the declaration of "clean and unclean" is seen to be problematic. Jesus' own teaching on the matter of defilement in Mark 7:18-23 recognizes the problematic that has caused Christians to view the matter in a way different from traditional Judaism. This critique of the conventional rules of defilement, moreover, is reenforced by the narrative of Peter's dream in Acts 10:10-16 that led, subsequently, to the decisive decisions of the "Jerusalem Council" in Acts 15. Thus Christian interpretation in general (and the Reformed tradition in particular) raises difficult questions about these sorts of disciplines. It is to be noticed, nonetheless, that the New Testament continues to appeal to "disciplines of purity" in the Christian life.

But one can also see that the early church employed the language of holiness in a different way. Perhaps the classic case is the great appeal of Paul in Rom 12:1-2. To be sure, Paul's agenda for what is "holy and acceptable" goes in a very different direction from the old disciplines of holiness, but he shares the view of the older traditions that the church's status as God's holy people must issue in visible, concrete distinctions. The early church appeals to similar language in its articulation of the importance of baptism (Eph 4:22-24).

Difficult as it is, this text may pose questions about the visible disciplines that are necessary to maintain and exhibit the distinctiveness of the community of faith in its work of maintaining the good order of creation. Christians are endlessly vigilant against "legalism" and "works righteousness." Such a one-sided vigilance, however, has surely led to "conformity to this world" in the interest of not being excessively odd and punctiliously different.

As a consequence some Christian communities are perhaps not so attentive to the prohibition of alien symbols in the very heart of the community. For example, one may ask, should a Christian community host "a Coke machine" in its midst? There is no doubt that a "Coke machine," in addition to supplying sugar water, betokens an entire world of self-indulgence, a market economy, and a global passion for "development" that eschews local culture. Of course, in most characteristically innocent Christian communities, the logo of the Coke machine is not read so seriously, for it is, after all, simply a Coke machine. One can imagine an argument in the circles of Deuteronomy concerning verse 21 that it is, after all, simply "a boiled kid." It may well be that the "YHWH alone" position of Deuteronomy is overly rigorous and excessively vigilant. The text nonetheless leaves open the issue of daily, visible disciplines and prohibitions that bespeak a peculiar destiny. It is a very old issue in the community, but for being old is no less urgent and immediate.

The Beginning of Social Legislation (14:22-29)

The statute on the tithe concerns the public management and distribution of funds under a covenantal impetus. This statute is arranged in three distinct commands, the basic law of tithe (vv. 22-23), a provision for those at a distance from "the place" (vv. 24-27), and the third year tithe (vv. 28-29). The tithe is to be understood as a tax paid to an overlord in acknowledgment that the owner of the land has a due claim on its produce (see 12:17). Thus tenant farmers to this day regularly "owe" the landowner a certain percentage of the crop, a percentage often larger than the traditional 10 percent. When the tithe is understood as a tax, then the question is, to whom is it owed? It is likely that such a tax was paid to imperial overlords. (See 1 Sam 8:15-17.) In the horizon of Deuteronomy, however, neither the king nor any alien imperial power could claim a tithe, because none of them is the rightful owner of the land.

Exegetical Analysis

14:22-23: The primary statute concerning the tithe is quite simple and direct (vv. 22-23). In an agrarian economy there will be a yearly reckoning of produce, and therefore a determination of what is "owed" in payment to YHWH, whose land Israel occupies. (On the land as belonging to YHWH, see Ps 24:1.) The tithe must be brought to that place where YHWH's name is present as an acknowledgment of the unequal relationship of owner and tenant.

This tithe, however, is unlike any other tax or payment made to the owner, because this owner (YHWH) does not want or need the tithe that Israel offers (see Ps 50:9-13). Instead, the tithe brought to the place is promptly given back to Israel, who is to eat and enjoy the offering it has brought. The tithe owed YHWH is given over to the joy of Israel. YHWH does not want the produce, but insists on the gesture that acknowledges YHWH's generous sovereignty. (In Christian tradition, that YHWH takes and gives back the tithe is replicated in the rhetoric of the Eucharist about bread and wine, "He took . . . he gave.")

The tithe has a pedagogical function. The annual excursion of giving and receiving is to instruct Israel and its young about the peculiar character of YHWH. Israel will "fear YHWH," that is, acknowledge YHWH as the true owner of the land and giver of life, who takes even Israel's grateful tithe and turns it back in yet another wave of generosity.

14:24-27: In what must be a subsequent development of the statute, these verses reckon on the fact that as the territory of Israel expands, the transport of produce becomes inconvenient. In order to accommodate such a geographical reality, produce can be converted into cash that can then, at the place, be converted back into produce to be enjoyed by this community.

Verse 27 provides for the inclusion of Levites in the celebration, the priestly teaching community that has no land, and therefore no produce for the tithe. The Levites are the carriers of the Mosaic tradition (and perhaps the source of Deuteronomy). Thus their mention here assures that the tithe will be kept within the framework of the covenantal vision that is championed by Deuteronomy.

14:28-29: The third element in this statute provides for a different practice of the tithe every third year (vv. 28-29). This provision continues several elements from the preceding action: tithe as acknowledgment, inclusion of the Levites, and culmination in joy. But there are also two new features here. First, this tithe is not brought to the "place of YHWH," but it is kept "within your towns." That is a profound secularization of the practice in which the owner, YHWH, does not even insist on the visible gesture of presentation at the sanctuary, but wants the 10 percent set aside in the community for its use. Thus the religious rite is transposed into an act that concerns the local economy, a 10 percent infusion of extra goods into the community. Second, this tithe "within your towns" is to be deployed for those disadvantaged who have no land from which to bring their own tithe. The landed bring an offering that is for the joy and well-being of the landless. The text names the three traditional landless, vulnerable groups: resident aliens, orphans, and widows, those who depend upon the generosity of the community for their survival. The triad of YHWH-Israel-land is recharacterized beyond the conventional requirement of taxation for an owner.

Theological and Ethical Analysis

This remarkable covenantal provision enunciates the distinctiveness of YHWH and the consequent distinctiveness of Israel. The tithe is an extraordinary characterization of economic reality asserting that the land, its produce, and all its wealth ultimately belong to YHWH, who causes the land to be fruitful. The requirement of such a public acknowledgment of YHWH's ownership is in fact a challenge to all ancient and modern theories of the economy that authorize autonomous wealth and that imagine that the production and enjoyment of wealth can be the ultimate goal of one's life.

In this recharacterization of the economy are the seeds of a covenantal notion of stewardship. Users of the land are only managers who are provisionally entrusted with the land by its owner.

This recharacterization of the economy tells decisively about the bottomless generosity of YHWH. YHWH is not a needy God who relies upon the gifts and offerings of Israel, for YHWH has no needs that Israel can or must satisfy (see Ps 50:9-13). YHWH, moreover, is not a God whose cravings need to be satiated or who, in competition with other gods, collects to see who can have the most. Rather YHWH is constituted in a plenitude of gifts; YHWH characteristically gives and need not receive. An economy that is rooted in the generous character of YHWH is an economy in which there is more than enough, so that a YHWH-rooted economy gives the lie to all economic theory that is based in scarcity (Brueggemann 1998). The tithe dramatizes an economy of surplus (see Mark 6:41-44; 8:6-8).

The generosity of YHWH is matched by Israel's gratitude that results in its own derivative generosity. The peculiar turn of the tithe in verse 29 demonstrates the way that an offering to God is characteristically transposed into an offer for the neighbor. Crüsemann observes:

> We might call this the beginning of real social legislation; it represents *the first known tax for a social program.* With it, those who were landless and socially weak received a sure support which was guaranteed by law and public oath to bring agricultural produce (26:12ff.). (Crüsemann 1996:218)

The tithe is a transaction in generosity and gratitude. It can be reduced to parsimonious calculation (as in Matt 23:23-24). But Deuteronomy intends otherwise. Israel gladly contributes a tax to enhance the economy of the community.

The Social Safety Net (15:1-18)

This statute is perhaps the most radical summons to obedience in Deuteronomy. Some scholars believe this text to be the center of the corpus of commands in Deuteronomy (Hamilton 1992; Weinfeld 1995:152-74). The chapter is a single, coherent appeal, but it may be treated in the following sections: (a) the basic command stated tersely and without explanation or elaboration (v. 1), (b) an explanation of its implementation (vv. 2-6), (c) a persuasive appeal for enactment that suggests resistance to the radicalism of the initial provision (vv. 7-11), (d) a provision for the emancipation or retention of a slave (vv. 12-17), and (e) a final appeal for obedience (v. 18).

Exegetical Analysis

15:1: The background of this provision is the way in which debt was managed in that ancient economy, a way not very different from contemporary practice. Those who accrued debt had to work it off as bond servants; consequently, the length of bond service correlated with the size of the debt. Those who owed more had to work longer to pay off the debt. The logic of such an unexceptional economic practice is that those with limitless debts must work them off to perpetuity. The teaching breaks the endless pattern of debt and work by the abrupt limitation on bond service to seven years, no matter how great the debt (v. 1). It is not clear why the seventh year is identified as the year of debt cancellation, except that perhaps it reflects the rhythm of "sevens" in sabbath and jubilee. The important point is that it puts a firm limitation on *servitude* linked to *debt*. Such a provision is radical, for it shatters the conventional practices of loans, credits, interest, mortgages, and debt management by which any conventional market economy functions.

15:2-6: The commandment, in all of its initial bluntness, requires and receives elaboration, both explanation and persuasion (vv. 2-6). The explanation of verses 2-3 makes explicit that this regulation is in the interest of enhancing the Israelite community. The subjects of this regulation are named "neighbor" *(rēaᶜ)* and "brother or sister" *(ʾāḥ),* both terms referring to fellow members of the covenanted community who participate in the socio-economic experiment that is Israel. Creditors have a relationship to debtors in this community that transcends shared economic reality. Among members of this community, economic realities are not definitional; rather, what is definitional is a common memory of the Exodus, a common blessing in the land, and a common allegiance to the God of Exodus and land.

After this explanation, the text begins to offer motivations whereby Israelites might be persuaded to enact a provision that is against their short-term economic interest. The urgent tone of the persuasive effort suggests that the listening community readily recognized that the injunction to "release" (= cancel) debts seriously undermined conventional economic transactions and assumptions. The persuasions offered here are of two kinds. First, the provision has practical value—it will really work: "There will be no poor among you" (v. 4). The "war on poverty" will be successful! The second motivation is that the release is to be undertaken in a land where YHWH blesses, that is, in a land overflowing with YHWH's abundance (on which see 6:10-11; 8:7-10). YHWH's abundance is the ground from which Israel can afford to be generous to the neighbor. Parsimonious calculations toward neighbors are inappropriate in a land of such prosperity. The bid of the text is that Israel should conduct its finances according to the reality of its context. The overriding reality is that YHWH's abundance makes stringent economic pressure on needy neighbors inappropriate.

15:7-11: The basic command of verse 1 is lean. To it is now added a more extended motivational appeal. While the "year of release" is clearly in view in verse 9, it is noticeable that this paragraph begins in verse 7 not with reference to the statute but with reference to "anyone in need." Perhaps it is assumed that "anyone in need" is sure to be in debt and therefore is a proper subject of the year of release. Thus the opening phrase in this unit, "anyone in need," in fact does a quick "class analysis" of Israelite society, addresses the landed, and affirms the solidarity of the landed with the landless and vulnerable. The statute insists that the landed have in their economic horizon precisely the reality, the need, and the entitlement(!) of the landless.

The citing of "anyone in need" evokes from Moses a passionate appeal that includes both warning and assurance. The appeal in verses 7-8 warns against being "hard-hearted" and "tight-fisted." This happy translation refers to "hand and heart" tightened in reflexive fear, resistance, resentment, and indifference, the kinds of responses that the needy tend to evoke in the anxious comfortable. The rhetoric is sensitive to a bodily, emotional response of fear out of which economic defensiveness may arise. Such emotional, bodily fear if unchecked leads to antineighborly conduct and policy.

The warning that supports the appeal is that the needy neighbor may petition to YHWH against the unresponsive member of the covenant community (v. 9). The term "cry" is a judicial one here. It means to file a legal complaint with YHWH. Because YHWH is so committed to neighborly justice in the covenant community, the uncared for and needy may mobilize YHWH against the unresponsive neighbor who has resources (see Exod 22:21-24; Ps 10:8-16). The assumption of these texts is that social transactions in Israel are never between two parties, but always take place in the presence of YHWH, the third party who will powerfully sustain the entitlements of the poor against the rich.

The warning is matched by an assurance (vv. 10-11). Attentiveness to the poor through debt cancellation will evoke more blessing from YHWH. Generosity to the neighbor will result in greater generosity from YHWH. Generosity evokes generosity.

While the main points are clear, they are somewhat differently articulated in verses 12-17. It is instructive that the term "Hebrew" is used for the slave and not the characteristic "Israelite" of Deuteronomy. The term "Hebrew" is commonly understood not as an ethnic term, but as a sociological term referring to the socially vulnerable and marginalized. The Hebrew man or Hebrew woman who might be treated with contempt is a member of the community of covenant (*ʾāḥ* = brother/sister) and therefore has entitlements that must be honored. It may be that the rhetoric of this verse deliberately creates the oxymoron, "Hebrew slave," because "Hebrews" in Israel are emancipated persons and not subject to slavery.

The provision of verse 12 that parallels verse 1 is followed in verses 13-14 by a passionate appeal. The bond servant is now "free." The act of emancipation from debt is not enough, for an Israelite creditor owes an Israelite debtor more than debt cancellation. Debt cancellation by itself would send the poor person back on the street without any resources. Economic realism would dictate that such a person has no chance of economic survival or success if he or she begins "empty-handed," that is, without resources. The act of debt cancellation is followed by an imperative to give the poor person enough wherewithal from one's own wealth in order to give economic viability to the poor (v. 14). From the blessings of flock, field, and vineyard they have received from YHWH, the wealthy are to give enough to help the poor to start over.

The imperative cannot be mistaken. This is redistribution of wealth in an act of reparations, a transfer of wealth from those who have amassed it to those who have none. The tradition knows unambiguously that a person without economic resources is not a full, functioning member of the community and will not enjoy the dignity and security to which such a companion is entitled. The teaching is willing to override all conventional "commonsense" economics in the interest of creating and sustaining a viable social fabric in which all members have the means to participate effectively. The economy must yield to the viability of the community.

The supreme appeal for compliance with this regulation, apparently commensurate with serious resistance to it in the community of listeners, is the memory of the Exodus (v. 15). Deuteronomy 6:12 and 8:11-20 have already suggested the threat of amnesia in Israel in its prosperity. Amnesia permits the creditors to imagine, "My power and the might of my own hand have gotten me this wealth" (8:17). Amnesia invites the assumption that the current dramatic distinction between haves and have nots, between creditors and debtors, has always been this way, with no need to make an adjustment or concession.

To the contrary, the memory of Exodus makes clear that the entitlements of creditors is recent, that what creditors have is gift and not possession, that creditors and debtors have more in common than what may distinguish them. Finally, Exodus memory recalls that a cry to YHWH (as in v. 9, on which see Exod 2:23-25) evokes divine action that causes redress. It is this specific memory that creates a context and pressure for visible, substantive, prompt, durable redress of social inequity. Creditors are called not to act like Pharaoh, but to replicate the action of YHWH who overcame debt-slavery in Egypt.

The addendum of verses 16-17 allows for the prospect that some debt slaves, in contexts where there is a viable, humane relationship between debtors and creditors, may renounce freedom and remain bondaged out of loyalty and out of a sense of well-being in a viable relationship of subordination. This possibility is a clear exception to the main statute, but allowance is made (see Exod 21:5-6). It is important that the bond servant, in making such a decision, makes the choice freely and without coercion. Even this is, in context, a modest act of freedom in which the bonded person decides his or her future. The final sentence of verse 17 concerning a female slave pertains, it seems clear, to the entire provision and not simply to the option of remaining in servitude. Together with the references to freeing the enslaved Hebrew woman, this provision for the regularized practice of emancipation of female slaves no doubt considerably advances Israel's social vision (see Exod 21:7-10).

15:18: The final appeal in verse 18 indicates, yet again, that there must have been considerable resistance to this radical economic provision. The resistance is for the obvious reason that the statute rigorously limits how creditors may treat debtors, and thereby "takes money out of their pocket." The God of the covenant requires such limit on money making.

Theological and Ethical Analysis

This provision for debt cancellation is not an isolated act, but it is the centerpiece of an alternative vision of covenantal economics that is to define the covenant community. The primary implication of the text is that the economy must be seen as a subset of a neighborly fabric, and must be made to serve and enhance that neighborly fabric. The resolve of Deut 15 is to assure that there will be in covenanted Israel no permanent underclass that is hopelessly and perpetually in debt. It is impossible to overstate how radical and crucial this provision is in the larger pattern of the "sabbatical principle" of Israel's social ethic. It insists on nothing less than a neighborly vision of the economy in which creditors and debtors are bound together in a common covenantal destiny rooted in the purposes of YHWH and confirmed by a memory of YHWH's emancipatory commitments and actions.

This vision of a neighborly economy, moreover, understands that debt management is the defining mark of neighborliness. What a society does about debt, how creditors manage debt, and how debtors are respected or reduced to long-term despair and eventually violence are the most likely indicators about whether there will be a shared, common "peace and prosperity" or whether there will be "prosperity" only for the creditors surrounded by a restlessness among debtors that keeps the entire community in turmoil, under threat, and lacking in "peace."

It is clear, moreover, that the economic vision of a neighborly society urged here is a contradiction of the more conventional economic assumptions and practices that recur in every society. It was a contradiction to the economic practices of the state economy of Egypt, as remembered by Israel, in which debt-slaves evidently were so deeply indebted to the state that they were hopelessly and perpetually in bondage (on which see Gen 47:13-26).

No less so, this provision is a contradiction of the present ideology of the "free market" with its penchant for "privatization." The ideology of privatization is in fact an economic claim that private prosperity is possible and legitimate, without any obligation to the neighborhood or to the maintenance of the social fabric. Karl Polanyi has traced the ways in which the Western economy was dramatically and intentionally torn away from the larger fabric of society and given a kind of pretend autonomy (Polanyi 1957).

Finally, a comment is appropriate to the interplay of verse 4 and verse 11. It is commonplace to notice that in Mark 14:7 Jesus quotes verse 11: "There will always be poor among you." By itself that statement has been misread to sustain indifference toward the poor because nothing can be done about poverty anyway. Nothing could be more remote from this text, however, than passive indifference toward the poor. Rather, verse 11 insists that the practice of debt cancellation is urgent precisely because there are poor people. The recurring presence of debtors requires Israel to be willing to cancel debts. At the same time, verse 4 offers an assurance: "There will be no one in need." That is, poverty can indeed be overcome through debt cancellation. This is an affirmation that the practice really will work and really can make a difference.

Thus verses 4 and 11 are not, as is often suggested, in contradiction to each other. Verse 4 offers *an assurance* of the great potential of this practice that counters despair over poverty. Verse 11 issues *a great imperative* that counters the deception that refuses to notice poor people. Both together make indebtedness a primal agenda for Israel's social vision and a pivotal test case for obedience to a radical covenantal alternative. What Moses does in this assertion is to insist that Israel's faith and future turn on addressing the destructive force of poverty by focusing upon the entitlements of the poor, who are indeed the neighbors of creditors.

Give of Your Best (15:19-23)

The provision for sacrifice of a "firstling," that is, the first male lamb or calf, belongs under the general rubric of "right worship of YHWH" and has commonalities with the provisions of 14:22-29. Thus 14:22-29 and 15:19-23 form an inclusio around 15:1-18, so that the "year of release" is situated textually in the context of the public performance of acts of worship. Worship addressed to YHWH assures that the year of release is an intensely theological act as well as an economic practice. This stipulation is in two parts, the offer of a firstling to YHWH (vv. 19-20) and the disposal of a defective animal that is unsuitable for sacrifice to YHWH (vv. 21-23).

Exegetical Analysis

The sacrifice of the first animal is commonplace enough as an acknowledgment that the animal (and all fruitfulness) is a gift from YHWH to be returned to YHWH in gratitude and acknowledgment of sovereignty (see 12:6, 17; 14:23). Thus the provision is likely routine enough. Here we may notice five features that are characteristically covenantal and reflect an odd, Israelite perception of a common practice:

1. The animal is to be brought to YHWH's special place, a public performance that exhibits allegiance to YHWH, on which see chapter 12.

2. The annual routine of such a sacrifice means that YHWH is recognized as the creator God who presides over the agricultural process of reproduction through the regular change of seasons.

3. As seen in 14:22-29, the sacrifice brought to YHWH at YHWH's place is not needed by YHWH, but is for the joyous consumption of the worshiping community.

4. That the animal is not to be "worked" is expressed in the same Hebrew term that yields the word "slave." Looking back to the sabbath command of 5:12-15 and in proximity to 15:1-18, the tradition understands that an offering to YHWH belongs to the sphere of freedom that allows no bondage (work). Thus an unworked animal bespeaks sabbath, release, and Exodus yet again.

5. Not stated but perhaps implied is the connection made elsewhere between this offering and *the Exodus* (Exod 13:12-16). That connection is not reiterated in 15:19-23. But because Deuteronomy is thoroughly Exodus-oriented, the point is likely the same. The linkage of Exodus to the agricultural cycle makes clear enough the peculiar identity of this God who is both creator and redeemer.

Verses 21-23 appear to be a qualification that has a protective purpose, namely, to avoid inappropriate sacrifice. A firstborn lamb or calf of course may be less than perfect. Such an animal is incongruent with the character of YHWH, who has given generously to Israel and who cannot receive back from Israel an offering unworthy of that generosity (see Lev 22:20-25).

Theological and Ethical Analysis

The offer of a firstling and the ban on defective animals together constitute an affirmation that YHWH must have the best Israel has received. YHWH is not a God to be addressed by way of leftovers. YHWH comes first.

The contemporary bite of this rather routine statute becomes apparent when one reflects on the seemingly endless costs of secularization to a clear and primal commitment to the covenantal realities of YHWH. Consider the common mandate of Deuteronomy concerning "all your heart, all your mind, and all your substance" (as in 6:5): the claim of YHWH must come first. But as members of the community of faith in a variety of ways become autonomous or heteronomous, such a claim tends to lose its force.

1. Instead of "all your heart," in an emotionally draining, anxiety driven society, the claims of faith receive the leftovers of commitment, for one may arrive at YHWH emotionally tired with nothing left to give.

2. Instead of "all your mind," faith is increasingly a victim of "dumbing down," so that the claims of faith in relation to the hard issues of life in the world do not receive the best critical thought. Letting faith become a mindless, self-preoccupied enterprise is like bringing a defective animal for sacrifice.

3. Instead of "all your substance," in a self-indulgent, overspent, over-mortgaged society, investment in covenantal concerns too consists of leftovers. Family or corporate or public income is not deployed so that covenantal claims receive a generous share first, off the top.

A spent emotional life, a life of intellectual laziness and indifference, and a parsimonious self-preoccupied economic life are not unlike bringing defective animals to YHWH's place. They demean YHWH and compromise YHWH's vision of what counts. Those who live in this way imagine life on their own terms, yielding nothing, grateful for nothing, generous about nothing. The routine sacrifice of unblemished firstlings is a regular gesture of discipline that serves to keep Israel's priorities straight.

Take Time to Be Holy (16:1-17)

Deuteronomy 12:13-27, 14:22-28, and 15:19-23 provide isolated mandates for times of worship, but these references amount to no overall pattern of such practices. The present verses offer a more or less complete liturgical calendar. The several festivals mentioned here did not appear in Israel, first of all, in an orderly, schematized way, but arose ad hoc out of a variety of historical memories and agricultural festivals. Moreover, the "liturgical calendar" of Israel was not stable and constant, but was shaped and reshaped over time by a variety of lived circumstances and interpretive needs.

Deuteronomy 16:1-17 focuses upon a regularized pattern that enacts what seem to be the primary covenantal-liturgical interests of Deuteronomy. The unit divides into four sections, verses 1-8, 9-12, and 13-15 concerning the three great festivals, and a concluding summary statement as an imperative in verses 16-17. The festivals, presumably already well established and well accepted in Israel, are to be festal exhibits for the accents of covenantal theology.

Exegetical Analysis

16:1-8: While the Passover emerged as a defining festival in Judaism, the references to it in the Old Testament are sparse (see Exod 12–13; 2 Kgs 23:21-23). These texts together make a linkage to *the Exodus* and to worship in *Jerusalem*. Deuteronomy 16:1-7 is situated in the midst of these two accents on Exodus and Jerusalem. It begins with the affirmation that the festival is *"to [for in NRSV]* YHWH" your God (v. 1). This is matched at the conclusion with a "solemn assembly *to* YHWH your God" (v. 8). Thus the festival is kept focused upon the exclusive YHWH agenda that pervades the tradition of Deuteronomy. This singular focus on YHWH is reinforced in verses 2, 5-7 with an accent on *the place,* on which see chapter 12. Attention to the place is taken in Deuteronomy as an assurance of focus upon YHWH. The accent on YHWH and upon place provides two envelopes for the core statement of verses 3-5 concerning the actual rite:

YHWH (v. 1),   place (v. 2)   place (vv. 5-7),   YHWH (v. 8)

a   b   b'   a'

In the center of these statements primary attention is upon "unleavened bread" *(maṣṣôt)* that is the main carrier of the festival (vv. 3-4). The unleavened bread, well described in Exod 12–13, is bread that was eaten "in haste," without waiting long enough for the yeast to rise, in haste in order to escape by night before the forces of Pharaoh. The purpose of the bread—eaten *without rising, in haste, at night*—is to replicate the ominous moment of escape from Egypt and the glorious emancipation that resulted on that night that is like no other night. As much as is imaginable in Israel, the purpose of the festival is to replicate the experience and the emotional intensity of the original Exodus emancipation.

The primary purpose of the festival may well be pedagogical, that is, to inculcate the young into the defining memory of the community. Such a purpose is likely, both because of the explicit pedagogical interest of Exod 12:26-27; 13:8, 14-15, on which see Deut 6:20-25, and because of the deep concern for the children we have seen in chapters 6–8. The festival is to assure that there is continuity into the next generation of the Exodus memory and the Exodus vision that gives force and authority to the statutes and ordinances that intend a self-conscious ethic of covenantal neighborliness.

The final phrasing of verse 8 situates the festival in the rhythms of the sabbath. The culmination of this festival is a day of work stoppage. The phrasing is reinforced in the Samaritan text tradition that says: "no work or bondage." It is plausible that the text has especially on its horizon the "year of release" in 15:1-18, for Passover is indeed a "festival of release."

16:9-12: The "festival of weeks" is the second great festival in this "liturgical calendar" (vv. 9-12). Its name, "weeks," derives from the number "seven," so that the festival calendar is a complex rhythm of sevens, reflective of the sabbatical principle; perhaps behind that is the rhythm of the agricultural seasons. In Exod 23:16 the same celebration is termed a "harvest festival," so that there is no doubt that it is related to the harvest of crops which, in an agricultural society, is the make-or-break occasion when the entire income of the year is produced.

Four characteristic marks of Deuteronomy stand out in this presentation of the festival:

1. It is an occasion of *joy* (see 12:12, 18). The liturgical life of Israel is marked by unrestrained exuberance (see Isa 9:3).

2. The joy of this festival is *inclusive* of the entire community. In addition to the Levites (12:12, 19; 14:27), also invited are slaves (as in the sabbath provision of 5:14), and the triad of stranger, widow, and orphan, all of whom are included in the bounty of celebration, all entitled to share when they have no produce of their own.

3. The celebration is at *the place,* under the kind of supervision that will keep the festival firmly devoted "to YHWH your God."

4. Verse 12 links the festival to *the Exodus memory,* a statement closely parallel to 15:15. The tradition of Deuteronomy cannot imagine any devotion to YHWH that is not Exodus-oriented, for this is the God "who brought you out of Egypt, out of the house of bondage." In this interpretive tradition, nothing falls outside this emancipatory memory.

Having noted all of these motifs, the great accent of the festival is upon *the blessing,* which here means the material abundance in the land, because of the productivity of the land. The original orientation of the festival and the focus upon the land do not easily link to Exodus; but the interpretive process of Deuteronomy readily draws all these matters together. The accent on *blessing* most broadly connects the festival to creation and the goodness of the creator (Westermann 1978). It is the creator God who has guaranteed fruitfulness that makes a bountiful harvest possible. Thus the God of the Exodus is the creator. The one who redeems is the one who creates. The prosperous land is a foretaste of the new creation that YHWH will surely bring in due course.

16:13-15: The third festival in the calendar is Booths (Tabernacles) (vv. 13-15). The characteristic notes of that festival serve much the same function as the previous ones. It is most likely that this festival was originally agricultural, perhaps with arbors built to protect jeopardized crops from the hot sun. The accent on harvest (v. 13), and the blessing for produce (v. 15) point to such an agricultural origin. But because the historical memory of Israel in Deuteronomy is so powerful, it is not surprising that the booths become replications for the tenuous living quarters of the Israelites in the wilderness (see Neh 8:13-18). Thus the combination of land blessing and historical memory is again readily held together, all in the service of generating a great public exhibit of gratitude.

16:16-17: In the symmetrical coding of Deuteronomy, these festivals constitute a fixed pattern, regardless of what the antecedent practices may have been (vv. 16-17). In this summary statement that names the three great festivals, this tradition specifies three duties related to the holy days. First, the festivals concern all the males in the community. In light of Deut 31:12 and Neh 8:3, for example, one may wonder why only males are mentioned, as the festivals elsewhere were more inclusive. This surely reflects the determined patriarchy of the tradition, but may at the same time be inclusive of households: "males," as "heads of households" may be representative.

Second, participation in the festivals is an act of gratitude, primarily preoccupied with bringing offerings (vv. 16-17). An offering is explicitly mentioned in verses 2 and 10, and is implied in the third festival. The offering signifies at the same time acknowledgment of YHWH's sovereignty (ownership of the land) and the gratitude of Israel. "Empty-handed" celebrants are precluded, because being "empty-handed" signifies a reluctance to acknowledge YHWH and an unwillingness to give public expression to gratitude. The festivals are designed as outpourings of gratitude by Israel, who lives completely by the power and generosity of YHWH and regularly cedes over to YHWH the credit and initiative for the well-being of life.

Third, all the males "shall appear." There is no doubt that this is a nonnegotiable requirement. Membership in the covenant community requires public participation. The festival is a visible public enactment, and what it most requires is "showing up," being seen to be engaged in Yahwistic activity, being seen by the young of the community, being seen by non-Israelite neighbors. Perhaps most crucially, it is a public act of responsible male adults who are unashamed and unembarrassed by an act of gratitude. They visibly announce their membership in this narrative of generosity and gratitude, and visibly declare a rejection and renunciation of other forms of life and other loyalties and sources of well-being. The festival is a declaration of a decision about life-and-death blessing-and-curse.

Theological and Ethical Analysis

These festivals in Israel represent a pure act, as pure as a communal act can be, of an alternative community. The alternative embraced and exhibited in the festivals is alternative to pharaonic brick quotas, alternative to Canaanite seductions, alternative to the deathly choices and ambiguous realities of daily life. Here Israel enters a zone where the durable emancipatory power of the Exodus and the awesome generosity of the earth are given full play. In the festivals Israel comes to a fresh realization that its freedom is not its own work, but is a gift gladly given by YHWH. In parallel fashion, Israel comes to a glad acknowledgment of the generous productivity of the earth so that grain, wine oil, herds, and flocks are given by YHWH in abundance without any productive engineering by Israel. Festival is the capacity to enter a way of life in which all other claims, pressures, and realities can be suspended.

It is precisely the glad suspension of all else in festival time that permits the singular sovereignty and unparalleled generosity of YHWH to generate an Israel not heretofore known, an Israel grateful, self-assured, ready for the rigors of covenant—on its way rejoicing.

In our time and place, it is a wonderment if festival can have such power and attractiveness, given pervasive complacency, self-indulgence, and individual autonomy. The ideology of complacency, self-indulgence, and individual autonomy, to be sure, has its regular, incessant festival in Hollywood, sports, and on television. The cogent question growing out of Deuteronomy is whether the vision of covenantal neighborliness rooted in YHWH's generous sovereignty can have festivals that are credible and compelling amidst other festivals that are better funded. The liturgical calendar of the church revolves around its three great festivals of Christmas, Easter, and Pentecost. Pondering the festivals of ancient Israel may lead to reflection on how these Christian festivals are moments outside time for,

- the totally *other* God who comes in flesh (Christmas)
- the totally *other* Crucified, raised to new power (Easter)
- the totally *other* Wind defying control (Pentecost).

Gratitude is a condition dominant culture wants resisted. But it is that very gratitude that becomes the precondition to and access point for entry into festival. Gratitude is the entry point to the festival wherein the new community of God becomes reality. Small wonder that it is important to "show up." "Showing up" is clearly what Paul has in mind:

> Clean out the old yeast so that you may be a new batch, as you really are unleavened. For our paschal lamb, Christ, has been sacrificed. Therefore, let us celebrate the festival, not with the old yeast, the yeast of malice and evil, but with the unleavened bread of sincerity and truth. (1 Cor. 5:7-8)

Instituted by God (16:18–18:22)

With this text the corpus of statutes and ordinances turns from cultic order to civil order, in the conviction that civic as well as cultic order can be organized and practiced in covenantal ways. Thus the general theme of this body of texts is the covenantal deployment of public power. Dean McBride has observed that as long ago as Josephus the book of Deuteronomy was characterized as a "polity," a serious theory of power (McBride 1987). That usage pertains to the entire book of Deuteronomy as McBride considers it, but the notion of polity pertains, more directly, to our section of text that identifies four "offices" or functions of power and leadership. With more precise reference to these particular texts, Norbert Lohfink has considered this text to be a model for the distribution of public powers in a way that avoids any absolutism, a distribution that is essential in a covenantal community (Lohfink 1982:55-75). The offices that are here authorized for covenantal leadership include judges (16:18-17:13), king (17:14-20), priests (18:1-8), and prophet (18:9-22). While the deployment of each of these offices in particular is important, the larger pattern of governance here indicated is even more crucial for our understanding of a covenantal vision of public power.

JUSTICE, ONLY JUSTICE (16:18–17:13)

16:18–18:22: These verses provide a more or less inchoate sketch of what a judicial system might look like in a community of covenant. It begins with a fundamental statement of covenantal justice and the expectation of responsible, trustworthy "judges and officials" who will guarantee a practice of justice befitting Israel's vision of society (16:18-20). This is followed by a particular case, apparently presented in order to establish rules for valid testimony (17:2-7). Finally this sketch provides for a centralized authority to adjudicate difficult cases (17:8-13). It is not at all clear why 16:21 and 17:1 are placed here as they are. The first of these texts, 16:21, echoes the polemic against alien religious icons in 12:2-4, and the second, 17:1, reiterates 15:21-23, though with the rhetoric escalated by the term "abhorrent," on which see 7:25-26. It is possible that these two seemingly isolated verses are a reminder that responsible civic power is grounded in an uncompromising theological vision. Covenantal social power derives from and is guaranteed by the singular worship of a covenant-making, covenant-keeping God.

Exegetical Analysis

16:18-22: The elemental vision of court justice in 16:18-20 parallels the provision in 1:9-18 that in turn may be informed by Exod 18:13-27. It is important that of all of these authorizations for public leadership, a commitment to justice and a reliable administration of justice are elemental to covenantal society and are listed first among the offices ordered by Moses. Two matters are of particular interest in this provision. First, verse 19 lists three defining qualities of judges by way of prohibition:

> Do not distort justice;
> Do not show partiality;
> Do not accept bribes.

The concern is that justice must be genuinely disinterested and not influenced by the special pressure that the rich and powerful are able to exercise, for it is the rich and powerful who characteristically are able to offer bribes and purchase partiality. This regulation, moreover, echoes the older text of Exod 23:6 that explicitly mentions "the poor," who must be protected by the court, because the poor are likely to have no other social guarantee or advocate.

Israel understands that in the liturgy the poor and destitute may "cry out" to YHWH in prayer (see Exod 22:21-26). In civic society, the court is the analogue to YHWH. As the poor may cry out to YHWH, so the poor may cry out to judges who enact YHWH's will for justice in actual cases (see Luke 18:1-8). It is the conviction of Deuteronomy that the disadvantaged have an inalienable entitlement in the covenant community; it is the business of the court to protect that entitlement.

The notion of "distorting justice" by failing to protect the entitlements of the vulnerable is at the heart of the anguish voiced by the prophets. Phrasing parallel to 16:18–17:13 occurs in prophetic indictment of the economic system (Amos 5:7; 6:12; Isa 5:22-23). The prophetic tradition, perhaps informed by the tradition of Deuteronomy, knows that a distorted judicial system makes a neighborly deployment of power impossible.

Verse 20, using a different term for "justice" *(ṣedeq)*, makes the practice of justice the condition for occupying the land. Without justice, Israel loses its entitlement to the land, a conviction that was seen to come to fruition in the great deportation of the sixth century.

17:2-7: The second section of this law works out procedures for reliable testimony (17:2-7). The case cited is, oddly enough, not a matter of economic justice, as 16:19 might lead us to expect, but a case of theological compromise in "serving other gods." Both the affront and the severe punishment in this case have most in common with 13:6-11. It is evident in both cases that a theocratic vision of social power here makes no clear distinction between "religious" violations of loyalty to YHWH and other, civic affronts against neighbor. Thus the case cited here hardly fits the purview of 16:18-20.

In any event, it is provided, as in 13:14, that communal discipline is not to be based on rumor or hearsay. A careful judicial investigation is required to determine the facts of the case. The primary case law in this instance is organized around "if" (v. 2) and "then" (v. 5)—if guilty, then execution. Verse 6 establishes an important point of procedure that may be the new element that advances beyond the material in chapter 13. As in 13:9-10, it is provided that the one who makes accusation is the one who must initiate the execution, supported by the participation of the entire community. But here the witness of the accuser must be supported by other testimony. The rules of procedure are no doubt reflected in the Gospel requirement of two witnesses (Matt 18:16) and in the invitation to "cast the first stone" (John 8:7). The book of Deuteronomy is committed to a rule of law even if it is a severe rule of law. The concluding formula of purgation, echoing 13:5, indicates the purpose of such judicial activity is the protection of the community from distortion.

17:8-13: The third section of this authorization of a court system provides for a centralized court. The paragraph divides into two parts concerning authorization (vv. 8-9) and compliance (vv. 10-13). The authorization is to provide for a court that will relieve local village courts of cases of excessive difficulty. The example of difficult cases in verse 8 is rather open-ended and is not limited to homicide and assault. What counts the most here is that the hard cases will be heard at "the place" (see 12:11) where YHWH is intensely present and where YHWH's public officials are most informed about Yahwistic justice. More specifically, along with "judges and officials," now the Levitical priests are involved in adjudication, which means for this tradition a move toward sacral authority and direct appeal to the covenantal will of the covenant-envisioning God.

The amount of space and rhetorical energy in this provision that are used to insist upon compliance is surprising (vv. 10-13). Compliance to law is a make-or-break issue in the community, and no departure from exact compliance will be tolerated. These verses make clear that in the rulings of the centralized court supervised by Levitical priests, the tradition of Deuteronomy has reached the bottom line of covenantal order. A court that cannot enforce its decisions is no court at all, though apparently enforcement here depends upon persuasion and intimidation. The punishment of those who do not comply is pedagogical, to discourage in the most dramatic and decisive ways resistance or indifference to the court from others in time to come.

Theological and Ethical Analysis

This provision, as the ones to follow in 17:14–18:22, makes clear that biblical faith cares about public power. It specifically intends that public power shall be in the interest of justice. This is an important accent, particularly in an environment of both church and society wherein faith is characteristically reduced to personal, privatized matters of a romantic, therapeutic kind. The Bible is about the reordering and reconstitution of public life under the vision of the rule of God and under the hope of the coming kingdom of God. It insists that public power is an arena in which the deepest claims of faith are operative.

That conviction about justice envisions a community of clear "law and order" that will not tolerate deviation. This is especially evident in the severe sanctions of verses 5, 7, 10-13, though perhaps the more telling sanction is the awareness that the land can be forfeited. Having recognized the severity of this justice, it is equally clear that the justice here envisioned is justice rooted in the vision of YHWH, who is known in Israel to be the generative power of emancipation. The "law and order" assumed here is not conventional positive law that defends the status quo or a bland system of sanctions. This is, rather, justice that is legitimated by the God of widows, orphans, and sojourners who authorizes a year of release rooted in the Exodus. The urgent Deuteronomic commitment to "law and order" has a theological dimension, insisting that it is the God of covenant (see v. 2), the God of social solidarity, who evokes judicial practice. At the same time, the references in verse 19 indicate that this justice has an important economic dimension; the Deuteronomic theory of justice contains the seeds of "distributive justice," which in our modern time takes the form of reparations for the disadvantaged.

Finally it is to be noted that this justice admits of no strict constructionism. It is the work of the central court to "interpret" *(yārâ)* (v. 11), that is, to convert social vision to particular cases. The practice of justice is not a series of fixed codes and automatic sanctions. It is rather a practice of covenantal interpretation that serves the larger vision of society. This text might be an invitation to the church to take up afresh the deep commitments of faith to affirmative social justice. Beyond that, there is no doubt that the moral passion to be found in the judicial traditions of the United States is deeply rooted in this notion of justice. The text may indeed invite a recovery of a central commitment of Deuteronomy that continues to be indispensable for contemporary practice of justice.

POWER WITHOUT ACQUISITIVENESS (17:14-20)

Provision for a second public official concerns the king. With the possible exception of Exod 2:28 (Heb. v. 27), this is the only Mosaic statute on kingship in the Torah. Such a lack of comment is remarkable in light of the dominant presence of the monarchy in the life of ancient Israel. The institution of the monarchy in Israel was a source of much dispute in that ancient community because (a) there were models of exploitative kingship prior to and all around Israel, (b) there were internal tensions in Israel motivated by competing political and economic interests, either for village autonomy or for centralized power that assured both military strength and economic concentration, and (c) these internal tensions were readily given theological articulation, so that human monarchy is variously interpreted as the will of YHWH for a new social circumstance in Israel or as disobedience against the sovereignty of YHWH who is Israel's true and only king. It is important to recognize that the statute of 17:14-20 does not exist in an interpretive vacuum or as a statement of the obvious choice of Israel. It is, rather, one advocacy among many advocacies on a deeply disputed issue, on which see especially 1 Sam 8:10-18.

The textual unit divides into three brief statements concerning Mosaic authorization of an Israelite king (vv. 14-15), a prohibition against royal policies of acquisitiveness (vv. 16-17), and an insistence that kingship in Israel be Torah-based (vv. 18-20).

Exegetical Analysis

17:14-15: The question of royal power only arises when Israel is in the land. The overriding issue in Deuteronomy is how to manage the land covenantally, so that it can be retained according to the promise of YHWH. Moses anticipates Israel in the land will want to be "like all the nations" (see 1 Sam 8:5, 20), with centralized economic power and strong military potential. The tone suggests a reluctance in the tradition that is congruent with the reluctance of Samuel and the ambiguity of YHWH in 1 Sam 8. Moses' hand is forced by the reality of circumstance; his work is to provide a monarchy that will maintain the distinctiveness of Israel as YHWH's chosen people, that is, a monarchy *"like* all the nations" for a people that is to be *unlike* all the nations. The first provision for such a tricky matter is that the approved king must be an Israelite and not a foreigner (v. 15). While such a provision may make an ethnic appeal, it more likely requires a candidate for kingship who is inculcated into and committed to a covenantal vision of community, one who remembers and does not forget, who will not imagine the importance of his own might and power (on which see 8:17).

17:16-17: The positive requirement of a covenantal horizon for governance is strongly reinforced by the three negations.

Do not multiply horses. The reference is to the development of a strong military force, for horses are a symbol and measure of such power. Moses already knows that a strong military power is much less likely to be covenantally alert and responsible. The explicit danger of such an investment is "a return to Egypt." The phrase is richly ambivalent. Taken theologically and in light of the Exodus accent in Deuteronomy, the injunction warns against the undoing of the Exodus and the reduction of Israel once again to slavery, so that the king in Israel, with an insatiable military budget, taxes his own people into economic dependence. Taken historically, this provision may reflect Solomon's "horse trading" whereby Israel was drawn into commercial practices as an "arms dealer," a practice surely inimical to a covenantal vision of reality (1 Kgs 9:26-29). Either way, "horses" signifies the undoing of covenantal Israel.

Do not multiply wives. This is likely not a comment on monogamy or adultery. More likely it is a belated reflection on the intricate political network of Solomon, who cemented political alliances through marriages so that his marriages were political arrangements, as for example, his marriage to the daughter of Pharaoh (1 Kgs 3:1; 7:8; 9:16). The Deuteronomic theology reflected in 1 Kgs 11:1-8 declares that it was precisely these foreign wives, seven hundred of them plus three hundred concubines who "turned away his heart" (v. 3). The danger of accumulating royal wives is that they, with the alliances and political commitments they signify, become an impetus and occasion for compromise of Yahwism. The phrase "his heart will turn away" is one common to this statute and to 1 Kgs 11.

Do not multiply silver and gold (v. 17). Silver and gold in large quantities signal a state that is committed to opulence and self-aggrandizement, an achievement possible only by the transfer of tax moneys in exploitative ways. There is no doubt, yet again, that Solomon is indeed the model here, for his Jerusalem establishment became a showcase for "conspicuous consumption" (Brueggemann 1998). The dispute after his death in 1 Kgs 11, moreover, makes clear that Solomon's economic policies, dependent upon heavy taxation, were intolerably exploitative. Solomon's regime had become completely self-serving, predictably to the neglect of the kind of neighborly concerns that lie at the heart of the covenant. Thus, quite explicitly, these verses of prohibition seem to take Solomon as the "worst case scenario" for what happens when concentrated power disregards the covenantal foundations and commitments of its power.

17:18-20: Moses offers an alternative to self-serving power and opulence (vv. 18-20). The alternative to aggressive acquisitiveness is that the king, the one granted reluctantly by Moses, should spend primary energy on the study of the Torah, instructed and tutored by the Levites, the proponents of Mosaic Torah. The provision is that the king shall have a "copy of this Torah." The term "copy," in Greek *deuteros,* means a second version. It is from this verse that the book of Deuteronomy takes its popular name as a second version of the Torah of Sinai. Thus the book of Deuteronomy is not the document of Sinai, but it is a second, derivative, more expansive vision from the God of Sinai. The Deuteronomic tradition urges that what will protect kingship from avarice and self-destructiveness is precisely the Torah of Deuteronomy. Deuteronomy makes the institution of monarchy subordinate to the Torah, dependent upon and responsive to the regulations of Moses. By making it subordinate, Moses seeks to assure that monarchy in Israel is never autonomous, always penultimate and subject to Torah.

This statute is the theoretical basis for the narrative of 1 and 2 Kings, a study of how the several kings in Israel do or do not adhere to covenant, with the cumulative judgment made in the narrative that it is the disregard of Torah by the kings that leads to land loss and deportation. Thus the final verse of the law of kingship is a leitmotif for the royal history. The durability of monarchy depends upon preoccupation with Torah. That durability is given up in Judah by default, so that in the end the dynasty ends in a deep pathos (Jer 22:30).

Theological and Ethical Analysis

This statute is not to be understood as the naive suggestion that reading a scroll will change public matters. It is rather that reading this scroll is emblematic of an alternative vision of social power that makes long-term, stable, productive governance possible. The text is an invitation for a community of faith to rethink public power and the relationship of the governed to the governors. Deuteronomy insists that the powerful (in state and in church) are subject to a will and purpose other than their own that concerns the just deployment of economic resources and political power among the governed. Three facets of this issue merit further attention.

First, it is clear in the Christian tradition that Jesus, the crucified, is exceedingly vulnerable and selfless in his exercise of dominion. In Matt 6:25-33, after his either/or teaching of verse 24, Jesus enjoins his disciples against anxiety. Even in the circles of the most extravagance, it is anxiety for "more." more power, more wealth, more security, more pleasure, more beauty, more influence, that propels arrogant power. It is not an accident that in verse 29 Solomon is cited by Jesus as the quintessentially anxious one who, in all his power and wealth, turned out to be second rate (see also Mark 10:42-44 on power).

Second, this provision is a strong word to the community of faith. In the United States, there is no doubt that free market ideologies of self-advancement deeply beset the church. Those who are summoned to leadership in the Church do not worry about horses and wives as much as about silver and gold, though perhaps the widespread scandal of sexuality among clergy bespeaks a need for accumulation of more than wealth. It is evident, moreover, that in a society of affluence, local congregations are sorely tempted to extravagance in buildings and programs in the expenditure of Torah funds that might be otherwise deployed.

Third, it is, however, public leadership and not church leadership that might be most in the purview of this statute. When government increasingly becomes the monopoly of the wealthy and Congress "a club of millionaires" supported by corporate management that cares only about profit, then a Torah-based social vision that invests in neighborly entitlements is difficult to keep in focus. In the United States, moreover, the cynicism of self-serving power may be as deathly, even if not in such dramatic ways as elsewhere in the world. Plain and simple, Moses asserts that leadership devoted to the accumulation of wealth, power, influence, prestige, in the public or the corporate domain, is a way to land loss, social disintegration, and death (see Ezek 34:1-10). The Torah keeps the managers of power fixed on the social fabric and the neighbor who has no horses, no silver, no gold, and perhaps only one wife or one husband who is underfunded.

A PRIEST WITHOUT PROPERTY (18:1-8)

The third office provided for in this "constitution" for covenantal Israel is the Levitical priest. Deuteronomy is thought to be profoundly linked to that priestly teaching tradition, so that the provision for them here may be something of a "signature" by the producers of the book left in their product (Weber 1952:174-87 and *passim*; von Rad 1953:60-69; Cross 1973:195-215).

This text divides into two parts. The first part concerns a general provision for the maintenance of the Levitical priests (vv. 1-5). The second part perhaps reflects a particular crisis and the guarantee of the legitimacy of this priesthood in the face of dispute (vv. 6-8).

Exegetical Analysis

Israel must have, so this text insists, Levitical priests for the sake of its life in the land of promise. In order to have such priestly leadership, Israel must be prepared to pay for their maintenance (vv. 1-5). These verses assert a primal theological characteristic of the Levitical priests (vv. 1-2), and then a quite pragmatic requirement in response to the theological reality (vv. 3-5).

The theological reality is that the tribe of Levi was left out of the division of the land of promise among the several tribes. (See Josh 13:14 in the context of Josh 13–19.) The tribe of Levites was an enduring ruling force in Israel even though it lacked an identifiable patrimony. These verses use the term "inheritance" four times, reinforced once by "allotment," thus indicating the issue of the regulation. The term "inheritance" of course is of primary importance in Deuteronomy, as the tradition ponders the land and Israel's title to it. More specifically, every tribe as part of Israel has entitlement, and by implication every Israelite as a member of a tribe has a secure inherited place in the people of God. That is what it means to be an Israelite.

Except for the tribe of Levi, the Levitical priests—they are omitted from the land process and so are excluded from the economic-political-legal dynamics of Israel. The text is insistent on this point. As compensation for that odd and costly status, these verses make two provisions. First, YHWH is the inheritance of the tribe of Levi, not YHWH's goods or properties, but YHWH's own self. Thus the phrasing of verse 2 suggests a peculiar intimacy with YHWH that is regarded as a great gift, perhaps greater than a parcel of land. Gerhard von Rad (1966:243-66) has noticed the phrase, "YHWH is my portion," and proposes that the peculiar phrase is an affirmation of the special spiritual Levitical legacy (Pss 16:5-6; 73:26).

Von Rad concludes that Yahweh is the giver of life, that Yahweh saves from death, that Yahweh is Levi's portion: all this and much more was made explicit in the cultus from the earliest times (von Rad 1966:265). At its best such a provision is a preference for *communion with YHWH* rather than a *commodity in Israel.*

But second, the immediate problem left by such an affirmation is that one cannot turn YHWH to food. The tribes that have land will produce their own livelihood (see Josh 5:12). Levi may "have" YHWH, but that is no "visible means of support." For that reason the statement of intimate communion with YHWH in verse 2 is matched in verse 1 by a statement of greater material realism. The offerings to which YHWH is entitled are in fact a means of maintenance for these priests. Thus the theological rhetoric of "offering to YHWH" is understood pragmatically as livelihood for the priesthood.

Verses 3-5 are an explication of the "LORD's portion" that the priests are to receive. The term "due" in verse 3 is a rendering of *mišpāṭ,* that is, *"just* due," to which the priests are properly entitled. The specificities of offerings in verses 3-4, including firstfruits, may suggest that the priests had generous provisions, though it is not possible to determine why in verse 3 certain parts of sacrificed animals are identified for the priests. The concluding verse 5 is a general formula of legitimacy of this priesthood "for all time," just in case any should imagine that such a priestly allowance might be terminated. The final phrase, which has a hint of polemic to it, leads to the following section.

Verses 6-8 seem to hint at a displacement of Levitical priests from "any of your towns" to "the place." This anticipated transition is frequently taken by interpreters as a reference to the vigorous reformist activity of King Josiah in 2 Kgs 23:8-9. The purpose of the reform seems to have been to shut down the "high places," that is, the rural shrines, in order to concentrate all liturgical activity in Jerusalem under royal supervision. Such a maneuver would have put many rural priests out of work if they remained "among their kindred," far away from the new place of liturgical concentration. These verses insist that displaced priests who come to "the place," presumably Jerusalem, are fully entitled to minister there. More than that, they are entitled to income commensurate with the better paid urban priests already on the scene. The prescription of Ezek 44 concerning the Levites (vv. 10-14) and the Levitical priests, descendants of Zadok (vv. 15-27), is an indication of the dispute and ongoing rivalries among the priestly orders in Jerusalem. Whatever may be said about that historic rivalry is largely speculative. It is enough to notice that 18:6-8 is one voice in a larger dispute. If the claim is correct that the Levites are connected to the teaching tradition of Deuteronomy, then these verses are an assertion of the legitimate claims of the Levites' perspective in a highly contested interpretive situation where other theological traditions vied for dominance.

Theological and Ethical Analysis

This special provision for the priesthood suggests the following:

1. The anticipated covenant community requires priests at its center in order to resist the profanation of life. It is apparent that the Levitical priests, while not limited to such functions, were Torah teachers who enabled Israel to reflect upon its pecu-

liar identity and its demanding covenantal ethic. These priests embody the practice of imaginative symbolization out of the normative tradition that prevents social life from being flattened into commoditization. It belongs to priesthood to handle the core symbols of faith in imaginative and artistic ways. The nurture and practice of such an authorizing presence in the community is deeply important.

2. That the priesthood lies outside the economic processes of land results in a life of freedom and dependence. These priests enjoy freedom from normal, social entitlements, a freedom that has the prospect of creating genuine disinterest. This is no small matter in a secularized society in which the priestly office is increasingly vulnerable to the standards and visions of a profaned economy. Along with disinterest, the Levitical priests, who have no assured stake in the economy, are cast in a position of dependence upon YHWH and upon other Israelites who bring offerings. This dependency is perhaps to be celebrated, for it offers a model of living by the generosity of others and finally living by grace.

3. At the same time, the text asserts that the agents of such imaginative symbolization are entitled to communal maintenance, a proper and legitimate deployment of YHWH's own offerings. These two positions together, a disinterested placement due to the lack of normal entitlements and the legitimacy of maintenance, suggest a way of situating priesthood and its symbolic imagination in a society not very responsive to such symbolization.

4. Though the text concerns priesthood, it is worthwhile to ponder the phrase, "YHWH is my portion" more generally. The Levitical priests are mandated to an extreme form of the covenantal living that in fact concerns all members of the community. The acceptance of YHWH as "portion" to the exclusion of all other "portions" is a remarkable check upon the attraction of commoditization. Extreme consumerism—the mad pursuit of a portion—is both the cause and the consequence of a lack of intimacy with YHWH, who is a true portion for those in covenant. YHWH as portion, in contrast to all other portions,

suggests a radical either/or for the priests who are to guide Israel in its own inescapable either/or, a choice fully between "portion" as *communion* and "portion" as *commodity.*

A FAITHFUL WAY TO THE FUTURE (18:9-22)

The fourth "office" in the anticipated covenant community to come is a prophet. The text places the prophet alongside judges, priests, and king, suggesting that the prophetic function is as crucial to a viable covenantal society as are the other offices that are more "common sense" for ordinary society. In the study of the prophets of ancient Israel, it is more generally correct to say that they are preoccupied with the present and not with the long-term future. It is only the most popular understandings of prophecy that treat them as predictors. Here, however, the prophet is considered precisely as one who will anticipate the future.

The authorization of the prophet "like Moses" is introduced with a negative declaration against the possible substitution of divination for prophecy (vv. 9-14). In the paragraph on the prophet as such (vv. 15-22), the material is divided into an authorization of the prophet (vv. 15-18) and an evaluation of and response to such prophets (vv. 19-22).

Exegetical Analysis

18:9-14: It is clear that knowing about the future is an important matter for a viable society, for it has to do with planning as well as hoping. In this text, knowing the future will be even more important in the new land, for the issue arises "when you come into the land." Perhaps the matter reflects the anxiety of an agrarian economy that is always at the mercy of "the elements." The control of the future is a highly contested matter, for whoever can control the future will have great power in the present.

The text delineates ways to control the future that are not admissible in Israel, for which the strong pejorative "abomination" ("abhorrent") is used (vv. 9, 12). These prohibited alternative practices are everywhere available, and perhaps were attractive to Israel. The text offers an inventory of seven different forms of divination. While scholars have used great energy in trying to determine the exact point of the different labels for different practices, Deuteronomy has no particular interest in and likely no expertise about such distinctions. All forms of divination are grouped together as strategies for learning about the future that are not permissible to Israel. Specifically these practices include consultation with "the spirit world" and "the dead"; such practices suggest that there are agents elsewhere, beyond YHWH, who have special knowledge, a claim mightily resisted by the YHWH-alone party in Israel (see 1 Sam 28:3-25).

The prohibited practices challenge YHWH's monopoly of authority in what might later be termed heterodoxy. This challenge to YHWH may include three elements:

1. These several practices likely were in some way defined by manipulative techniques as though some secret knowledge would give access to the future.

2. This approach to the future assumes that the future is fixed, stable, and settled, that is, that persons, communities, and world are all subject to a fate that is once for all decreed. From the angle of covenant, such a perspective is completely mistaken, for the future under the rule of YHWH is a zone of freedom. The future is not a settled fate but an open destiny partly given and partly chosen, still to emerge. The entire weight of Deuteronomy is to insist that Israel may indeed *choose* its future (30:15-20). Techniques that presume a settled fate, if embraced by Israel, would lead to a collapse of the theological premise of covenant.

3. These techniques are objectionable because they are void of any ethical dimension. The fated future, it is assumed, is given no matter what. Such a view nullifies both freedom to shape the future and responsibility for shaping the future. Obviously Deuteronomy believes that whether one offers right sacrifices and whether one cancels debts and loves sojourners is decisive in determining what the future holds.

Divination would deny the freedom of responsibility; in the same way YHWH is denied both covenantal freedom and covenantal responsibility for a partnership, albeit an asymmetrical partnership with Israel. Thus these "abominations" are based on assumptions that cut the covenantal nerve of Yahwism and produce a society of apathy and manipulation in which human choice, human freedom, and human responsibility are rendered null and void. These practices are to be shunned in order to attend both to the sharpness of divine imperative and to the freedom of choice belonging to Israel

The positive alternative to these rejected practices is given in the succinct statement of verse 13. This verse is conventionally and misleadingly translated, "You shall be perfect." The NRSV, to the contrary, has it exactly right, "You shall be completely loyal." The Hebrew term *tāmîm* means "integrated, whole, undivided, as one unit." Israel's commitment to YHWH shall be total and without reservation. The practices of verses 9-12, 14 would indicate a divided loyalty, an attempt to secure one's life on other terms without full trust in YHWH.

The same term is likely reflected in Jesus' teaching in Matt 5:48, which NRSV renders, "Be *perfect*, therefore, as your heavenly Father is *perfect*." That translation is unfortunate, because the term "perfect" may suggest a kind of moral perfection that is remote from the text and the point of discipleship that Jesus enjoins. In both Deut 18:13 and Matt 5:48, the summons is of another kind, namely, unreserved loyalty to one who genuinely gives life and summons responding obedience. Israel is called to be fully dependent upon YHWH without seeking to manage its own future.

18:15-22: The opening declaration of verse 15 provides that this new "officer" in Israel, the prophet, will be "like me," that is, like Moses. It is assumed that the function of Moses as the mediator of the covenant will continue to be crucial for Israel after the "historical" Moses is gone. The primary requirement for the prophet, like the king in 17:15, is that he or she must be a member of Israel, thoroughly situated in the traditions and claims of the Yahwistic covenant. The text seems to assume a single prophet in time to come, though it is possible in the perspective of Deuteronomy that the verse envisions a succession of prophets, each of whom reenacts the role of Moses. (See 2 Kgs 17:13.) The conclusion of this lead verse is "heed" *(shema^c)*. The text uses this crucial imperative to suggest that the prophet shall be one who issues covenant requirements, statutes, and ordinances. That is, the prophet is the one who will assure that Israel remains "completely loyal" to covenant.

In verses 16-18 the text reflects on the authorization of the prophet whose legitimation is a replication of the authorization of Moses. The tradition remembers the fearful need of Israel at Sinai to have a mediator and YHWH's agreement to accept Moses as the single legitimate mediator of divine revelation (Exod 20:18-21; Deut 5:22-33). That is how Moses became pivotal to the covenant. Now, in something like "apostolic succession," Moses will in turn "raise up" a prophet to continue his singular function, to mediate covenant, more specifically, to summon Israel to obedience (vv. 17b-18). In verse 19 as in verse 15, the key word is again *shema^c*. Israel is to obey what the prophet says as if it were the word of Moses, the authorized speaker of YHWH.

The tradition then reflects upon the complexity of response to the prophet (vv. 19-20):

1. The real prophet must be fully obeyed (v. 19).

2. A false prophet may arise, but such a one shall die, that is, be executed (v. 20; see 13:1-5). That false prophet may either summon to "other gods" or may falsely represent YHWH, either way distorting YHWH's true character and will. The particular wording of verse 20 appeals to the notion of the prophet being in the "divine council" to receive the divine word as signaled in the formula, "Thus says the Lord." The false prophet is one who has not been given such a word, but pretends he or she has and so speaks his/her own word (see Jer 23:21-22; 27-28).

3. The matter of sorting out true prophet and false prophet is difficult but urgent (vv. 21-22). The criterion offered here for the true prophet, unlike that of 13:1-5, is curious. In 13:1-5, the criterion is that true prophetic summons is to "follow YHWH" (13:4), that is, to adhere to covenant. Here the criterion is whether the prophet speaks truly about the future, thus

transforming the prophet from one who commands Torah to the one who anticipates YHWH's future. The affirmation about prophetic utterance concerning YHWH's future is that the prophet knows what YHWH will do because the prophet has been in the presence of the divine council where the future has been determined, or alternatively, the prophet knows the future because the prophet is intimately aware of YHWH's intentions. Either way, the prophetic figure is the carrier of YHWH's will and purpose in a most direct and unmediated way.

Theological and Ethical Analysis

This authorization of the prophet is a remarkable recognition that a voice from outside normal channels and protocols of governance is definitional for Israel. Its life and well-being depend upon a voice "from the outside," a voice that sounds the peculiar cadences of Yahwistic "metahistory" (Koch 1982:70-76). There is an important tension in the work of the prophet who (a) announces covenant commands and summons to obedience and repentance in the present tense and (b) anticipates the future that YHWH will enact. Perhaps this tension is a declaration that present obedience and anticipation of the future actions of YHWH are connected to each other and the prophet presides precisely over that connection. By holding *present covenantal obedience* in connection with *the future of YHWH*, the prophet makes clear that Israel is never fated, but is always situated in the freedom and responsibility of covenantal interaction.

The notion of prophetic freedom for the future is an important issue in ethical reflection, for it asserts at the same time that the community of faith (and by extrapolation the larger society) is neither *autonomous* to do what it wants nor *fated* without freedom. The presence of the prophet makes clear that the community is not autonomous, because the ethical imperative of Torah keeps insisting upon accountability. The ideology of autonomy (expressed just now as free market claims and the practice of privatization) tends to assert that those with power and wealth and knowledge, individuals, corporations or nation states, are freed to do whatever they want.

The presence of the prophet asserts that the community of faith (and by extrapolation the larger community) is not fated to a closed future in which it has no options. It is possible to imagine fatedness because of gender, race, class, or the vagaries of one's family of origin. Of course social practice and social stratification are powerful in the enactment of an inchoate "natural law" that keeps people "in their place."

The twin temptations of *autonomy and fatedness* share in common the premise that there is no God with the authority to command and to transform. In the face of two such powerful assumptions, powerful in contemporary society as in that ancient world, the prophet "like Moses" bears witness that human life is under the aegis of a covenantal sovereign. After the verdict of the *judges*, after the rule of the *king*, and after the sacrifices and instructions of the *priests*, Israel with the *prophet* comes to the verb "listen." In listening comes human responsibility for a just present. In listening comes human possibility for the future. The prophet permits Israel to hear . . . and to do.

Breaking the Vicious Cycles of Violence (19:1-13)

This unit of text begins a series of texts in seemingly random arrangement. The present text is concerned with the danger of homicide and an ensuing cycle of homicide. The provision for cities "set apart" as places of sanctuary is a remarkable feature of a covenantal vision of society. The provision for such cities is an attempt to curb the violence of murder within the fabric of the community, thus a parallel to the way in which 15:1-18 seeks to curb and frame debt within such a framework. More important is the idea of curbing the vicious cycles of violence in the community. This provision is yet another instance in which the bold vision of society in Deuteronomy is given concrete implementation through special institutional arrangement.

Exegetical Analysis

The initial provision is given in verses 1-3. The designation of cities of refuge is to be enacted so that such places for asylum are readily accessible. The murderer may be pursued and needs to be able to reach protection promptly. Two other matters are to be noticed in these verses. First, the stipulation pertains to the "inheritance" given by YHWH. The offer of asylum is appropriate only to this land, because it is congruous with the character of YHWH who is the ultimate refuge of Israel. Second, the initial notion of asylum is an offer for "any homicide," that is, all murderers. While distinctions over guilt and innocence will be addressed subsequently, the idea at the outset is an unconditional welcome to any comer, without any initial questioning. Such an openness may indicate how crucial asylum is, in turn suggesting how intense was the danger of blood feud and retaliation.

The statute now proceeds to explore different "cases" of homicide. The first "case" concerns an accidental death (vv. 4-7). The statute specifies that there must have been no "bad blood" between the two parties before the incident of death. In an agrarian tribal society, families have very long memories of grievances that are not readily overlooked. For that reason any death where there is already bad blood must be suspected of being intentional. The most interesting phrase here concerns "the avenger of blood," elsewhere rendered "redeemer of blood." This phrasing refers to the "next of kin" of the slain person who must, in the interest of family honor and solidarity, kill the murderer in revenge for a slain kinsman or woman. It is evident that in the heat of family honor, the "redeemer" does not stop to ask if the initial death is accidental and indeed, does not care, for blood requires blood. Thus the provision for asylum is an antidote to blood feuds that are endless in their retribution, an endlessness that in turn endlessly destabilizes any attempt at ordered gov-ernance (2 Sam 2:23-28). The hot blood of revenge is expected to stop at the edge of the designated city of asylum. The purpose of such an institution is not to curb the *feeling* of vengeance, but to limit the *act* of revenge in order to make a stable social fabric possible.

Verses 8-10 would seem to be a parenthetical comment, for they come between the comment on an *innocent* killer (vv. 4-7) and a *guilty* murderer (vv. 11-13). This provision for extension of the institution of cities of refuge does two things. First, it appeals back to verse 3 and recognizes that such sanctuaries must be easily available at a close range. Thus the more territory, so the need for more such refuges (see 4:41-43). Second, this paragraph grounds the institutional practice theologically. The institutional protection of innocent life is an act of obedience to YHWH, with the characteristic terms of Deuteronomy, "love and serve."

The important point is not protection of the innocent but protection of the land. "Bloodguilt" is understood as an almost substantive, palpable danger as a residue of wrong killing that will contaminate the land and make it unlivable. The asylum is to preclude more bloodguilt and so to keep the land livable. One need not however, have such a substantive notion of bloodguilt in order to see that an unchecked cycle of hate and violence will make the rule of law impossible and eventually make the land unlivable.

As verses 4-7 concern an innocent killer, so now verses 11-13 take up the opposite, the guilty murderer. One is judged guilty if there has been "malice aforethought," a preexisting condition of hate. In that case, the elders who manage the process of adjudication and asylum willingly let the killer be killed by blood revenge. That is, the adjudicating powers of the elders, required by the provision for cities of refuge, have only a judicial, not an "executive" function. When the condition of guilt is satisfied, the elders cease to function and the old processes of family vengeance are permitted to operate.

The focus of the entire paragraph is on the management of bloodguilt, a matter much more serious than the emotive energies of family vengeance. The killing of an innocent creates bloodguilt. The "execution" of the guilty ends the power of bloodguilt by answering it, and therefore the adjudicatory function is of crucial importance in determining innocence or guilt. The purpose of the procedure is to protect the land that can be placed in jeopardy by the mismanagement of bloodguilt.

Theological and Ethical Analysis

It will be seen that the law itself has a very narrow agenda. It is not "soft" on punishment and in its own context vigorously affirms "capital punishment," albeit the rough procedure of a tribal society. Notice that in contrast to 13:9, the community does not join in the execution, which is left to the parties to the dispute. "The state" makes an intervention into the workings of blood feuds, but it is a careful, disciplined, circumscribed intervention. Four lines of extrapolation from this institutional proposal may be suggested:

1. The issue of vengeance is a huge matter in any society, because vengeance run loose makes life unlivable. Therefore every society that intends to be stable—let alone covenantal—must face the problem of vengeance and must devise mechanisms for its limitation. The theological effort of the Old Testament is an insistence, finally, that vengeance belongs to God, and human persons and even the human community are not free to enact what belongs to God (see Deut 32:35, 41-43; Ps 4:1) (Brueggemann 1982, 67-80). The remarkable ethical reflection of Paul in Rom 12 deals with a conciliatory alternative to vengeance. Susan Jacoby has traced the ways in which failed institutions of justice and vengeance have invited freelance, vigilante vengeance when there is no more widely shared confidence in the institutional forms of vengeance. In a sharp critique of (Christian) romantic notions of forgiveness without a serious practice of revenge, Jacoby makes a strong case for the deep necessity of vengeance that may be channeled and restrained but not denied:

Revenge, in both its constructive and destructive forms, is an expression of the aggressive drive. . . . It will not do to classify vengeance as merely childish, because it is decidedly adult. (Jacoby 1985:163)

Advocates of the death penalty are absolutely right, however, on one point: popular support for capital punishment is grounded in the conviction that criminals ought to be paid back for their violent crimes and that they are not now [in 1985] being punished in sufficient measure. This conviction is neither illegitimate nor childish; to deny it the respect it deserves is to encourage the boundless outrage that generates demands for boundless retribution. (Jacoby 1985:289)

2. This law seeks to break the vicious, apparently self-perpetuating cycles of killing. Thus if it should happen that the

"blood avenger" kills an innocent neighbor in retaliation, it is required by "honor" that the avenger should in turn be killed as a wrongful killer, and on and on and on. It would be nice to think that the "modern world" has "evolved" beyond such practices. And yet the sectarian killings in Northern Ireland that are finally inexplicable to outsiders, or the ethnic cleansing in the Balkans or in Central Africa or the endless retaliation in the Mideast indicate that where there are no public institutions that compel trust and confidence, the ancient thirst for honor is unquenched and will have its way. Thus the interface of *real human inclination* and *protective public institutions* is an important one. Institutions of restraint are crucial, because it is clear that the savage, elemental hunger for vengeance is unchanged. The rule of law that curbs tribal inclination is indispensable, as this tradition well understands, may attest to the importance of larger institutions of restraint in the face of stronger energies for hate.

3. The matter of blood feud assumes social relationships in which both parties (tribes or clans) have power to retaliate. The matter of asylum pertains to other social relationships not directly on the horizon of this statute, namely, situations in which the powerful pursue the powerless who never have enough leverage to permit retaliation. Consider, for example, defenseless refugees and political fugitives who seek sanctuary from aggressive regimes or immigrant workers hunted down by ruthless governmental agencies, or in U.S. societies, gays and lesbians who in many places have no "safe place" in a society still bloodthirsty. The offering of sanctuary or, as current rhetoric says, "open and affirming spaces," is of critical importance if society is to honor humanness beyond the satiation of rage, hatred, and vengeance. "Cities of refuge" is an ancient notion but one no less pertinent in a society that has not "evolved" beyond elemental violence in the name of honor and justice.

4. While it lies beyond the scope of this text that is focused on public institutions, the matter of sanctuary and asylum cannot be considered without a final reference to YHWH. In its prayers and songs Israel finally has confidence that YHWH is

the ultimate sanctuary for those who have no other help or defense (Pss 14:6; 46:1; 62:8; 91:1-2; 142:5).

The vocabulary is different from the provision of public institutions in Deuteronomy, but the resolve is the same. Human life is life at risk, pursued and exposed by destructive forces. Therefore to have a "safe place," close at hand, is essential for living a viable human life. The psalms of lament and complaint repeatedly speak about life at risk that finds its antidote in YHWH, who is close at hand and reliable. It is YHWH who breaks the vicious cycles of death, who by forgiveness disrupts the patterns of punishment, and draws lines against violence that violates (see Rom 8:37-39).

Don't Move the Markers (19:14)

This isolated verse belongs under the general rubric of "protected life," but its particular concern is unrelated to what precedes or follows. The law is an absolute prohibition against moving a boundary marker, for such a maneuver will damage the neighbor whose property is thereby usurped and so put common life in jeopardy. While the law is a defense of private property, it concerns private property situated in and guaranteed by a communal fabric in which each on his/her own land is a member of the larger "inheritance" of Israel. Moving boundary markers is a most elemental violation of the community, a fact signaled in the absolute formulation of the prohibition "You must not . . .," an echo of the absolute prohibitions of the Decalogue. The cohesion of social relationships depends upon the inviolability of the placement of persons in community (see the curse in 27:17; Fensham 1963).

Exegetical Analysis

In this simple, undeveloped form, the prohibition precludes neighbor acting against neighbor. This is the point of Prov 22:28 as well, though that teaching appeals to the oldest, most settled tribal practice. The other uses of the same theme, however, introduce an important dimension of social criticism, suggesting that the law concerns not simply neighbor versus neighbor, but the strong against the weak. Seen in that light, the statute is to protect the landowner in the retention of family land when preyed upon by more powerful economic agents, thus a statute that has the same point of view as the stipulation we have seen on widows and orphans (see Hos 5:10; Job 24:2; Prov 23:10-11).

In this little text two theories of land are in conflict in the life of Israel. The tradition of Deuteronomy advocates an old tribal theory of entitlement that makes personally held land sacrosanct and beyond challenge, guaranteed by tradition and reinforced by Yahwistic sanction. That tradition is challenged by an alternative theory of land, here condemned, that sees land as a commodity to be bought, sold, taken by the powers of acquisitiveness, by the free operation of economic leverage unencumbered by communal restraints.

This dispute over land theory is most dramatically voiced in the Old Testament in the narrative of Naboth's vineyard (1 Kgs 21; see also 2 Sam 9:9-11; 16:4; 19:29-30; 2 Kgs 8:6). Naboth embodies the ancient entitlement of land through tribal guarantees that need not yield even to royal avarice. Jezebel, seconded by King Ahab, operates on a different theory that has no respect for tribal entitlement but that will seize land simply for convenience' sake. The abrasive intrusion of Elijah into that narrative, with his harsh Yahwistic denunciation, draws the dispute over land theory into the covenantal orbit of Yahwism, the same orbit signaled in Deuteronomy by reference to the land as "inheritance" given by YHWH. In the Naboth narrative and in 19:14, there is no accommodation to the "new economics" practiced by both princes and the wicked.

Theological and Ethical Analysis

The "new economics" of acquisitiveness, now as then, runs roughshod over ancient entitlements. It does so in the name of "progress" and "development," mantras that cover the passionate conviction that "there is money to be made." The making of money, moreover, is not to be slowed by the impediment of vulnerable people with ancient rights that can be run over by bulldozer or by court writ. The examples are numerous:

1. The right of "eminent domain" that intends that public process can prevail, but which more often is an excuse for "developers" to have their profitable way.

2. The incursion of "supermarkets" into settled neighborhoods in ways that change traffic patterns, disrupt old businesses, and violate neighborly culture in the service of greed

3. The capacity of large economic, political, and even military operations to be heedless about what is local, readily destroying the local infrastructure in the service of greed.

4. The large-scale disruption of environment by moneymakers, as in the case of the Brazilian rain forests.

The rationale for such enterprise is of course always readily in place:

1. The Olympic committee will make jobs and rebuild homes.

2. Business is the survival of the fittest, and those who do not subscribe to new patterns have no right to exist.

3. The rising tides of business will raise all boats, and so on.

This little text invites critical reflection on economic practices that array big financial power against the small and vulnerable. The kingdom of God is not and will not be a place where powers overrun the entitlements of the vulnerable. The "developers" are on notice!

Due Process (19:15-21)

This regulation is concerned with responsible, trustworthy courtroom procedure. Its presence in the corpus of statutes is a reminder that Deuteronomy advocates a polity, that is, a pattern of public order that manages public power in responsible ways in order to enhance community.

The statute divides into two parts. The first part concerns a basic guideline that no one can be convicted of a crime on the testimony of one witness (v. 15). This general concern for valid evidence, already seen in 13:4 and the need for multiple witnesses (as in 17:6), indicates the importance of judicial procedure for this community. The second part of the text concerns a more specific case of an unreliable witness who willfully misleads the court (vv. 16-21). Obviously such false testimony will distort and discredit the entire judicial procedure.

Exegetical Analysis

It is important to notice that the horizon of this law is any offense. The point of verse 15 is the simple recognition that adjudication of the truth in court cases is problematic, and the best test of truth is the corroboration of several witnesses. Both the Torah of Moses (Deut 5:20) and the prophets (Amos 5:7, 10) understood that truth-telling in judicial procedures is the most elemental guarantee of a viable community, the last resort of the aggrieved. Where there is convergence of testimony, the community may be satisfied that the court has approximated the truth, and therefore justice, as closely as possible.

Major attention is given in this statute to perjury on the part of malicious witnesses who come to court to do damage against another member of the community (vv. 16-19). The offense of the malicious witnesses is not simply that they *lie*, as though the appeal were to a settled, available norm of truth, but rather that *by* lying they willfully do *damage* to a neighbor. Thus one may suggest that the norm of perjury is a pragmatic one, not a principle of truth, but a principle of protecting the neighbor.

The most interesting feature of this statute concerns the dispatch of the false witness who sets out to do harm. If the witness is determined by the central court to be malicious, lying in order to do damage, the court proceeds to punishment. The punishment is not set out in terms of exact measure, but is simply a statement of proportionality. What this malicious witness sought to have done to another by lying will be the perjurer's punishment. In verse 21, then, the "law of retaliation" is clearly enunciated, so that the punishment fits the crime, or more precisely the punishment fits the intended damage to the community. The factoring out of potential costs, life for life, eye for eye, and the like, reflects an ancient system of penalties in which offenders were penalized an eye, a tooth, a hand, depending on the affront. The commendation of such punishment at the same time reflects severity and restraint.

Theological and Ethical Analysis

The basic concern of corroborative testimony needs no additional comment; it is enshrined in the theory of law in the West. Two other matters may be considered in this statute.

First, the test of truth and perjury is a pragmatic one, whether the witness seeks to do damage to the community or someone in it. Thus truth is linked to neighborly justice; the court is not in pursuit of truth as may be controlled by excessive punctilious rules of evidence, it is concerned about the well-being of the community. Such a measure of truth or perjury gives focus to the work of the court and gives it great latitude in deciding what is malicious.

Second, the law of retaliation that led to a precise *quid pro quo* of affront and penalty warrants careful, sustained reflection. The community introduced such a formula of proportionality in order to curb excessive barbarism among those bent on vengeance. There is no doubt that this principle of proportionality is deeply embedded in Israel's sense of justice (Miller 1982).

Nonetheless it is clear that the principle of precise retaliation is a license for approved violence. In the current bloodthirsty passion for capital punishment in the United States, there is no doubt that a formula of "a life for a life" is a bid for state-sanctioned violence. The ethical traditions of both Judaism and Christianity have understood the problem of the principle. In Christian interpretation, the principle of retaliation is criticized and overthrown in the teaching of Jesus:

> "You have heard that it was said, 'an eye for an eye and a tooth for a tooth.' But I say to you, Do not resist an evildoer. But if anyone strikes you on the right cheek, turn the other also; and if anyone wants to sue you and take your coat, give your cloak as well; and if anyone forces you to go one mile, go also the second mile. Give to everyone who begs from you, and do not refuse anyone who wants to borrow from you." (Matt 5:38-42)

This teaching of Jesus directly challenges the old law of retaliation (Betz 1995:275-93).

Deuteronomy intends to create an alternative community that practices justice that is measured and not driven by bloodthirstiness. In turn Jesus is summoning a community that is an alternative to violence, even publicly sanctioned violence. Jesus' teaching moves beyond the exact proportionality of the Deuteronomic statute. The tension leaves open as future work the question of how to resist evil in a way that is genuinely transformative.

Faith, War, and the Environment (20:1-20)

This chapter provides impetus and rules for, and limitations upon the conduct of war. The chapter makes clear, yet again, that the tradition of Deuteronomy lives in the real world. In chapter 15, it moves in the world of *real debt* and works to relate debt to a Yahwistic vision of reality. In chapter 19, it moves in the world of *real murder* but seeks to subsume murder under YHWH's characteristic concerns. Here it acknowledges the world of *real war* and all its hatred of the enemy and its ensuing violence, and makes only a start on relating war to the claims of covenantal faith. This tradition knows that "war is hell." It is no less "hell" if it is fought in the name of YHWH. It would be preferable if one could say that in this chapter on war, the habits of war are in deep tension with the claims of YHWH. But alas, to the contrary, YHWH is presented as deeply enmeshed in barbarism. If anything, the barbarism is escalated by the certitudes Yahwism provides for combat.

The text can be divided into four parts: (a) preparation for war that is constituted by speech (vv. 1-9), (b) permissible strategies for combat implemented toward an enemy "very far from you" (vv. 10-15), (c) possible strategies for enemies "close at hand" (vv. 16-18), and (d) a concluding coda alert to the environmental costs of war (vv. 19-20). It is evident that in every part of this chapter, the presentation of war procedures is linked to the reality of YHWH, so that YHWH is understood here as the authorizer of Israelite violence toward its neighbors. An articulation of YHWH as a moral agent who stands outside the judicature of war and functions as a critical perspective about the ravages of war still awaits development outside the world of Deuteronomy.

Exegetical Analysis

20:1-9: The statute begins with preparation for war, with the wide-eyed recognition that there will be wars and Israel will be engaged in them (vv. 1-9). This account of preparation is framed by an introduction (v. 1) and a conclusion (v. 9) that together bracket two speeches by a priest (vv. 2-4) and by the officials (vv. 5-7). The first verse sets the premise for the entire preparation. The normal circumstance of war in Israel is that Israel may expect to be outnumbered and "out-gunned." The enemy will characteristically have more troops and more horses and chariots, and therefore Israel will characteristically respond in fearfulness. It is not clear why this assumption is voiced. Certainly in Israel's stylized memory of war—first with Egypt and then with "the inhabitants of the land"—Israel was ill-prepared and ill-armed. The judgment may be rooted in some historical sense of Israel's past, suggesting an appeal to very old traditions, certainly well before the impressive arms programs of the monarchy under Solomon.

It is plausible, however, that this casting of Israel as an inferior military force is not so much an appeal to historical memory as it is a theological ploy for the second part of the verse. The "natural" response of fear in battle is inappropriate and is overridden by the reality of "the LORD your God," who more than overcomes any deficiency on Israel's part (see Judg 6:2-8). The assurance appeals to the Exodus memory in which YHWH proved more than a match for Pharaoh (see Exod 14:13-14). Thus the initial bid, "do not fear," has as its unspoken positive counterpart, "have faith," trust in YHWH who will be adequate and will prevail. Without YHWH, Israel is militarily at risk and hopeless. With YHWH, Israel may be confident of victory (see Phil 4:13). Thus the tradition resituates the practice of *war* in *faith*. The issue is not arms or troops; it is rather a decision for fear or faith, once again the radical "either/or" of Deuteronomy concerning the rule of YHWH in the real affairs of the world. Even the fearful practice of war is reshaped by the claims of YHWH's sovereignty over the process, of which the Exodus is the prime example.

In terms of troop preparation, this recharacterization of war is accomplished by two preliminary addresses. The first by a priest is perhaps not unlike the address of a military chaplain before combat. The role of the priest is to accent that the "either/or" issues are theological and not military. The priest's stylized address is in three parts:

1. There is a characteristic summons, "Hear O Israel," the same phrasing as 6:4, suggesting that this decision before battle is about the power of YHWH.

2. This is followed by four parallel assurances stated as negative imperatives: "do not . . . do not . . . do not . . . do not" (see 1:21). While the intent is assurance, the tone is imperative (see 1:29). The priest encompasses the troops in an enactment of faith, "makes" the troops trust in YHWH.

3. The ground for assurance parallels the observation of the Egyptians in Exod 14:15 (and see v. 14): YHWH is seen to be a decisive figure in combat. The ground of confidence is the assurance that Israel is not alone in the battle but has as ally the formidable power of YHWH, who in the past has been victorious.

This simple, stylized speech reflects core convictions of the tradition of Deuteronomy. It asserts that YHWH is a real player in Israel's conflict. By YHWH's engagement, historical battles are never what they seem, because the unseen force of YHWH is decisive. The ground of assurance has nothing to do with technology, strategy, or "military preparedness." Such a claim for the power of YHWH is made most effectively, not by a highly ordered, technologically sophisticated military establishment but by "freedom fighters" with guerrilla techniques who have no rational chance of victory but who may prevail because of the "theological energy" they sense and in which they trust.

After the priest, the "muster officer" addresses the troops (vv. 5-7). This speech outlines four conditions for which one may be exempted from combat. The first three perhaps appeal to old taboos of unfinished business that might detract from a single-minded investment in the battle:

1. a new house still undedicated;
2. a vineyard not yet enjoyed;
3. a marriage not yet consummated.

These three provisions reflect Israel's conviction about the entitlement of living a good life; the location of the community must protect the rights of its members to enjoy and complete the material processes of life. The exemptions are cast with an awareness that if a man is not exempted for these reasons, "another man" will enjoy them. Thus the exemption protects male honor in the community of competing males. The same measures of "the good life" that needs to be protected are reflected in both the blessings and the curses found elsewhere (Deut 28:30; Amos 5:11; 9:14; Isa 62:8; 65:21-22). The curse is that the normal processes of life shall be disrupted and fall into the hands of another man.

4. The fourth provision in verse 8 is given a different introduction and may be added to conform to the double "do not fear" of verses 1 and 3. The tradition knows that fearlessness (faith) cannot be commanded and fear cannot be prohibited by mandate. It knows, moreover, that cowardice is contagious. The provision, however, should be understood theologically and not psychologically. This battle is not for "the brave," but for those who trust YHWH (see Judg 7:3). Those who do not submit to the reassuring sovereignty of YHWH have no place in YHWH's combat.

20:10-15: What may be an older rule of war—lacking the pious rhetoric of verses 1-9—is a regulation for how to proceed against an enemy (vv. 10-14). The regulation is simple. In its approach to any enemy town, Israel must offer terms of surrender. The text has the term *shalom,* "terms of peace." It is to be noted, however, that the terms of "peace" suggested here are harsh. Peace requires surrender and submission to a condition of forced labor (see Josh 9:21). Presumably an enemy would only submit willingly to such conditions if it were self-evident that Israel could not be resisted or defeated.

If, on the other hand, the enemy resists the harsh offer of peace, Israel is then to unleash a formidable siege. In this rhetoric, it is not doubted that Israel will prevail over every enemy because the tradition has complete confidence in YHWH as the key factor in battle. The presentation of war is here highly synergistic: Israel lays siege; YHWH gives victory (see Prov 1:31). The real interest in this unit is not the benefit of the imposed terms (forced labor to do Israel's lackey work), but the gain of booty upon victory. Israel is to kill all the opposing soldiers, but is to take and enjoy as war booty everything else, including women (on which see 21:10-14), children, and cattle. This procedure likely reflects the reality of war in which the death of enemy soldiers is "common sense." The confiscation of "women and children" may be regarded as a "taming of war" if the alternative is death for all. One should not, however, miss the barbarism implied in the permission to take women and children as captives of war. All of the certain cruelty of such a procedure is understood, in uncritical fashion, as a gift of YHWH's sure victory.

That basic rule of war probably is a procedure common to the ancient world and is surely reflected in modern warfare with its technologically enhanced brutality. The rule, however, is emended in verses 15-18, under the stringent ideology of Deuteronomy. What had been a rule of procedure for all war (surrender or defeat and submission) now is applicable only to distant towns and cities with which Israel is to have no continuing contact. There is a harsher requirement for towns close at hand, in the land of promise.

20:16-18b: Deuteronomy now zealously ensures Yahwistic monopoly in war. The harsh provisions of verses 17-18 authorize the killing of all enemies, even women, children, and cattle, which were exempted in verses 10-14. (See 2 Kgs 10:14; Hos 10:14 for such military brutality.) The powerful ideological force of Deuteronomy is evident in three rhetorical signals:

1. The list of enemies echoes 7:1, though the absence of the Girgashites from this list reduces the conventional number seven to six enemies. In any case the list is an ideological signal of comprehensiveness, referring to the entire antecedent population of the land of promise.

2. The governing verb, "annihilate" *(herem)*, stated in an emphatic form, recalls the harsh rhetoric of chapter 7, and intends the destruction to be a theological act in the interest of preserving the distinctiveness of Israel's faith.

3. The use of the term "abhorrent things" (abomination) echoes 7:26, and concerns anything that threatens or challenges the "pure" Yahwism of Israel.

The convergence of these fierce ideological factors introduces a new distinction between *far* and *near* enemies of Israel. It suggests, moreover, that annihilation of the enemy is not an act of "devotion" to YHWH, but is a pragmatic step by an exceedingly anxious community to eliminate all threats and seductions that might provide an alternative to YHWH. It is possible to understand this provision as the rhetoric of faith gone hysterical and see it simply as ideology that is never intended to be embodied in actual war. One cannot, however, miss the brutality that is assured in such ideology. Whether in fact such rhetoric ever intended actual implementation or not, it is evident that in the service of convinced theological monopoly, a rhetoric of violence the tradition does not object to.

20:19-20: After the ferocity of verses 6-18, one is scarcely prepared for the final statute of verses 19-20, which takes a first step in making war "environmentally friendly." Siege of a city must have been a widespread practice, and siege weapons require lots of lumber. This requirement of lumber is one case of the characteristic ways in which war savages the environment and leaves it desolate and unproductive long after "affairs of state" have been resolved and forgotten (see 2 Kgs 3:19-25).

In the face of Deuteronomic realism about war, these final verses provide an astonishing limitation upon combat procedures.

The purpose is to protect the food chain, even leaving a food supply for one's enemies after the battle when Israel's troops have withdrawn. Such a provision may be subsumed under an inchoate creation theology in which it is recognized that the created world has its own rights and privileges, and there are important limitations imposed on human intervention. It is noteworthy that the statute gives no rationale for the limitation, but only offers a lat injunction that stands against the wholesale brutality of verses 15-18.

Theological and Ethical Analysis

In a way characteristic of Deuteronomy, this chapter on war combines passionate Yahwistic faith and exceedingly harsh social policy. There can be little doubt that it was the pressure and anxiety of real circumstance that initially produced the severity; in any case, this is a harshness into which YHWH is fully drawn. YHWH is implicated as initiator and legitimator of the harshness that Israel is thereby compelled to enact.

The chapter exhibits deep trust and confidence in YHWH. In the development of the tradition, the thirst for war is transposed into a summons to faith (as in Isa 7:9; 30:15), a readiness to trust YHWH in every circumstance. Even at the level of brutality, this tradition believes and risks everything on the will and capacity of YHWH. Israel will triumph because YHWH is committed to the battle (vv. 13, 16). The speech of the priest is an affirmation of YHWH's sovereignty over the military process and an invitation that Israel's troops should rest their future in YHWH's reliable care.

Confidence in YHWH, however, becomes a warrant for brutality. Whatever may be said about confidence in YHWH's sovereignty and providential care, there is no escape from the reality of this text: war is hell; it remains hell when conducted by Israel. Moreover, it remains hell when conducted by Israel with the authorization of YHWH. In times of emergency, confidence in YHWH readily spills over into justification for one's own cause, which is easily read as the cause of YHWH (see Ps 149:6-9).

It is easy to regard such an uncritical linkage of YHWH

and brutality as primitive and ancient. But that same self-serving, self-deceiving legitimization is as powerful in contemporary life as in the ancient text. Thus in World War II, rhetoric made the war into moral crusade, each side claiming, "God with us," while church choirs were not very different from popular songs in offering "Praise the Lord and Pass the Ammunition," surely a modern echo of Psalm 149. More recently, United States military power has been deeply linked to theological claims, so that seemingly endless waves of violence are justified as God's goodwill against demonized embodiments of evil that must be "utterly destroyed."

There are, to be sure, mitigations of brutality in the text, the list of exemptions and the protection of trees. At the same time, however, it must be recognized that as long as the rhetoric of violence is employed in order to summon faith, the texture of violence is undeniably at work, no matter how noble the summons is intended. Thus the rhetoric of the church—for example, in its martial hymns—continues to carry subliminal nuances of violence, even when the violence is no longer intended. The long abusive history of the church is evidence that this durable rhetoric of violence continues to do its legitimating work, even where it is employed by those who intend no such message. The upshot of such usage is that the God of the Bible remains implicated in the thirst for violence even when the testimony of suffering love keeps speaking against it.

In the end this text is a summons to faith in YHWH, to trust the future to YHWH's good assurance. In its particular rhetoric, it is a summons to have enough faith to fight. Noting the problems of that connection of *faith and fight,* the text may leave us with a question about faith enough *not* to fight, but to risk other actions in obedience, thereby creating a new future.

An Ordered Neighborliness (21:1–22:12)

This extended body of statutes is rather random and admits of no compelling structural analysis. It seems best to take up the laws one at a time. In this section of text, the longest regulation is at the outset (21:1-9), followed by three shorter laws (21:10-14, 15-17, 18-21), which in turn are followed by laws that are for the most part very brief (22:1-12). The general intention is to bring every phase of Israel's life under the governance of YHWH and under the practice of a certain notion of covenant.

Exegetical Analysis

21:1-9: The first and longest statute in this section of text fits well under the rubric of "protection of human life" (that is, "do not kill") (21:1-9). It is more or less a continuation of the concern of 19:1-13, which is preoccupied with bloodguilt and the shedding of innocent blood. In 19:1-13, the case was simpler and admitted of adjudication because the killer was known. All that needed to be decided in that case was the murderer's motive. In the present case, the matter is more problematic, because there is a body evidently murdered, but no possible identification of the killer. In 19:1-13, the purpose of adjudication is to *properly assign bloodguilt* that is like a substantive lethal force in the community. The issue then is to protect the community against the threat of unanswered blood.

Here the problem of bloodguilt, the enduring threat of a wrongful death, must be handled differently because there is no known perpetrator to whom bloodguilt can be assigned. The problem is laid out in verse 1, and the matter of jurisdiction is settled in verse 2. The key players are the "elders of the town," thus reflecting a small agrarian community that must take responsibility for its own well-being with the procedures it has at hand. The elders manage the process of bloodguilt by action and by two speeches, one of declaration and one of petition. The action of the elders is likely a very old, traditional practice, surely older than Yahwism (and without any reference to Yahwism), a "nonrational" strategy for *expunging bloodguilt* from the community (vv. 3-4). The action involves a heifer, a young female cow, which has considerable value in an agrarian community, plus running water in a wadi. Both the heifer and the water are at their best; the heifer has not been worked *(ʿābad)* and the wadi has not been worked *(ʿābad)*. Both are elements of creation in a free, unspoiled, unclaimed state offered as an act of unrestrained investment in a process commensurate with the threat. It appears that "good blood" is offered to overcome the threat of "bad blood," blood made bad by being violently poured out.

The gesture of washing is matched by a declaration of innocence. The elders assert that neither they (nor any they represent in the village) have shed the blood nor have they witnessed its shedding, that is, been an accomplice. The statement distances the elders and their village from the bloodguilt. This declaration is matched by a petition. The petition centers on the imperative "absolve" that bids expiation for "your people Israel." The verb used by the elders, *kipper,* is more familiarly translated "atone" (best known from the Hebrew "Yom Kippur," Day of Atonement). The NRSV rendering "absolve" may suggest a more judicial nuance, but the term likely combines cultic and judicial dimensions. The point is to remove the threat of bloodguilt from the community by the sacramental act just completed and by a statement of innocence.

It is remarkable that the priest in fact never says anything in the text. The priest grants absolution to the village and its elders. The process thus is completed and the emergency is overcome. As in Lev 6:1-6 (Heb. 5:20-26) two quite distinct actions are required. The first is a secular, economic act of *reparations.* The second act, done by a priest is *absolution.* Both acts, lay and ordained, are necessary. The lay act is a precondition, but the authoritative act with the verb of absolution is by the priest. This well-ordered protocol is a process in which the community may have confidence that will give security and well-being in the face of ominous forces that are beyond the ken of the community.

21:10-14: The next law concerns yet another rule of war and continues the agenda of chapter 20 (vv. 10-14). In its present context, however, the case concerns matters after the war. For that reason, Carolyn Pressler (1993:9) has grouped together this statute with the two that follow (vv. 15-17, 18-21) as concerns for authority and order in the household.

This statute authorizes the dominating power of the male in the family. The statement is restrained, but the tone and gist of it are clear. Warriors are free to "want" and to "take" foreign women in war (see 20:14). The verb "take" suggests forcible action (see 2 Sam 11:1-5). The woman has no voice in the matter, either to resist or to comply. She is acted upon by the man, who has all the rights. The final assertion of male power affirms that the one he has forcibly seized, he is now free to divorce (v. 14). Pressler concludes:

> The law clearly assumes a male dominated situation. It addresses the male. It assumes that the male is the primary actor: he desires and takes, he no longer desires and sends out. While it defines the woman's legal status (wife) and provides her protection in that status (she may not be sold), it does so by limiting the man's actions. (Pressler 1993:15)

Deuteronomy has not yet transposed gender relationships into covenantal categories as it has been able to do in some other matters such as the economy.

21:15-17: The second statute in this trilogy of family ordinances concerns the right of inheritance (21:15-17). This provision is designed to protect the custom of primogeniture, the privilege of the firstborn son in the inheritance of family property. In that ancient world and well into the modern world, that custom is intended to protect family property, to prevent endless quarrels about inheritance of land, and to preclude the fragmentation of such property with a multiplicity of heirs. The statute, moreover, underscores the privilege of the firstborn son in a quite traditional social ordering by guaranteeing him a double portion of inheritance.

The issue of the statute arises because the landowner, the one now bequeathing his property, loves a wife who is the mother of a younger heir. Out of preference for the wife whom he loves, he wishes to privilege her son; and by privileging the younger son to throw over social convention and propriety. But he cannot, says Moses, because such an act would "not be right." It would violate the "just entitlement" *(mišpāṭ)* of the older son. This is a teaching that supports traditionalism against any emotional deviation, even by the male head of the family. While these family laws have a high view of male, patriarchal authority, here the freedom of the head of the family is curbed. The authority of the father is regulated in the interest of social stability, so that he cannot do what he wants with his own wealth and property. The circumstance reflected in this statute closely parallels that of Esau and Jacob in Genesis 25–27. In the ancestral narratives of Genesis, the claims of primogeniture are regularly overturned (see Gen 48:13-20).

21:18-21: The third in this triad of family ordinances concerns the discipline of a recalcitrant son (21:18-21). The statute affirms traditional authority of parents over children in the interest of maintaining social order. The son is a disturbance in the family because he will not "listen," that is, accept authority. The verb *shema^c* is used three times, in a recognition that as Israel's life depends upon heeding Mosaic command, so the life of family and of society depends upon heeding proximate authority. The "not listening," which is generic in verse 18, is made explicit in verse 20: "a glutton and drunkard" (see Prov 23:20-21; 28:7). Such misconduct brings shame on the family and eventually economic jeopardy.

The statute asserts that such a family crisis is a public concern. A child who places the family at risk must be dealt with by the authorities when the parents have exhausted their own capacity. The action of the elders—the dominant officials in village life—indicates that the community will close ranks to deal with any unsettlement that disturbs the economic (and therefore moral!) coherence of the community. The act of public execution is designed to purge the threat to the community and to make the violator an example to any other who may want unrestrained freedom. This statute reflects a customary village order that is ready to give community order priority well before any personal freedom, and in which the parental order is equated with God's own will for the community.

21:22-23: This brief and isolated law of 21:22-23 reflects the concern of Deuteronomy for the land. The key term is "defile" (*ṭamēʾ*, v. 23). The land is not to be polluted, for if that happens it will cease to produce, and Israel will eventually forfeit the land.

It may be the case that the "powers of death" that swirl around the body are thought to be a special threat at night, and therefore burial is required. Or it may be that "sundown" sets a limit on the time of exposure, because a decomposed body is intrinsically a threat. In any case, a dead body, certainly a dead body of one executed for a crime, is an affront to God and a threat to the community. There are, no doubt, all sorts of possible meanings to "death, night, and curse" in this text. For our purposes it is enough to see that "YHWH's holy people" must keep the land "clean," so that it may function as God's good creation (see 14:10-21).

22:1-4: Now follows a series of statutes that reflect a neighborly responsibility for private property. These stipulations reflect the concerns of a small, agrarian community (see Exod 21:1-15). Such a community is composed of small landholders who are daily dependent upon each other for cooperation, assistance, and vigilance. The first four statutes concern loss of property and the responsibility of the neighbor to return what is lost when it is found; neighbors are bound together in mutual care and protection. The most remarkable aspect of this statute is the last imperative urging. The NRSV translates "You may not withhold your help." The verb is "conceal, hide," stated in reflexive form. You may not hide yourself. You may not withdraw from neighborliness. Perhaps in a more contemporary context, you may not live behind high walls in a gated community, as though you are not obligated to be a neighbor. The fifth statute is somewhat different, but with similar concerns for the same sphere of neighborly obligation (v. 4; see Matt 12:11). Again the verb "hide yourself," this time rendered in NRSV "ignore," reinforced by the emphatic infinitive absolute, "surely lift." The claims of covenantalism extend to the most mundane realities of daily life.

22:5-12: This miscellaneous section concludes with seven statutes that reflect three concerns we have already seen elsewhere:

1. Verse 5 is a prohibition against cross-dressing, an act that comes under the general rubric of mixing things that must be

kept apart, on which see 14:1-21. The prohibition clearly intends that everything, including man and woman, shall be kept distinct, "after its own kind," here "male and female he created them" (Gen 1:27). The mixing of even the slightest matter is apparently taken to be an act that has a huge ripple effect, a "domino theory," that will eventually result in chaos and destabilize all of creation. Anyone who knows about small village life knows that a "domino theory" of disorder is always available to support resistance to change. The triad of prohibitions in verses 9-11 concerning the mixing of crops, animals, and clothes (on which see Lev 19:19) belongs together with verse 5, each statute in turn reflecting anxiety about the destructive power of mixing and contaminating. (Verse 12 is a regulation that in form is not unlike the preceding, though it is positive and not prohibitive. It is possible that tassels, like "signs and emblems," specify a distinctive Israelite identity [see Num 15:37-41].)

2. The provision on the mother bird and her young is to be subsumed under a theology of the land (vv. 6-8). It is permitted to take bird eggs or young birds. It is prohibited to take the mother bird. One must not interrupt the food chain, so that "every winged bird of every kind" might continue to "be fruitful and multiply" (Gen 1:21). The use of "good" in Gen 1:21 (and repeatedly) is the same term as "well" in verse 7. Israel knows that the creation (the land) has been ordered for fruitfulness by YHWH and that the good order of blessing willed by YHWH must not be disrupted. One must not overstate the environmental awareness of this text (and 20:19-20). Nonetheless, it is evident that care and respect for the land is a more vital dimension of this covenantal horizon than had been noticed in the past.

3. The brief statement in verse 8 requires the erection of a protective barrier (railing) in the construction of a balcony on a house. The rule is particular, and seems likely a building code requirement. The point for Deuteronomy, however, is that the code requirement is linked to a large anxiety about *bloodguilt* (on which see 19:1-13; 21:1-9).

Theological and Ethical Analysis

To the extent that one may generalize at all from the miscellaneous material, these regulations are concerned with construction and maintenance of an infrastructure of neighborly interactions that summons members of the community to pay attention to the well-being of the community in ways that may, at the least, be inconvenient and, at the most, be costly. Under that general rubric:

1. The provisions on bloodguilt mean that attention must be paid to keep the powers of death at bay by careful ritual (21:1-9), by attentiveness to proper procedure (21:22-23), and by careful consideration that does not count costs (22:8). Unresolved and unanswered death can continue to work to jeopardize a community.

2. The family provisions surely would strike a contemporary reader as variously barbaric (21:10-14), inexplicable (21:15-17), or as unbearably harsh (21:18-21). There is no need to affirm or appreciate these statutes in order to understand that they are attempts to regulate family life in the interest of a stable community. The interplay of established authority, personal freedom, and the dignity of all of human life is here unsettled and unfinished.

3. The rules of neighborly obligation are essential to a viable community, and tell against excessive privatization (22:1-4).

4. The rules against mixing (22:5, 9-11) and ecological respect (22:5-6) in different ways concern the prospect of a viable, stabilized created order.

One does not need to resonate with all of these laws to see what is at stake in the community. Three dimensions of the matter of *viable infrastructure* at work here are:

1. *The God-given order of reality* in relation to initiatives that persons in community may take.

2. *The power of traditional authority*—male, elder—in the imposition of order upon underlings in harsh and hierarchal ways.

3. *The obligation of neighborliness* against a privatization that does not want to be inconvenienced.

A reader at the beginning of the twenty-first century in the United States might especially notice the insistence on investment in the community. The ideology of privatization that tends toward self-indulgence, the unwillingness to commit energy to the neighbor or to tax money for the common good—all indicate a pervasive yearning to be done with neighborly reality. This tradition offers a wholesale insistence that the future depends upon sustained, intentional commitment to the public good.

A Disgraceful Act in Israel (22:13-30 [Heb. 22:13-29, 23:1])

These six statutes seek to regulate sexual relationships between a man and a woman. It is clear that the regulations governing sexual relationships are intensely patriarchal, written from a male perspective to protect male entitlements and privileges. Indeed, even the violation of a woman is characteristically because she is related to "another man," so that the affront is to the man. In this area of covenantal ordering of social relationships, the horizon of Deuteronomy has not advanced very far from traditional patriarchy toward a covenantal practice of mutuality. Both Carolyn Pressler (1993) and Washington (1998) view these laws as authorizations of male domination and, where "necessary," violence.

Exegetical Analysis

22:13-21: The first and most extended of these six statutes concerns a case of properly ordered marriage that does not work (vv. 13-21). The statute may be divided into three parts, the presentation of the problem (vv. 13-17), a penalty for false charges (vv. 18-19), and punishment when the charges are true (vv. 20-21).

The case concerns a disappointed husband (vv. 13-17). The statute moves quickly to the problem in verse 1: "He disliked her" (Heb. "hate"). The law assumes that the husband is "entitled" to a virgin wife, that the wife is obligated to be virgin, and the parents of the wife must guarantee it.

As seen elsewhere in this corpus, the statute is concerned with clear and fair judicial procedure. The parents of the wife apparently have to refute the charges; they do so by appeal to the village elders who, as previously noted, are the appropriate judiciary body that is to verify the claim of virginity. It is evident that the charge is a most serious one that warrants public attention and review. The matter is not simply a private issue between two parties or even two families. In the context of Deuteronomy, the matter of loss of virginity is apparently both a threat to proper social order and a cause for familial shame.

It is assumed (and not stated) that the charges are false. The husband is seen to be a false witness who must be punished (vv. 18-19). Two matters in the punishment of the man are to be noted. First, the penalty is simply a cash payment to the father for slander. While the sum of the fine is considerable, a mere cash payment is a "light sentence" in view of the penalties that follow in the subsequent statutes. This is a "man-to-man" deal, with the woman simply a passive party to the financial transaction, because the real affront would seem to be of one man against another man. The additional "punishment" designed to assure social stability is that the husband forfeits his normal right to any future divorce. He is "locked in" to a marriage with a woman he has despised—punishment indeed! But so is the woman! What counts is the social standing of the two men and the stability of the community.

In what must be a further development of the statute, verses 20-21 are willing to entertain the alternative case that the husband's charge is true and the woman in not a virgin. In that case, severe reaction against the woman is authorized:

Indictment: She has done "a disgraceful thing in Israel" by violating her virginity, bringing shame on her family, humiliation on her husband, and jeopardy on her community (Philips 1975). Every cohesive village society knows about the scandal of such an act and the deep shame that comes upon the entire household for a daughter's failure to be a "good girl."

Sentence: In front of her father's house, in her own town, all the men (n. b., not the elders) will execute her. The text conjures a scene of unrestrained male violence against a woman who has dared to disrupt a social order that guarantees a network of male power.

22:22: The second, brief statute takes up yet another case of "disordered" sexual intercourse. The statute is terse. Both parties to the adultery are to be executed, because such an act creates destructive futures for the community. One need only notice two matters. First, the law is framed concerning the man who is the initiator of the illicit action: "if a man . . ." Second, the affront is that the woman is the wife "of another man," that is, the act of the man violates the prerogatives of another man. The entire matter is among men.

22:23-24: The third statute in this series, to be paired with the fourth, is yet another case of illicit intercourse. In this case, the woman, a young virgin, is mentioned first; but she yet again belongs to a man as his betrothed. The crucial matter for the process of adjudication is the setting of the violation, "in the town." Because the act was "in town," around other people, it is presumed that the woman consented and did not cry out in protest or seek help, for others would have heard her. That she apparently consented in the act includes her in the violation, even though it is a violation of a man by another man. The two of them are stoned at the gate, she because she consented, he because he violated the privilege of another man. The order of the community will be maintained in a most ruthless way.

22:25-27: The fourth statute is linked to the case of verses 23-24. It assumes all of the same facts except the location of the affront that is now "in the open country," away from other people. She is still an engaged woman. Among all these laws, only here the woman is given the benefit of the doubt. She might have cried out for help in protest and resistance; she might have, because no one was close enough to hear her. Therefore she is presumed innocent and is acquitted of any wrongdoing. She is given no compensation or protection, but is left "ruined" in the eyes of this patriarchal community.

22:28-29: As the laws proceed in a movement toward less severe affronts, the fifth case is, from the perspective of the text, the least severe (vv. 28-29). This case involved an unengaged virgin, that is, a woman not yet possessed by a man other than her father. The man is aggressive and seizes *(tāpaś)* her, though the verb here is less harsh than that in verse 25. The case is contrasted with the two preceding cases. In this case, neither party is executed, because there is no other man who is affronted by the act. Thus social pressure is off; nothing much is at stake. The settlement of the case is not unlike the first case in which charges are found to be false (vv. 18-19). The man is fined and forfeits his right to a future divorce. Again the settlement must be made between the two men. The woman has been raped, but she is not even acknowledged in the settlement, except that she is assigned to a lifelong partnership with her rapist.

22:30: The final statute here is not in fact a part of the series, but appears to be placed here because it concerns family regulations. Unlike the others in this series, this statute is a prohibition against incest (see Lev 18:6-19; 20:11-21; Gen 9:22-27). It is again worth noticing that it is not so much a violation of the marriage as it is the violation of the father's honor, because the mother belongs to him and must not be taken from him (see the royal version of this act in the seizure of the father's concubines [2 Sam 16:20-23; 1 Kgs 2:21-25]).

Theological and Ethical Analysis

This tedious body of statutes seeks to regulate family life and sexual relationships according to the Torah. The apparent purpose of these laws is to ensure social stability and order and, in doing so, to protect the status quo arrangements of social power. The uncriticized form of male power encased in these statutes indicates that family law has not moved very far toward covenantal mutuality. Rather these laws operate on the assumption of male domination and prerogative: "There is an unshakable basis in these texts for the inferior position of women in a patriarchal society" (Crüsemann 1996, 250; see Pressler 1993, 43; Washington 1998, 23-24).

This characteristically patriarchal formulation of power, voiced with the claim of divine authority and enshrined in this holy book, has exercised huge influence upon the formation of Western law, habit, and perspective. Indeed, the maintenance of order, the protection of honor, and the guarantee of property in a patriarchal society have derived terrible strength from this textual tradition that has for the most part gone uncriticized.

In broad sweep, one may notice cultural leaps that illuminate the ongoing power and ongoing problem of this vision of sexual relationships:

1. In both Judaism and Christianity there has been, over time, the development of a critical stance against such unrestrained patriarchy. The emergence of feminist consciousness has made it possible to see a growing attentiveness to these matters.

2. It is sorry for the credibility of the church that it has been largely the secularized Enlightenment that moved decisively in the Western world to acknowledge that women are fully adult, fully responsible, fully free partners with men in the human enterprise. It is a source of awkwardness and cause for repentance in the Christian community that the church has been unable, in light of the gospel, to be more critical of its own traditions. Characteristically the church has followed and not led in the emancipatory awareness now at work in the world.

It is clear that by the end of the century, Western society has arrived at a very different crisis concerning family life and sexual relationships, the temptation to reduce relationships of loyalty to transactions of convenience that are powered by a notion of detached freedom that is expressed and enacted largely in utilitarian and consumerist categories. Deuteronomy has erred in the matter by its *authoritarian disregard of mutuality,* even as dominant contemporary practice errs in its determined *disregard of fidelity* in the interest of autonomy. It is no easy thing to find a way to covenantal fidelity, freedom, and respect that is a third way, a way that differs from abusive authoritarianism and detached autonomy. At its best, Deuteronomy reached toward such covenantal fidelity, but it did not reach very far or very effectively.

The Jewish and Christian communities have contributions to make in a dehumanized society, but they cannot be made by direct appeal to texts such as these. What is required, as Deuteronomy at its best understood, is a continuing interpretive practice that moves always between traditional inheritances and faithful innovation of a covenantal kind. Deuteronomy in general is headed down that road of fidelity and innovation in the interest of covenant. On this theme, however, it has not gotten very far.

Rules of Access (23:1-8)

Deuteronomy authorizes a community that is devoted unreservedly to YHWH as a holy people of trust and obedience. Given that aim, the question of access to the community is an important one, for the affirmation of being an "insider" to the covenant community generates, in turn, a sense of the "outsider" who must be excluded in order to maintain the integrity of the community. The present text presents a statement of guidelines for exclusion. The emergence of ethnic consciousness in the list indicates the unsettled way in which the "Holy People of YHWH" is variously understood covenantally (theologically) and ethnically.

Exegetical Analysis

The first two principles of exclusion pertain to Israelites who might expect to be admitted to the holy community but who are rejected (vv. 1-2). The first case concerns one with a "crushed testicle," or cut-off penis (v. 1). Reference to male genitalia not only indicates a horizon of male membership in the covenant community, but evidences how closely covenantal membership is related to sexual generativity, a pervasive concern of the ancestral narratives in Genesis. The preoccupation with male genitalia here brings the notion of the holy people unsettlingly close to the rules of a sperm bank, albeit a holy sperm bank.

The second rule of disqualification of an Israelite concerns someone born of an illicit union, that is, a bastard born out of wedlock (v. 2). This rule of exclusion reinforces the rules on illicit sexuality in chapter 22. The only other use of the term used here for the subject, *mamzēr,* is in Zech 9:6, rendered in NRSV "marginal people," or more simply in the Greek *allageneis,* that is, "others." This term suggests alarm about "otherness" in the prohibition.

The second group of exclusions is ethnic and concerns in turn the Ammonites, Moabites, Edomites, and Egyptians (vv. 3-8). While these exclusionary rules are stated apodictically and absolutely, it is most plausible that they represent convictions of a certain moment of articulation, suggesting that on the larger horizon of Israel's self-construal, the exclusions are not stable and fixed. In another circumstance, the rules might have come out differently. While they may be recognized as contextual, these exclusions are given in the tradition as absolute.

The first case concerns Ammon and Moab, who are treated as a pair. These peoples, Israel's cousins (see Gen 19:30-38), are permanently excluded from the assembly. The exclusion, moreover, is underscored by the final accent of the paragraph in verse 6, which precludes forever any concern for the *shalom* of Moab and Ammon. The particular justification of this exclusion turns on two very particular memories. The long-term negative effect of one remembered affront is striking. It was a violation of hospitality to refuse food and water, and Israel, so this tradition suggests, established a pattern of permanent hostility on the basis of one simple affront against hospitality. But of course, given ethnic self-consciousness, such affronts are enduringly productive of hostility.

Curiously, the harshly negative attitude toward Ammon and Moab here is in obvious tension with the more affirmative line in 2:9-21. The tension indicates the instability of enmities that may, in other circumstances, be different.

The terse affirmation concerning the Edomites in verse 7*a* is quite in contrast to the tone of verses 3-6; moreover, it is not clear why Edom is differently regarded and is no longer the object of Israel's intense religious rejection. This is still short of welcome and acceptance, but the changed tone marks a conciliatory attitude. The reason given is that Edom is a "brother" (on which see Amos 1:11), which coheres with 2:4-8.

Finally comes the astonishing affirmation of the fourth people mentioned, the Egyptians (vv. 7b-8). After the abusiveness of Pharaoh one might have expected hostility toward Egypt. But against that expectation, any "abhorrence" toward Egypt is vetoed. Apparently Egypt is here remembered simply as the host country of the ancestors and not as an abuser (see Gen 46:28–47:12). The memory of "sojourn" opens Israel to a more liminal perception of its past and a more open posture toward its present. It need not label people enemies forever.

Theological and Ethical Analysis

The six guidelines, four exclusionary and two affirmative, exhibit a community struggling with its identity and integrity. It is characteristically a major task of such a "sectarian" community to know when and how and on what grounds to exclude or include (Mullen 1993).

There is no doubt that in post-exilic Judaism the question of exclusiveness was an acute one. It is evident that Ezra and Nehemiah, surely in an appeal to texts like this one, sought to protect the community in its purity by the purgation of foreigners who are disqualified simply because they are foreigners (Neh 13:1-3, 23-30).

While exclusion has been a primary posture in shaping Judaism, it has not been without important challenges. In the book of Ruth, the Moabite Ruth becomes an Israelite and eventually a mother to the later king David (Ruth 4:13-22, on which see Matt 1:5). More important Isa 56:3-8 affirms that all eunuchs and foreigners are welcomed into the community of covenant if they subscribe to covenant and practice sabbath. This text represents a remarkable challenge to the old exclusionary tradition (Donner 1985).

The same critical question that occupied emerging Judaism in the time of Ezra inevitably surfaced in early Christianity (see Acts 15). This old tension of exclusion and inclusion is a continuing project in the church. In current church circles it is evident that the issue again is invested with great intensity (Gaiser 1994). The arc of inclusiveness in the church community is open and embracive. The intensity of the current church issue may illuminate the interpretive struggle that surely is present in this text, not only about the four exclusions, but equally about the two inclusions that would not have come easily to Israelites with long memories.

Purity and Justice Intermingled (23:9-25)

This section of texts includes a series of brief statutes on a variety of subjects, a series that appears to be randomly ordered. It is possible to suggest something of a patterned arrangement of these laws:

purity in camp (vv. 9-14)	justice to slaves (vv. 15-16)
purity from "cult prostitutes" (vv. 17-18)	justice with interest (vv. 19-20)
reliability of vows (vv. 21-23)	justice with neighbors (vv. 24-25).

Such an arrangement (that may be completely happenstance) exhibits the major emphases of the Torah of Deuteronomy and shows that issues of *purity* and *justice* stand side by side in this interpretive tradition.

Exegetical Analysis

23:9-14: The first of these statutes concerns a rule for the conduct of war, and so is topically related to chapter 20 (vv. 9-14). The regulation exhibits the way in which this corpus attends to detail, for the issue here is the maintenance of a "clean" military camp and the disposal of human waste that, if left unattended, would make the camp "unclean." The use of categories of "clean/unclean" with reference to human waste might be understood in terms of hygiene. However, cleanness here is linked to holiness, that is, a habitat that is appropriate to the holy God. Thus the concern is cultic, ritual purity and not hygiene.

The appeal is that YHWH is in the camp of Israel in order to "save." The negation of YHWH's presence by uncleanness means the loss of YHWH's saving presence and power. Thus the practice of holiness is a precondition of Israel's military success. Conversely, carelessness about human waste will jeopardize military fortunes. The conviction that "uncleanness" will cause a departure of YHWH's presence becomes the basis of Ezekiel's theology of glory (Ezek 8–10, 43–44).

23:15-16: The second, brief statute concerns runaway slaves (vv. 15-16). This regulation is congruent with the "year of release" in 15:1-18, but is even more radical. The regulation is remarkable because it accepts the legitimacy of a slave's escape. Conventional "law and order" might insist that such a runaway should be captured and returned to bondage, for that is the only way to maintain an economy of careful, controlled, debt management. This law urges noncooperation with slave laws, the recognition of the right for a slave to "choose" where to live as an escapee, and the practice of hospitality for such a runaway. The statute commits to the dismantling of slave laws and therefore the disruption of conventional economics. It asserts that the humanity (and therefore freedom) of the slave is a covenantal reality that overrides conventional economics.

23:17-18: The third statute concerns cultic practice and, as in 18:9-14, regards non-Israelite practices as an abomination to be strictly avoided in Israel. It appears that this statute aims to delineate Israelite distinctiveness by rejecting a non-Israelite practice. But it is not possible to determine what it is that is condemned. The Hebrew term in the first two lines translated "temple prostitute" is simply a nominal form of "holy," feminine and masculine. The terms themselves do not suggest sexual practice, a notion derived from the different term in verse 18, "prostitute." It is important not to present a caricature of non-Israelite worship. Scholars have been unable to find any documentation supporting the notion that other religions in the region engaged in a practice of "temple prostitutes." Because evidence for such practices is not found elsewhere, one should not be overly eager to explain Israel's prohibition (Oden 1987:153; Bird 1997:219-225).

23:19-20: The fourth statute, like the second, concerns a remarkable economic insistence (vv. 19-20). This prohibition of interest among members of the covenant community envisions a radically alternative economy, a vision that is voiced characteristically in Israel's statutes (Exod 22:25 [Heb. v. 24]; Lev 25:36-27), in the wisdom traditions (Prov 28:8), in the prophetic tradition (Ezek 18:8, 13, 17; 22:12) and, perhaps most spectacularly, in one of the oldest liturgies (Ps 15:5). Given the recurrence of the subject in a variety of traditions, the prohibition against interest on loans emerges as one of the most elemental teachings of the ethics of covenant (see Neh 5).

The teaching makes one allowance and offers one assurance. The allowance is that the limitation on interest applies only to covenanters and not to outsiders (see 14:21). This allowance has provided an opening for a variety of interpretations. It has been argued, on the basis of this allowance, that this is not a universal principle for commerce. The assurance is that when the community practices a neighborly economics, prosperity comes. The explicit negation is that when neighbors treat each other as occasions for profit, then the "natural environment" will be less responsive and less productive, because YHWH will not grant abundance to those who live an antineighborly existence.

23:21-23: The fifth statute in this series concerns the keeping of vows (vv. 21-23). It is important that the regulation pertains, in the first instant, to vows to YHWH and not to neighbor (see Num 30:2). Verse 22, as a qualifier, leaves a way out of such obligation: don't pledge! Apparently because there was no obligation to make such a promise, there is no opprobrium in withholding pledges, but when adhered, it must be performed (see Pss 61:5 [6]; 22:25 [26]; 61:8 [9]; 65:1 [2]; and 116:14 [18]).

The addendum of verse 23 appears to interpret the original cultic stipulation by drawing it out to a more general principle that applies to all such utterances, to neighbor as to God.

23:24-25: The sixth statute in this series concerns neighborly access to produce. The teaching both permits and limits. The permission is that one may enter the vineyard or field of a neighbor and help one's self to what is grown there. The limitation imposed is that such free food is only for the moment of eating: one cannot use containers to harvest produce beyond what one can take by hand. This balance of permit and limit envisions a neighborhood in which the owner is not grudging toward a neighbor and the user is not exploitative toward the owner, but both are respectful of the other.

Theological and Ethical Analysis

These laws, in a variety of quite specific ways, trace out the ingredients of a viable community in Yahwistic covenant. In the rhythm of six statues, two major emphases emerge:

A viable covenant community must *host the Holy* and maintain conditions whereby holiness is willing and able to abide. These rules for hosting holiness may seem not terribly important. And yet if one considers the violation of them in terms of cheap indecency (vv. 9-14), manipulative sexuality as an ultimate (vv. 17-18), and a breakdown of fidelity (vv. 21-23), one can see that holiness, a presence of ultimate power for well-being that gives life its buoyancy, is easily discarded. Community becomes nothing more than transactions of convenience in which the strong will always defeat the weak.

The second theme concerns the practice of *economic justice*, which is here articulated in small but radical requirements:

1. The freedom of slaves in ways that will break the debt system (vv. 15-16). This law asserts that the humanity (and therefore freedom) of the slave is a covenantal reality that overrides conventional economics.

2. The prohibition against interest on loans to neighbors (vv. 19-20), a prohibition against reducing neighbors to poverty. There is no doubt that the history of charging interest is a sorry tale of exploitation, reflecting the fact that finance is a major zone of covenant obligation and a major opportunity for

covenantal obedience. Benjamin Nelson (1994) has traced the history of the practice of usury in the West. It is his well-argued judgment that the prohibition on charging interest was a conscious ethical position in the West until the time of the Reformation. With careful documentation, Nelson demonstrates that the Reformers, Luther and especially Calvin, with the rise of the commerce-driven bourgeois, found a way to justify interest and therefore changed the most elemental economic restraint of the West (Nelson 1994, 73-74). Nelson's play on the terms "other" and "brother" is derived from the pairing of "brothers" (which in the Hebrew of Deuteronomy includes "sisters") and "foreigners" in the statute and are particularly telling. As long as one is a "brother or sister," that is, a member of the community, interest is a problem; when the borrower is an outsider, an other who is to be treated at a distance as an alien, then the law of Moses permits interest. Nelson's aphorism is, "In modern capitalism, all are 'brothers' in being equally 'others'" (Nelson 1994, xxi).

3. Society depends on fiduciary relationships in which people are as good as their word. It is clear that such fiduciary ways of relating are an oddity in a mass culture of anonymity that relies upon the manipulation of images. Indeed a cynical judgment, in such a social context as contemporary consumerist society, might be made that to be trustworthy is foolish, for one is sure to be exploited. But the threat to human well-being in the absence of reliable relationships is nearly unbearable (Berry 1983:24-63; Fukuyama 1995:26-27).

4. The access of neighbors to produce that precludes privatized enclosure (vv. 24-25). This rather innocent looking guideline for neighborly accessibility in an agrarian society has within it the seeds of resistance to "laws of enclosure." Karl Polanyi has traced the precise moment in English history, to cite one case, when legislation was enacted whereby established landowners earned the right to fence their property and to make foraging by needy people a crime with severe sanctions (Polanyi 1957). That enactment of laws of enclosure, preventing the use of grazing land or the collection of firewood was a

massive move toward privatization and the breakdown of social bonds between owners and needy neighbors. The begi ning of laws of enclosure, resisted. in our text, contributed to contemporary extremity in such steps of privatization as "gated communities" in which one can "hide" from a neighbor (on which see 22:1-4).

Taken together it is clear that economic transactions concerning debt, interest, and access become crucial ingredients in a society where neighbors count along with the holy God.

Holy Identity Enacted Concretely (24:1-22)

The predominant concern of this chapter is neighborly justice (vv. 6, 7, 10-13, 14-15, 17-18, 19-20, and 21-22). Interspersed among these statutes, however, are other requirements for covenant that relate to themes and subjects already considered. Thus verses 1-4 pertain to family regulations and are linked to 22:13-19. Verse 5 concerns war exemption and is reflective of the allowance made in military service in 20:7. Verses 8-9 concern ritual purity and link to the general concern for purity seen, for example, in 14:1-21. Verse 16 stands by itself as a remarkable development in the administration of justice. This series of statutes provides an opportunity to notice the several ways in which a large covenantal vision of social reality is brought down to the specificities of daily life.

Exegetical Analysis

24:1-4: The opening statute is a case law on marriage. As already seen in 22:19, 29, the male forfeiture of the right of divorce is against the common male prerogative of divorce in this patriarchal society. This present statute assumes such a male privilege that can normally be undertaken easily and without challenge. The statute shares with 22:13-19 a case in which a man rejects a wife. She is put out from the house of the man. She marries a second man, and her second marriage also ends in divorce or widowhood. The statute provides no details; it is not concerned with either the first or the second divorce. That is all taken as routine in a patriarchal society.

The issue is not either marriage or the status of the woman. It is the status of the land (v. 4). The issue turns on the characteristic terms "defile" and "abhorrent." The second marriage has made the woman a "used" woman as far as the first husband is concerned. For the first husband to reengage with her sexually would be to relate to a "used" woman, which could only bring *contamination* to the community and to the land. Thus the entire regulation concerns a patriarchal judgment about protecting the purity of the land of promise by exclusion of the now "defiled woman." The law operates on the assumption that anything "out of order" will threaten the order of everything else; a sequel of sexual interactions that is not "normal" is a disruption and a threat.

The statute, however, is used metaphorically in Jer 3:1-5 and is dramatically overturned. In Jeremiah, YHWH is the first "husband" of wife Israel. Wife Israel leaves her first husband, YHWH, for a second husband, Baal. When the second husband, Baal, is found to be inadequate, wife Israel wants to "return" to her first husband, YHWH. It is precisely the return that is precluded by the statute of Moses. That, however, is only a setup for the announcement of the prophetic poetry. The surprise, according to the poetry, is that YHWH is eager to violate the statute in order to have Israel return in faith. (See the term "return" in vv. 12, 14, 22; 4:1.) YHWH in great passion overrides the Torah, risks the defilement, and embraces the wayward, "used" wife, Israel. This poem effectively undermines the stringency of the statute, though the benefit of such subversion pertains to the future of covenantal theology and not to the old family law.

24:5: The rule on military exemption in verse 5 (to which reference is made in Luke 14:20) is linked to the series of exemptions in 20:5-7. In this earlier series, as Washington has observed (1998:15), the exemption is to guard against the competing rights of "another man." This lean regulation more simply seeks to make time for the marriage itself and its "joy," without explicit reference to particular male privileges.

24:6-7: The prohibition of verse 6, like the regulation of verses 10-13, concerns a limitation on what can be taken as collateral for a loan. The short, apodictic prohibition concerns two millstones between which grain is ground. The use of a millstone is menial work and presumably is done by those who are reduced to poverty and servitude (see Exod 11:5; Isa 47:2). Thus the rule prohibits taking as collateral for loans to poor people their means of livelihood. The poor are not to be denied their limited "means of production," their capacity to live at all. There are limits to what lenders can expect from needy debtors in the community.

The prohibition of verse 7 concerns kidnapping, or literally, "stealing a man." We do not know the circumstance or extent of selling people in "slave trade." Obviously such economic transaction treats such a person as a commodity and not as a neighbor. The statute concerns an extreme infringement on neighborliness and asserts yet another insistence in this tradition that neighborly responsibility cannot be subordinated to economic interest. Kidnapping may here be understood as any maneuver or economic practice that reduces human dignity and human freedom to cause human persons to become an instrument or a statistic in economic management. The seriousness of the prohibition is signaled by the concluding formula of purgation.

24:8-9: The series of "justice regulations" is interrupted in verses 8-9 by the only mention of leprosy in Deuteronomy. It is clear that leprosy is a "social disease" which, among other things, makes one ineligible for participation in the worshiping community (see Num 13–14; 2 Chr 26:16-21). Thus the case is not medical but cultic, a worry about ritual capacity that would threaten the community and endanger the land. The rule stipulates a procedure and cites a precedent. The best protection against such ritual contamination is *full compliance* to Levitical instruction. The admonition to heed the Levitical priests seems to support the initial imperative; it may be that the reference to leprosy is simply a device for underscoring Levitical authority. The reference concerning Miriam is to the narrative of Num 12, in which Miriam, sister of Moses, was smitten with leprosy for challenging Mosaic authority (Trible 1989). The concern for purity appears to be a stratagem used for the enhancement of the authority of Moses and derivatively of the Levites.

24:10-22: The remainder of this chapter constitutes a series of brief regulations designed (except for verse 16) to ensure neighborly justice:

1. A concern for collateral for loans expressed in verse 6 is taken up again in verses 10-13. It is assumed, as in verse 6, that in the process of granting a loan the creditor has social leverage over the debtor. Such leverage must be restrained because the creditor also has an obligation to protect the dignity of the debtor in two ways. First, a debtor's home "is his castle," a safe place where the creditor may not enter (vv. 10-11). This law prevents voyeuristic confiscation. Second, the vulnerability of the debtor is even more if the debtor is "poor." In such a case the creditor might insist on more substantive collateral to secure a risky loan, and take everything the poor person has. The most extreme collateral imaginable is the poor person's coat, needed for warmth at night; if the coat is seized by the creditor, the debtor is left completely exposed by an exploitative creditor (see Amos 2:8). Such a coat as collateral, the statute mandates, must be given back to the poor person every night, for safety and comfort in sleep, while the loan continues. This requirement perhaps intends to make the daily pick up and return of collateral so inconvenient that the need for collateral is waived. In any case, the rights of the creditor are curbed and the dignity of the poor debtor is affirmed.

2. The parallel statements in verses 14-15 seek further to curb the wealthy employer in relation to the poor laborer. The statements insist that wages must be paid the day earned (as in verse 13). Creditors are wont to withhold and use other people's money, however briefly, to their own advantage. (An

analogue might be the exorbitant interest rates on short-term loans offered for poor people who are without bargaining power.) One cannot say to the poor worker, "The check's in the mail," for the poor must have their money promptly. The point is that the poor employee is a neighbor and not an economic pawn.

3. Verse 16 is a remarkable statement in context. Whereas the other statutes seem to be case law, this verse enunciates a principle for capital offenses, seeking to contain sanctioned retaliation for a capital affront. Certainly in a society of uncurbed raw power, a capital affront might evoke a wholesale retaliation, so that the entire family or village of the murderer might be wiped out. This statement seeks to break the pattern of vengeful, disproportional retaliation by limiting retaliation to the perpetrator. According to the narrative of 2 Kgs 14:6, royal vengeance is restrained precisely by Torah teaching. The same principle of proportionality is stated for different reasons in Jer 31:29-30 and Ezek 18:2.

4. The statute of verses 17-18 returns to the issue of collateral for loans already voiced in verses 6, 10-13. Here the debtor who is identified only as "poor" in verse 12 is now specified according to standard Deuteronomic rhetoric by the familiar triad of those vulnerable because they are landless: the alien, orphan, and widow. In verses 12-13, the garment of the poor could be taken only in the daytime, but here restraint on the creditor is further advanced—no collateral at all! The motivation of verse 18 parallels that of 15:15. This motivation belongs together with the affirmative sanction of verse 13 and the negative sanction of verse 15. The three statements of verses 13, 15, and 18 together lodge economic transactions in the context of YHWH's good governance.

The three parallel regulations of verses 19, 20, and 21-22 are related to 23:24-25. The difference is that in 23:24-25, the laws give to the needy neighbors permission to glean. In the present verses, the statutes issue a *restraint* to creditor-owners that matches the *permit* of 23:24-25. That is, restraint and permit share the same class analysis of how the powerful and the powerless are related as neighbors. The owner, in harvesting grain, olives, and grapes, cannot go through the field, orchard, or vineyard a second time for what was dropped and left the first time. The residue, which might be considerable, is for the needy. Thus the restraint on the owner is to ensure a modest welfare allotment of produce to those who have no land of their own.

Theological and Ethical Analysis

The great emphases of this collage of brief instructions are purity and justice. The two major rules for purity here are concerned with avoiding contamination that will jeopardize the land and endanger the community. While verses 1-4 (5) and 8-9 may seem offensive because of their authoritarian cast, they do raise an important concern: pollution and contamination are a deep threat to the life of Israel and to the life of the world. The land (earth) is not given as an unconditional guarantee of well-being, but is exceedingly fragile and requires attentiveness. The regulation in verses 1-4, moreover, understands that distorted human relationships do "pollute" and endanger, so that the interrelatedness of the human and the environmental is affirmed (Berry 1993).

The cumulative effect of this cluster of statutes on justice is impressive. The rules concern quite concrete matters of loans and collateral, payment of poor workers, and welfare provisions for the landless poor. It remains, however, to take up these modest "village requirements" and transpose them by re-imagination as neighborly economic practices and policies in a mass culture where the power of the propertied and the vulnerability of the property-less still play out together in destructive ways. The "class analysis" done here is itself important because it insists upon recognition that the poor—widow, orphan, alien—are different, have different needs and entitlements. Beyond class analysis, the social dynamics of "haves" and "have nots" are framed Yahwistically by sanctions (vv. 13, 15) and by motivations (vv. 18, 22). The neighbor—especially the neighbor in need—lives in a world governed not by the ruthless "iron law" of the market or by the unencumbered autonomy of the powerful, but by the same God who curbed Pharaoh.

Variations on Covenantal Themes (25:1-19)

This final chapter of stipulations consists of six distinct instructions. While each of them makes its own statement, it may be useful, after this long exposition of statutes, to pay primary attention to the cross-references that these particular texts exhibit in relation to other texts that deal with the same themes.

Exegetical Analysis

25:1-3: The first regulation provides a limitation on sanctioned punishment. Two provisions are given for such judicially determined punishment. First, it shall be conducted in the presence of the judge, that is, under court supervision. Second, it shall be proportionate to the offense. The comment of verse 3, moreover, provides that no matter what the offense, the limit of proportionality is forty lashes. The reason for the limitation is crucial, that the guilty member of the community not be abased in public. Punishment is in the context of neighborly respect. The regulation is not unlike the aim of the year of release in 15:1-18, that the poor shall be able to resume a full place in the community. This law seeks to establish "a rule of law" that will "guard each one's dignity and save each one's pride."

25:4: The second brief provision is a remarkable example of the prevention of cruelty to animals (v. 4). The regulation concerns the treatment of oxen, which do the drudge work of threshing grain. The animal was muzzled to prevent it from eating grain while working. The law insists that the animal is entitled to a modicum of satisfaction while working and is not merely a production machine (see 1 Cor 9:9; 1 Tim 5:18). Along with 20:19-20 and 21:6-7, this text allows a modest opening toward environmental issues.

25:5-6: The third stipulation is a part of family law that governs marriage and family matters (see 22:13-29; 24:1-4). This particular law—that has its narrative complements in Gen 38 and the book of Ruth—provides a standard procedure in the event of the death of a husband who has no son (vv. 5-6). A brother of the deceased man is obligated to marry his dead brother's widow, and so to provide a son for the deceased. The provision reflects the intensely patriarchal concern that the "name" and line of the deceased should be perpetuated. Family continuity is an overriding agenda, as is evidenced in the ancestral narratives of Genesis.

The statute has in view an ideal "Israel" that takes care of its own and does not permit an "outsider" to marry one of its widows. The premise of the law is a well-ordered, self-conscious community with all members committed to its well-being, "When brothers reside together" (see Ps 133:1).

25:7-10: That idyllic state of community is jarred by the recognition that not all "brothers" "dwell in unity," not all are prepared to accept an obligation that would dictate the marriage of the surviving brother, no matter how he himself may regard the matter. The statute does its best to promote its vision of "brotherliness" by suggesting that to renege on such family obligation is a cause for communal deliberation. The widow can file a charge, and the elders can intervene with the brother to urge compliance to this demanding ordinance. If the brother still resists, then the abandoned widow is free to engage in two acts of humiliation of the brother, spitting in his face and removing his sandal. While the exact meaning of the second act is not clear, it is the more durable act, because it gives the reneger a lasting "nickname" that keeps his resistance to social obligation visible in the community. Verses 7-10 indicate how difficult this ideal "brotherhood" is to sustain, and how problematic enforced compliance is. The verses suggest that the ultimate weapon against such a brother who will not "act for the family" is shame. Communal coherence is a large agenda in this corpus, but it did not everywhere prevail. The shame was apparently bearable for the brother who reneged. He could live well enough, even if labeled and despised.

25:11-12: The fourth brief statute in verses 11-12 concerns a dispute among men, perhaps the litigation of verses 1-3 carried into the streets. Thus the regulation is to be understood as part of the family law that guards and enhances patriarchal primacy. The physical dispute among men is taken for granted; what interests the regulation is the "inappropriate" intervention of a woman on behalf of her husband. The case cites a knowledgeable woman, for when she intervenes, she goes for the genitals of her husband's adversary, his most vulnerable part. The term used for genitals, *(měbūšāyw)* based on the root *(bôš)*, recognizes that the genitals are the part of the male anatomy most exposed and most vulnerable, and therefore most private and not to be touched by the wife of another man. Her contact with his genitals humiliates him.

Her hand has offended and must be cut off (see Matt 5:29-30). The formula "no pity" is reserved in this corpus for the most extreme and dangerous affronts (see 13:8). This is evidently one of those most extreme affronts. The priority of men and the irrelevance of women are unmistakable in this case. That ordering of social power is preserved with harshness and unblinking severity.

25:13-16: The fifth stipulation in this chapter concerns equitable economic transactions, and so relates to the fundamental and concrete insistence on justice in 16:18-20. "Justice" is not simply a "good idea" in this vision of society, but comes down to quite concrete practices. This stipulation consists in two prohibitions and two corresponding positive statements, plus a motivational clause introduced by "in order that." The two negatives concern commercial fraud of rigged weights and measures. The two parallel positive statements require that weights and measures should be "full and honest," that is, as claimed and represented, so that customers receive what is allegedly sold. The term "honest" *(ṣedeq)* is twice used in 16:20 where it is conventionally rendered "justice, justice." The most remarkable feature of this statute is the way in which fair commercial practices are treated as a condition for sustainable life in the land. The nonnegotiable condition of well-being is intentional neighborliness in every dimension of life, including daily dealings in the marketplace (see Amos 8:5-6).

25:17-19: The sixth and final stipulation in this chapter concerns enduring hostility toward the Amalekites, Israel's perennial enemy. This final, passionate urging in the corpus of statutes relates to the "Rules of Exclusion" in 23:1-8, but escalates the rhetoric well beyond any of those formulations. The statute begins with an extended historical allusion in verses 17-18, looking back to Ex 17:8-16 [see also Num 14:43-45].

With that grounding for "eternal hatred," the final verse issues its imperative. It is simple and unqualified: "blot out" the memory, everywhere, in every way, for all time. The mandate is re-enforced by the final, "do not forget"—ever! The locus of this durable hostility is for a time when Israel will be "at rest" in the land and safe from all enemies and threats (Deut 12:10; Josh 21:43-45; 2 Sam 7:1).

In that context without any threatening enemies, however, Israel's adrenalin is to be devoted to hatred toward the Amalekites. The juxtaposition of *rest* from enemies and this mandate for *hate* is highly ironic. The harsh statement is no doubt rooted in some concrete memory. What was apparently a concrete and compelling memory has become an ideological slogan that perhaps has a purpose other than hatred. Its function in this location is to remind Israel at the end of the legal corpus that *Israel is different,* unlike all other peoples, especially unlike its enemies who are the enemies of their God, the quintessential one being the Amalekites (on which see also 1 Sam 15). This durable hatred is a defiant way to affirm that "through many trials and snares we have already come." The function of this slogan may be better understood if one recalls parallel slogans that have a similar function:

- "Remember the Alamo"
- "Remember Pearl Harbor"
- "Never again" [at Masada]

The main intention of these slogans is not to evoke hatred or destruction of, respectively, the Mexicans, the Japanese, or the Romans. Rather they summon, respectively, Texans, Americans, and Israelis to take account of their special place and role in the world, given providentially and enacted diligently. Thus this concluding law is not intended to be enacted. It is rather a bid that Israel not forget its blessed, painful past that has culminated in gifts, assurances, and entitlements. None of that, to be sure, minimizes the harsh, ruthless formulation that finally loses none of its ominous tone, a slogan kept ready for the mobilization of violent adrenalin in any future emergency.

Theological and Ethical Analysis

The six "statutes" reiterate themes already known elsewhere in the corpus: a concern for due process (25:1-3); an acknowledgment of the dignity and entitlement of nonhuman creatures (25:4); family law that preserves patriarchal preeminence (25:5-10, 11-12); the practice of neighborly justice (25:13-16); and rules of exclusion now escalated (25:17-19).

This strange but characteristic sequence exhibits an intentional community at work seeking to regularize and make coherent its own sense of itself. The two regulations in 25:4, 13-17 accent a caring ethic of justice. That ethic, however, operates within a settled patriarchal order sustained by harsh sanctions (25:3, 9-10, 12) that draw rigorous, even inflammatory lines against outsiders. To an observer of the tradition, such a collage of requirements and sensibilities seems fraught with incongruities. Nevertheless, the incongruities altogether add up to a community of intentionality, obeying YHWH as they understood the God of the Exodus and caring for neighbor as they were able in an environment saturated with threat and anxiety.

A DECLARATION UNASHAMED (26:1-19)

With the end of the corpus of statutes in chapters 12–25, the "Second Address of Moses," begun in 4:44, now moves to its concluding statement of sanctions and appeals in chapters 26–28. The present chapter has been understood, since the defining work of Gerhard von Rad (1966:2-33), as an oath of allegiance whereby Israel accepts its identity as YHWH's holy people and swears to abide by the statutes and ordinances just given in chapters 12–25.

The chapter readily divides into three rhetorical units: the presentation of offerings with an appropriate verbal affirmation (vv. 1-11), an oath of innocence (vv. 12-15), and a declaration of covenant commitments (vv. 16-19).

Exegetical Analysis

The presentation of firstfruits is here situated as a pivotal liturgical opportunity to enact and declare Israel's peculiar identity as YHWH's people. The text begins with a proper location of the rite at the shrine when Israel is securely settled in the land (vv. 1-2). The basket of firstfruits is a gesture that creates the context for the formal liturgical utterance of verses 3-10. This utterance is given in two parts. Verse 3 is a terse acknowledgment that the land is a gift and that the present worshiper is a recipient of all YHWH's promises in Genesis. The second, longer statement to the priest lines out Israel's most treasured memory that decisively defines Israel's present-tense life (vv. 5-10). Scholarship has largely followed Gerhard von Rad in his hypothesis that these verses preserve Israel's primal liturgical declaration of its identity as YHWH's people (von Rad 1966:3-8). The recital draws together the major facets of Israel's memory preserved in the Torah, and the present speaker positions the community so that the memory shapes the future. The memory consists in three themes:

1. The past of Israel is rooted in an at-risk ("wandering") Aramean semi-nomad. The reference is apparently to Jacob in Genesis 25–36 and the providential power of YHWH that transformed Jacob's situation of risk to one of profound well-being.

2. The second theme concerns the Exodus (vv. 6-8). The rhetoric of this assertion moves through three phases, a situation of abuse, a desperate petition, and YHWH's transformative response. This confession of YHWH as the God who enacts public transformations is at the heart of Israel's claim for

YHWH and is, properly, what the Bible means by "miracle" and "mighty deed." The rhetoric works so that the speaker who is a belated rememberer of an old event becomes a present-tense participant in that old event. In "liturgical time," the gap between past time and present time is overcome, and present-tense characters become involved in remembered events. The recital, moreover, makes clear that the initiative for this deliverance is not with YHWH but with the pained petition of Israel. Israel speaks first and mobilizes YHWH into action. YHWH is decisively responsive to Israel's need. The irresistible power of YHWH is exhibited in the assault on Pharaoh. YHWH has done for Israel what it could not do for itself.

3. The recital culminates in verses 9-10 with an affirmation of the gift of the wondrous land as the fulfillment of both the ancestral promises and the deliverance from Egypt (see already v. 3). The presentation of the firstfruits is an avowal of this narrative account of Israel's past with YHWH. At every point, it is YHWH who is the decisive actor.

26:12-15: The second part of this chapter concerns the third year tithe and seems especially connected to 14:28-29 (vv. 12-25). Thus the two offerings are here placed back-to-back but with no evident relationship to each other: *firstfruits* (on which see 15:19-22) and third year *tithe* (on which see 14:28-29). The third year tithe is special because it is "in your towns," not brought to the sanctuary or to a priest, but kept for the needy in the community.

As with verses 1-11, this unit of text consists in act and word. The act entails genuine solidarity with the poor and needy (v. 12). The text is dominated, as in verses 5-9, by the utterance of the worshiper. The offering provides opportunity for a public attestation of singular, uncompromised devotion to YHWH, an attestation that is given as a "statement of innocence" in a series of declarations:

> I have removed,
> I have given,
> I have not transgressed,

I have not forgotten,
I have not eaten,
I have not removed,
I have not offered (given),
I have obeyed (listened).

In every way, the speaker has diligently and scrupulously kept the covenant and obeyed the Torah commandments. The entire assertion of fidelity and innocence articulates a contrast between Torah obedience and other alternatives that were surely available and that required intentional denial. The outcome is a life that is completely shaped and disciplined by the commands of YHWH. This is indeed "a righteous man" who has meditated on the Torah "day and night" (see Ps 1:2; Deut 17:18-19), and who finds joy in such attentiveness.

The recital of innocence forms the ground of appeal that is uttered in the imperative of verse 15. After the statement of qualification, the speaker has earned the right to petition YHWH as a devoted adherent. The imperative is in two parts:

1. "Look down"; the verb assumes that YHWH is high above and not in "the place." The term regularly bespeaks both YHWH's transcendence and YHWH's attentiveness (Gen 19:28; Ex 14:29; Pss 14:2; 102:20; Lam 3:50). The petition wants YHWH to notice.

2. The second, more forceful imperative is to "bless" both Israel and its land. The term "bless" appeals to the creation tradition of the God who infuses the earth with abundance. The term affirms that YHWH has willed the habitat of Israel to be fruitful. The petition asks that in special, particular ways this land of promise may enjoy the intense generosity that YHWH has decreed for all of creation. While the recital of verses 3-10 looks to the *past,* the recital of verses 13-14 looks to the *future* and the blessing for which fidelity qualifies Israel and its land. The speaker is fully committed to a Deuteronomic theology of *choosing* life and of *receiving* life from the Lord of life.

26:16-19: The conclusion of the chapter reflects mutual promises of loyalty that effectively bind YHWH and Israel into an exclusive covenant relationship of fidelity (vv. 16-19). The statement three times asserts "today" (vv. 16, 17, 18), suggesting a cultic, liturgical exchange of vows undertaken with great intensity. The term that NRSV renders "agreement" refers to formal verbal assertions, that is, solemn vows that commit the speaker to certain obligations to the partner. Israel binds itself in this agreement to *full obedience* "to walk, to keep statutes and ordinance and commandments, to obey, with heart and soul." The requirement on YHWH's side is to be the God of Israel and to establish Israel's singular well-being and prominence over the nations in "praise, fame and honor," that is, to establish Israel's superiority to all other peoples (see Deut 28:13).

The taking and receiving of vows yields the status of Israel as YHWH's "treasured people," a people "holy to YHWH your God" (on which see 7:6; 14:1-2, 21). These mutual vows create in the world a relationship of covenant and an entity (Israel) that did not exist until this moment of formal utterance and solemn declaration.

Theological and Ethical Analysis

Chapter 26 brings together several liturgical acts that were originally independent of each other. The three sections of this text together yield a liturgical, and subsequently textual, pivot point in the formation of covenantal Israel and in its periodic reformation. The rite of firstfruits provides an occasion when Israel attests to *what YHWH has done,* a series of transformative acts that has brought a "wandering" (= at risk) people to the land of well-being. The rite of the third year tithe, in turn, provides an occasion when Israel can attest to *what Israel has done,* a series of claims, generic and concrete, that Israel has been singularly and consciously loyal to YHWH. These two declarations provide the basis for the mutual declaration that concludes the chapter in vv. 16-19. The mutual declarations are oaths that bind each party to the other in uncompromising fidelity: Israel will be *utterly obedient* to YHWH and thereby enhance YHWH as YHWH's only treasured people. YHWH will be *utterly devoted* to Israel and thereby assure Israel a spectacular, visible, political success in the world. This resolve to live through the vagaries of life together leads to the following observations:

1. The mutual giving and receiving of promises of fidelity has its closest analogue in wedding vows—"for better, for worse, in sickness and in health." The analogue of the wedding vow suggests the profound intimacy of this mutual commitment, the deep risks it entails, and the profound pain caused by infidelity and betrayal.

2. The thrust of Deuteronomy makes clear that this relationship of mutual fidelity is conditional. It depends upon Israel's readiness to honor its vow of obedience, for obedience is the condition of YHWH's devotion to Israel.

3. *And yet* this same tradition of covenant produces poets (Hosea and Jeremiah) who voice the deep grief of YHWH and the yearning of YHWH to have the covenant with Israel restored, even though it has been terminated in infidelity.

It is clear that newness in covenant that is rooted in YHWH's unconditional love for Israel, newness voiced by the prophets, runs well beyond the harsh conditionality of Deuteronomy. And yet it is possible to see that such generous unconditionality is a development of and extrapolation from the passion of YHWH for Israel that is already inchoately present in Deuteronomy. Newness from YHWH is inchoately present in the inception of the covenant. It is this God who has "set his heart" *(ḥāšaq)* on Israel (7:7; 10:15), who wants Israel for a treasured people, and who wills steadfastly to be Israel's God.

YHWH, in deep passion, acts the terminator when Israel disobeys. This relationship, however, will not stay terminated. It keeps reemerging as YHWH reengages Israel beyond every *quid pro quo* upon which Israel has reneged. Thus Deuteronomy and the entire covenantal tradition of YHWH has as its core dynamic the endless capacity for newness in the relationship just when it has sadly failed. This mutual declaration, stated in the present text once-for-all and repeatedly restated in new contexts, causes the emergence of a radical newness in the world that makes the world irrevocably different, a newness grounded in mutuality and concretely enacted as fidelity.

BECOMING THE PEOPLE OF YHWH (27:1-26)

27:1-10: While the materials of this chapter were no doubt independent pieces, in their present location and configuration they serve to give liturgic implementation to the mutual declaration of 26:16-19 that constitutes the covenant. This chapter consists in two independent but related units. In verses 1-10, careful preparation is made for the "furniture of the covenant" in the new land across the Jordan, in order to make covenant a visible, public phenomenon in Israel. The remainder of the chapter (vv. 11-26) "scripts" a ceremony of blessings and curses that is to enunciate the sanctions that support and enforce the covenant.

Exegetical Analysis

27:1-10: The covenant propagated by Deuteronomy is not just a good idea or a theological commitment. It is a relationship constituted publicly and initiated through liturgical enactment as a form of life.

These verses are framed in verses 1 and 9-10 by solemn appeals for obedience. The opening imperative, "keep," is in emphatic form that is answered in verses 9-10 with the double use of *shema*[c] ("hear, obey"). These imperatives pertain to the large obligations of covenant.

Within that framing verses 2-8 give detailed guidance for making the covenant process highly visible in the new land, so that Israel is consistently aware of its peculiar gift from YHWH and its peculiar obligation to YHWH.

"This law," presumably the statutes of Deut 12–25, is to be visibly exhibited in plaster-covered stones that are written "very clearly" (v. 8). The plaster billboards may be parallel to advertising that seeks to win consumers as converts to a certain brand of

product. Alternatively, one is reminded of the large billboards in contemporary China where the government dispenses highly supervised news. The purpose of all such billboards is to nurture and administer public opinion and public loyalty to persuade for "this claim" against all other claims.

An altar is to be erected to YHWH, a different kind of public exhibit to direct public energy to the God of the covenant. The central liturgical enactment whereby this people "becomes the people of YHWH" (v. 9) is to be conducted on Ebal and Gerizim, perhaps an ancient place of covenant making (see Deut 11:29-30; Josh 8:30-35; 24:1-18). The drama of blessings and curses, sanctions for covenantal obedience, involves all twelve tribes in the ideal system of Israel in Deuteronomy. The drama, however, is conducted by the Levitical priests, the apparent supervisors and guardians of the Mosaic covenant. One can imagine a liturgical antiphon among the two groups of six tribes on the two mountains, except that the only utterance is of curse; the negative sanctions are given primacy, again indicating the nonnegotiability of this covenantal tradition.

27:11-26: The list of twelve curses constitutes a set liturgic piece that has been crafted in a stylized way and likely was used over time (vv. 15-26). That it is stylized and includes twelve elements suggests it functioned not unlike the Decalogue in Deut 5:6-21 as a charter teaching for covenant. These twelve curses are one version of the "bottom line" concerning practices that are intolerable in Israel because they will jeopardize the community. By this recital and the regular communal response of assent ("Amen"), Israel accepts its peculiar status as the people of YHWH and the uncompromising requirements and prohibitions that go with that status.

It is not necessary to comment on each of these acts, because a number of them have already been considered earlier as their themes have been anticipated elsewhere in the book of Deuteronomy. Thus I will indicate the ones that are cross-referenced elsewhere and then consider those not already commented upon:

v. 15 concerning idols and images	*5:8-10*; 4:15-20
v. 16 dishonoring parents	*5:16*; 21:18-21
v. 17 on moving boundary markers	19:14
v. 18 misleading the blind	new
v. 19 widows, orphans, aliens	14:29; 16:11, 14; 24:19-21; 26:12-13
v. 20 lying with father's wife	22:30 (Heb. 23:1)
vv. 21-23 lying with any animal	new
v. 24 striking a neighbor	new
v. 25 bribery	10:17; 16:19
v. 26 concluding generalization	new

Of the twelve curses, the first two are present in the Decalogue; six have appeared elsewhere in the corpus. It remains to consider the four not heretofore mentioned.

1. Misleading the blind (v. 18), a prohibition paralleled in Lev 19:14, is a characteristic way of protecting the vulnerable in the community. The blind belong socially among the more general category of the vulnerable on the horizon of Deuteronomy and are guaranteed communal protection (see Job 29:15-16).

2. The three prohibitions of verses 21-23 are not elsewhere present in Deuteronomy, and verse 20 only with reference to 22:30. This community, as we have seen, intends to be holy, pure, and clean. Disordered sexuality is regarded as a primal threat to such a community; see Lev 18:6-23; 20:10-21 for a fuller, more detailed expression of this concern. The prohibited actions are taken to be "disgraceful acts" (see Deut 22:21) that jeopardize the community.

3. The prohibition against striking a neighbor is not else-where mentioned in the tradition; it is nonetheless congruent with respect for the neighbor that pervades Deuteronomy. "Neighbor" here as elsewhere refers to a fellow member of the covenant community. An Israelite must curb anger and vio-lence, because violence toward a neighbor will jeopardize the entire community. The qualification "in secret," here as in verse 15, reflects an awareness that the community cannot supervise

all such acts. The weight of theological sanction is an alternative to community scrutiny, designed to protect against undetected endangerments to the community and its members. YHWH can see in a supervisory way where the community cannot.

4. The final curse of verse 26 is a generic conclusion, perhaps included to complete the number twelve.

The tone of this recital is one of deep conviction, prone to authoritarianism, intolerant of deviation. It reflects the sense that the community may be put in jeopardy by these prohibited actions that are, in the most severe way, precluded.

Theological and Ethical Analysis

Covenant must be regularly, intentionally enacted in a public way. The mood of this text indicates that being the holy people of YHWH is no obvious, natural, or easy matter, but requires daily resolve in order to be a different kind of community. In a social environment that is marked by easy complacency and self-indulgence, the maintenance of an intentional alternative community is indeed an endless challenge. That intentionality, moreover, does not concern thought or belief, but concerns actions that grow out of covenantal passion and show up in daily life. The odd mix of these sanctions concerns economic matters like bribes and boundary markers, neighborly acts toward disabled neighbors, cultic acts about images and idols, and family relations and illicit sexuality. That is, the sanctions concern every facet of life, a summons to love God in the concrete ways of loving neighbor.

THE "IF" OF HEADS OR TAILS (28:1–29:1)

The second speech of Moses (4:44–29:1) that constitutes the primary material of the book of Deuteronomy now draws to its close. The final material is a recital of blessings (vv. 1-14) and curses (vv. 15-68) together with a closing "historical" note (29:1). This recital of covenant sanctions, as Delbert Hillers has shown

(1964, 30-42), participates in a common stock of blessings and curses used all over the ancient Near East and, given variations, is expressed in a conventional, highly stylized form. That is, the material is not particularly original to Israel and its connection to covenantal Yahwism is loose and secondary. More specifically, a recital of such sanctions, placed after "covenant stipulations" as a mode of enforcement of the stipulations, is a characteristic arrangement of international treaties that were especially prominent in the eighth to seventh centuries, which is perhaps the time of the formulation of Deuteronomy.

The enunciation of blessings and curses can be understood primitively as the enactment of a "hex" with magical power, so that a word uttered takes on a lingering, looming power before which the addressee is helpless. More likely, however, the blessings and curses are understood not as free-floating magical words that cast spells, but as a system of rewards and punishments that are the covenant Lord dispensed according to compliance or resistance to treaty conditions. The importance of these sanctions is evident across the Israelite tradition, having different forms in the historical narratives, the prophetic poetry, and the sapiential instruction of ancient Israel.

Exegetical Analysis

28:1-14: The recital of blessing in verses 1-14 promises to obedient Israel all the well-being of peace, prosperity, and abundance in time to come. The sense of all of these blessings is "life" (life abundant as in John 10:10), or *shalom*. That gift, however, is conditional. It depends completely upon obedience, for this demanding sovereign does not give gifts readily to recalcitrant subjects.

It is important to notice two quite different modes of rhetoric by which the blessings are to come upon Israel. In verses 3-6, the term "blessed" is used six times as a passive participle in what is surely a highly stylized series of assurances. The use of the passive participle "blessed" affirms that Israel will be *acted upon* in this positive, life-giving way. The focus is upon Israel as the recipient. Obviously the passive voice means that no agent is named who will give such a good future; that is, the process takes place without explicit reference to YHWH, who here does not act. This way of speaking is important for, as Klaus Koch has shown, such grammar affirms that there are "spheres of destiny" created by acts of obedience, so that the blessing is a guaranteed and "natural" outcome and consequence of the action of Israel (Koch 1983). That is, obedient acts *produce* good outcomes.

Beginning in verse 7, the blessing recital shifts to a different form, in which YHWH is the active agent of blessing as the subject of a series of active verbs (vv. 7-13). These six statements portray YHWH as an actively engaged agent who personally and intentionally takes an initiative to establish Israel's preeminence among the nations, a preeminence visible in abundance. It may well be that the two kinds of rhetorical formulations, in the end, come to the same thing. They arrive here by very different routes, suggesting blessing first as "natural" *consequence* and second as intentional *reward*.

28:15-68: The recital of curses (vv. 15-68) is much longer than that of blessings and therefore more varied. The relative length of the curse section is congruent with the fact that in chapter 27, the recital of curses in verses 15-26 has no counterpart of blessing at all. The negative sanctions of curses occupied the primary energy of the tradition, likely reflecting its anxiety about the future.

As in the blessing recital, two rhetorical patterns are found in the curses. In verses 16-19, the series of six passive participles (the same passive participle as in 27:15-26) corresponds to the blessing formula of verses 3-6, though the third and fourth elements are in reverse order. Again it is affirmed that Israel's own actions generate curse as the inescapable consequence of disobedience. The second pattern of curse with YHWH as active agent is voiced in verses 20-28, 35-37. YHWH will be the active agent who intervenes in the life of Israel to cause Israel's life in every aspect to fail.

The recital of YHWH's active intervention is interrupted in verses 29-33, 38-44 by rhetoric that lacks such active agency and that simply articulates consequences of recalcitrant action. Thus the provisional conclusion of verses 45-46 attributes to the curses a life and force of their own, without divine involvement.

In verses 47-48, the text takes a remarkable turn that has no counterpart in the blessings. It focuses, in verses 47-57, upon an enemy invasion that will devastate the land. In the larger context of Deuteronomy with its connection to the Deuteronomic history that culminates in 2 Kgs 24–25, these verses surely have reference to the Babylonian devastation of Jerusalem at the beginning of the sixth century, even though the rhetoric could be understood more generically. This section of text that seems to move from the generic to the concrete develops in three stages (vv. 47-57):

1. YHWH as active agent will *send,* will bring (vv. 48, 49). That is all that YHWH does, but it is decisive. YHWH is presented as the sovereign of all the nations and empires of the earth. And therefore it is no stretch, as in Jer 25:9, 27:6, to see Babylon and its ruler Nebuchadnezzar, as agents (servants) of YHWH who are dispatched to implement sanctions against YHWH's own people.

2. That nation ("it") dispatched by YHWH will devastate the land, as occupying armies are wont to do, and will finally lay siege to the cities (of Judah). The imagery of the dispatched power is congruent with the poetry of Jeremiah concerning the invading power (Jer 4:13-18; 5:14-17; 6:22-25).

3. The purpose of the siege is to starve the inhabitants of the city, to deny food until they surrender. Now, in verses 53-57, the siege itself does the work of curse. These verses describe a desperate community that is completely without resources. In its desperation, moreover, the most basic dignities are abandoned; all that counts now is survival. Every person treats every other as a competitor for what little food remains. The graphic scenes portray in detail Israel's humiliating helplessness and degradation.

The final section of the curse recital turns from the specifications of the Babylonian siege to reflect upon the nullification of old faith traditions and the despair that such nullification will bring (vv. 58-68). The section again is governed by the "if" of Torah (v. 58). The "if" will produce YHWH's "dazzlement." The verb of YHWH's action, "overwhelm," is a translation of the verb *pl*, to do something extraordinary. This term characterizes the *miracles of YHWH* that are beyond Israel's understanding or explanation that can only be understood through doxology (see Ex 15:11; Ps 77:12; Job 37:14). Now the term is used with some irony to reflect on the prospect that YHWH will *undo* those old miracles in a way that will be as spectacular as the initial miracles themselves.

1. The dazzlement of the Exodus will be undone, so that Israel will again be subject to the diseases of Egypt (v. 60; see Ex 15:26), and will return to Egypt (v. 68).

2. The promise made to the ancestors to be like the stars in the heavens, a promise celebrated as fulfilled in Deut 10:22, will be reversed; Israel will again be few in number and "at risk," as in 26:5.

3. The community that prospered in the land, "prosperous and numerous" (v. 63), will lose its land, "plucked off" and "scattered" into exile, so that the great tradition of land entry is negated.

The sum of these statements is to deny Israel its most treasured traditions and memories that are the ground of its identity and its *raison d'etre* in the world. Israel will have lost its reason for being Israel. The depth of despair is expressed in two nice rhetorical flourishes. First, in verse 67, Israel will find the day unbearable and will wish for the night, and the night unbearable and wish for the day—no rest, no respite, no comfort. Second, the final humiliation is to be offered as slaves once more, as in long ago Egypt, and to find no buyer (v. 68). Israel now has become useless and worthless, not even suitable for menial tasks, not wanted for state slave projects, beyond any notice.

29:1: The conclusion of 29:1 is an allusion back to the beginning of 4:44-49. All of this, in the final form of Deuteronomy as given to us, is anticipation of the land. Israel will be *carried into* the land; now in its final flourish Israel is *removed from* the land.

Theological and Ethical Analysis

The notion of blessing and curse, as a framing idea, is problematic in a modernist, technological world, for it affirms that there are forces and agents that hover around us and impact our lives in ways we cannot control or resist. That is, the claim is that there is more to our lives than we undertake. In the theology of Deuteronomy, curse (or blessing) is not antithetical to choice, but it is a product of Israel's choices. Thus the "if" that governs this recital is indeed a celebration of choice. By its obedience or disobedience, Israel can choose its future. The "surplus" of blessing or curse beyond choice is simply the insistence that (a) choices occur in a frame of accountability and (b) choices have futures that are watched over by the vigilance of a faithful God. This theology of blessing and curse has no wish to deny the importance of human choice. What it wants to deny or resist with all its rhetorical capacity is a technical reductionism that treats choices as merely instrumental and without substantive fidelity connected to them that lasts far into the future.

The most immediate issue related to blessing and curse and any simple theory of rewards and punishments is the Jewish Holocaust in which innocent people of faith perished in mass slaughter. Given that and other barbarisms in the twentieth century, care must be taken not to be simplistic about ethical coherence in the world. Having said that, the baseline of covenantal theology, with its sanctions, continues to be the reference point and beginning place for serious interpretive reflection. The entire tradition of Jewish and Christian faith starts from the glad affirmation that the world is governed by a God who takes human choices with deep seriousness.

PARDON REFUSED (29:2-29)

This text begins the third address of Moses, which culminates in the great poem of 32:1-43 with a prose addendum in 32:44-47. The structure of this corpus is the dramatic movement of broken covenant (chap. 29), repentance (30:1-10), and summons to new covenant (30:11–31:13) that opens the way to a future in the land (31:13-39). Or put more simply, it is the movement of *rejection* and *renewal* that is geographically presented as *land loss* and *land entry*. This third speech takes as a given the brokenness of covenant and abandonment by YHWH. On that basis, its work is (a) to show why this brokenness has come about and (b) to assert a future beyond the brokenness. The poem of 32:1-43 takes up the same themes, articulating both the dismal failure of Israel and the determined action of YHWH to give Israel a new future.

More particularly the narrative structure of 29:2-28 on *brokenness* and 30:1-20 on *newness* pivots on the curious text of 29:29 that stands alone, between the two texts, as a pondering of the gift of the future that YHWH will give to this recalcitrant people.

Chapter 29 is presented as a speech of Moses, a preferred vehicle for theological instruction in the tradition of Deuteronomy. The speech develops as an historical review (vv. 2-8), a summons to renewed covenant (vv. 9-16), an indictment for covenant violation with a reflection on the reasons for rejection by YHWH (vv. 17-28), and the enigmatic verse at the end (v. 29).

Exegetical Analysis

29:2-8: The historical review of verses 2-8 follows the standard line of recital also found, for example, in 26:5-9. It begins in the wonders of *Egypt* (v. 3) and moves through the sustenance of the *wilderness* (vv. 5-6) to the conquest of the *land* east of the Jordan (vv. 7-8). The whole of the recital is taken as an inventory of "signs and wonders," whereby Israel can see that its lived memory is pervaded by the power of YHWH that has been mobilized on its behalf. The whole of the memory is "in order that" Israel may learn that "I am YHWH your God" (v. 6). The memory is a normative disclosure of YHWH, who is capable of sustaining Israel in every circumstance.

Verse 4 asserts that the miracles did not evoke faith. The reason is that Israel lacked, because YHWH had not granted, *hearts* to discern, *eyes* to see, and *ears* to hear. Israel is so obtuse through all these miracles that it does not recognize what a power YHWH is or what a gift YHWH gives to Israel. The triad of "heart, eyes, ears" calls to mind the despairing verdict in Isaiah 6:9 that Israel will not catch on enough to "turn." (See Mark 8:17-18.) Israel has failed to respond, and so has failed as of now to be YHWH's holy people. The speech of Moses thus voices a harbinger of the judgment that is to come later in this chapter.

29:9-16: It is on the basis of that long-term obtuseness that Moses issues a powerful summons that Israel should now, for the first time, embrace the covenant and become the people of YHWH (vv. 9-16). The imperative addressed to the assembled of Israel is remarkably inclusive. The meeting includes not only elders, officials, and all males, as in 16:16, but also women, children, and sojourners. Of special note is the inclusion of those who do the menial work of the community, those in Germany now called *Gastarbeiter* (guest workers).

The odd proviso of verse 15—those "not here with us today"—is parallel to the opening statement of 5:3 in Moses' long second speech. In that earlier reference, the phrase "all of us here alive today" focused on the *present generation* in distinction from the failed past. In the present verse, the parallel phrase has its eye on *future generations*—not here, not yet born—in distinction from the current generation.

29:17-21: This buoyant expectation for "those not here," however, is immediately sobered (vv. 17-21). The voice that speaks here is not romantic about Israel's future. Deuteronomy is deeply aware that Israel's faith is in a context of endless distraction and seduction, "detestable things" *(šiqqûs)*, filthy, objectionable distractions from covenantal faith. Not only is the environment filled with such alternatives to covenant, but some in Israel may succumb to them. The risk is a heart turned away to other gods, on which see 1 Kgs 11:3. The most likely candidates for such seduction are precisely those who are comfortable and complacent in Yahwism and who congratulate themselves over their *shalom* (v. 19). They are the ones most susceptible and most surely to bring disaster upon all of the community. Verses 17-19 are a psychologically acute analysis of how seduction from covenant happens among those who turn a little at a time away from YHWH because they are not vigilant. Their lack of vigilance is rooted in their self-congratulations, in which they presume upon their special status, and in their presumption bring disaster upon the entire community.

The heavy conclusion is that "all these curses" of chapter 28 will be enacted on Israel, until Israel's identity is completely undone (vv. 20-21). A wayward Israel will be a destroyed Israel. It cannot be otherwise. Thus the terrible scenario of suffering in Deut 28:47-68 has the crisis of Jerusalem in 587 BCE in purview. In verse 20, the speech of Moses sounds its final ominous note: "unwilling to pardon." The phrase has its only precise parallel in 2 Kgs 24:4 at the end of the historical narrative concerning King Manasseh. It is because of Manasseh that the harsh, irreversible verdict falls on the city. The covenant has run out and the life of Israel is exhausted, just as 28:58-68 anticipates.

It is important to notice the remarkable abrasion between the strong *appeal* of verses 9-16 and the devastating *judgment* of verses 17-21. The reason the appeal can be issued, given the judgment, is that there are those "not here with us today" (v. 15), that is, "the next generation" (v. 22). It is to them that the appeal is addressed. The tradition, for all its rhetoric of termination, has its eye on the coming generation that will arise "after you." It is this generation that is addressed in chapters 29–30, after the termination of all that failed is fully voiced and acknowledged.

29:22-28: The first task of this next generation "not with us here today" is theological reflection on the debacle in order to understand the cause of termination (vv. 22-28). The governing question of theological reflection, paralleled in 2 Kgs 17:7 ff., is stated in a twofold way:

Why has the LORD done thus to this land? What caused this great display of anger? (v. 24)

The evidence is unmistakable. The devastation is like Sodom and Gomorrah, all burned, devastated, flattened, emptied, like "the day after" of nuclear assault. In this stern explanation with a metaphor that allows no wiggle room, Jerusalem has become an embodiment of that old imagery of devastation. In the fierce portrayal offered by Moses, all could see and none could be mistaken.

But that still left the young with "why?" In the horizon of Moses, the answer is obvious, issued in a harsh, clear speech of judgment:

> *Indictment:* they abandoned;
> they went after;
> they served;
> they bowed down (vv. 25-26).

They refused to be the very Israel in covenant they had pledged to be.

> *Sentence:* YHWH responded in anger, fury, wrath . . .
> because YHWH is intolerant of rivals . . .
> YHWH uprooted;
> YHWH cast (v. 28).

YHWH deported Israel away from Jerusalem. The logic is as simple as it is devastating. Disobedience brings land loss, a theme everywhere affirmed in Deuteronomy. This chapter in substance is a speech of judgment that indicts and sentences, fully focused on the horrendous culmination of "covenant history" in 587 BCE. The tone is unrelieved.

The remarkable fact, with an eye on chapter 30, is that the argument is not as unrelieved as the tone intends to suggest. There are only hints of a future, but the hints are crucial in the total affirmation of this harsh covenant formulation. The chapter includes three hints beyond devastation:

1. In verse 15, "those not here with us today," alluding to those beyond the devastation;

2. The "next generation" in verse 22, clearly looks beyond;

3. These two explicit references are reinforced by what may be a third, remotely implied reference. If one engages seriously the metaphor of Sodom and Gomorrah, then it is important to notice that in that terrible narrative account, "God remembered Abraham, and sent Lot out of the midst of the overthrow" (Gen 19:29). YHWH remembered Abraham and, as a consequence, rescued Lot. Hos, moreover, is closely linked to Deuteronomy. In Hos 11:8-9, the terror of YHWH against Sodom and Gomorrah (Admah and Zeboiim) is withheld at the last moment because of YHWH's pathos-filled love of Israel. The "anger, fury, and great wrath" of 28:28 is fully felt by YHWH in Hos 11:5-7. And yet,

> I will not execute my fierce anger;
> I will not again destroy Ephraim;
> for I am God and no mortal,
>   the Holy One in your midst,
>   and I will not come in wrath. (Hos 11:9)

This assurance of survival beyond devastation, to be sure, is not explicit in our chapter. But it is there and it leads to verse 29.

29:29: Verse 29 clearly moves beyond the rage of verses 25-28 and looks toward chapter 30. Or said another way, it looks beyond the deportation of 587 BCE and toward homecoming and the emergence of Judaism. It attests to a future that YHWH will give to Israel, Moses knows not how. The verse makes clear a division of responsibility. What is revealed—made clear and available—is obedience to the Torah. That is given by Moses in Deuteronomy. There is no need for ambiguity or uncertainty about obedience to Torah (see 30:11-14). That is Israel's single task. Moreover, the task is given "to our children forever," a wondrous statement of an open-ended future.

What is not given to Israel is held in YHWH's inscrutable governance, completely secret from Israel. There is no hint of what this phrasing means, but it seems most likely, in context, that it refers to the future YHWH yet intends, and to the ways in which

YHWH will bring this rejected people into its undeserved future. What is hinted at in chapter 29 and fully clear in chapter 30 is that there is still life to be chosen by Israel, even after the deportation.

The division of labor in this verse is an assurance coupled with a summons. Israel may be at peace about YHWH's assured future. While *at peace,* however, Israel must be *diligent.* Quite practically, Israel is therefore freed for obedience, not needing to explain or understand anything else. How to get from verses 20-21 to a future is YHWH's mystery. The faithful need give no energy to explanation of the mystery. YHWH makes a way out of no way for Israel through its abyss.

Theological and Ethical Analysis

Together with chapter 30, this chapter constitutes a large-scoped articulation of the grand themes of *judgment and promise* from YHWH; in the tradition of Deuteronomy, the theological themes of judgment and promise are presented historically, so that judgment = exile / land loss and promise = Judaism beyond exile.

The judgment is severe, for the God of Israel will not be mocked. It entails the undoing of all that constitutes Israel and all that Israel held dear, as anticipated in 28:58-68. In a sixth-century context, that loss refers to the Jerusalem establishment that embodied all of Israel's best hopes. In that moment of undoing, YHWH is unmoved by pity or compassion toward Israel; the judgment is final, even as anticipated in the curse recital of chapter 28.

For the most part, the enactment of hope awaits the next chapter. In chapter 29 hope is indicated only in the enigmatic phrase, "the secret things." That is, there is *more.* There is more that YHWH knows, has at disposal, and will do; none of that future, however, is open to Israel's discernment. Israel must wait midst the judgment.

This chapter then is a remarkable theological achievement. It appears in its primary terms to be a statement of unmitigated judgment. In the end, however, the judgment becomes a matrix out of which YHWH's newness for Israel is announced. That future is held in secret by YHWH, and Israel *has access* to it only in anticipatory doxology. Finally this chapter moves even beyond "judgment and hope" to focus on the full, free governance of YHWH that is not in thrall to any choices of Israel. The insistence that YHWH holds for YHWH's own self the full range of the future is a marvelous celebration of YHWH's providential freedom.

ON RECHOOSING (30:1-20)

The present chapter is an appeal on the part of Moses to the "next generation" (that has a chance of being genuinely YHWH's holy people) to repent and rechoose life with YHWH according to YHWH's disclosed will. The chapter divides into three distinct units: (a) an appeal for repentance (vv. 1-10), (b) an assurance that obedience is indeed possible (vv. 11-14), and (c) a dramatic summons for a decision (vv. 15-20).

Exegetical Analysis

30:1-14: The first unit in this chapter bids Israel to repent and to return to full obedience to YHWH (vv. 1-10). The first verse sets the context of exile where Israel has been "driven" by YHWH, where "all these things," presumably the curses of chapters 27–28, 29:20-21, have been enacted on Israel. The dramatic presentation of Deuteronomy assumes the exile and addresses those in exile about life beyond exile. It is in exile that Israel is to "turn" *(šûb)* its heart to the blessings and curses, that is, "call [them] to mind" in order to "turn" to YHWH. The accent is upon repentance and reversal, which are the keys to the future.

YHWH will intervene, end the exile, and bring exiled Israel back home to its own land (vv. 3-5). These verses are freighted with YHWH's most characteristic promises to Israel, promises that dominate the core theological assertions of the Old Testament:

1. "Restore the fortunes" is a translation of the Hebrew *(šûb) šĕbût,* "turn your captivity," that is, reverse the "destiny"

of Israel. YHWH is powerful, loyal, and determined enough to intervene in exile and transform Israel's life from curse to blessing. The phrase "turn the turnings" is especially preferred in the related literature of Jeremiah where it also refers to the end of exile (Jer 29:14; 30:3, 18; 31:23; 32:44; 33:7, 11, 26).

2. This is a God of compassion (see 4:31) who notices the people in exile even as this same God had noticed the slaves in Egypt. Again YHWH is moved to extricate Israel from its current situation of powerlessness and despair.

3. The word pair, "gather/scatter" (on which see Jer 31:10), is a characteristic way of speaking of exile and homecoming, both of which are the work of YHWH. In this context, it is the "gathering" work of the compassionate God that is prominent (see Isa 56:8; Luke 13:34).

The interplay of verses 1-2 and verses 3-5 is as an "if-then" formulation: *If* Israel again becomes obedient Israel, *then* YHWH will be the God of all well-being. The "if" is Israel's enactment of the "revealed things" of 29:29; the "then" is YHWH's enactment of YHWH's "secret things." The future is a gift from YHWH, but it is a gift given only when Israel is in an obedient posture. YHWH's gift of the future will not be wasted on the unreceptive.

YHWH will do more (vv. 6-10). These verses are largely about YHWH's gift. But pervasive in these verses of generous grace is a repeated accent on "obey" (vv. 8, 10). Israel in its return to true covenantal obedience will receive a future it had little reason to expect.

1. YHWH will circumcise Israel's heart (v. 6);
2. YHWH will remove the curse from Israel and re-deploy the curse on its enemies so that Israel who was "tail" will become "head" (see 28:13). The full embrace of covenant by both parties means the end of all *quid pro quo* calculation and the full, unmeasured yielding by each party to the other.

The accent on Israel's role in this recovery of covenant in the land is crucial in the theology of Deuteronomy. Israel is to turn and obey (vv. 1, 2, 8, 10). The new covenant is not a free, unilateral gift, even though it is YHWH's initial summons that begins the process of recovery. Israel must play its intentional, substantial part in the restoration by becoming again YHWH's obedient people. That raises hard questions: Can it be done? Can Israel obey? Can Israel repent? Can Israel act differently? It is as Jeremiah asks, more pessimistically:

> Can Ethiopians change their skin
>   or leopards their spots?
> Then also you can do good
>   who are accustomed to do evil. (Jer 13:23)

Jeremiah's answer in his pre-exilic context is NO. Deuteronomy answers differently. The present text affirms that the "revealed things" of Torah are doable (vv. 11-14). These verses seem a response to the objection that Torah requirements are impossible, because they are too demanding, too obscure, too remote from Israel's daily life. The text, in refutation of such resistance, makes a negative and then a positive response.

The negative response is in four parallel statements:

> *not* too difficult;
> *not* too remote;
> *not* in heaven;
> *not* across the sea.

The accent is not on the elements of remoteness, but on the positive affirmation: Torah is *near,* as near as in your mouth that recites, as close as in your heart that remembers. The Torah is near and can be obeyed. Israel is without excuse. The nearness of Torah is a theme that echoes from 4:7-8. The Torah is a gift completely entrusted to Israel. Israel knows the Torah and can do it. Israel can keep its part of the rapprochement of verses 1-10.

30:15-20: With this affirmation, the third speech of Moses now issues its most formidable summons to Israel (vv. 15-20). Israel must choose. It belongs to Israel to choose. The choice, especially clear and congruent with the pervasive imperatives of Deuteronomy, is stated with a double "if-then" formulation:

The positive "if" concerns full obedience by hearing, loving, walking, and heeding (v. 16). The verbs are all familiar from the characteristic cadences of Deuteronomy.

The positive "then" concerns blessing in the land (v. 16).

The negative "if" concerns not listening and therefore forgetting covenant and serving other gods (v. 17).

The negative "then" entails perishing (v. 17).

The calculus is clear and pervades this tradition: obey . . . land, disobey . . . land loss.

It is on the crucial basis of that court-verified testimony (according to the metaphor) that Moses issues the first imperative in this paragraph, a simple, unadorned summons: choose life by keeping Torah (v. 19). The basic imperative, narratively enacted in Joshua 24:14-15, is supplemented by familiar verbs: love, hear, cleave. Such a choice will lead to life and well-being.

Theological and Ethical Analysis

If one stays with the corpus of Deuteronomy until this point, then the conclusions and options stated here are familiar. Deuteronomy contains no exotic disclosures, but gives the simple, plain "meat and potatoes" that obedience is the condition of life in the land. This simple and unqualified appeal is placed in intimate connection to chapter 29. That means that appeal, invitation, and summons are addressed to "the next generation" against a backdrop of deportation. It is thus a program for the refounding of Judaism based upon the sorry and difficult lesson of disobedience that has led to land loss.

The hard work of this chapter is to persuade "the next generation" that a future is indeed possible. Three themes may be noted:

1. The intricate grammar of verses 1-10 suggests a glad, unrestrained, uncalculating mutuality of two parties, YHWH and Israel, who are glad to be back together after the hiatus of exile. They are eager to make the new relationship work.

2. The "doable" character of Torah is important, because it frees the community of the faithful from excessive preoccupation and anguish about how and in what ways obedience might be done. The simple guide of "all your heart and all your mind" that includes within it "your neighbor as yourself" opens a first step that when undertaken opens more.

Illustrative of the "plain and simple" character of Torah obedience is the account of the evangelical Christian community of Le Chambon in France that hid Jews during World War II from the Nazi efforts at extermination (Hallie 1979). Among the remarkable features of that brave and faithful community was an inquiry after the war by a Jewish adult who was kept alive there as a child. When he interviewed his protectors about their reason for taking such risky actions on his behalf, they only shrugged their shoulders and indicated that it seemed obvious from their faith. They had no dramatic explanations or theological interpretations to offer him. It was rather a "habit" of neighborliness that was at the center of their embrace of the gospel; and it was enough! (See Rom 10:6-8.)

3. Finally, what is this *life* to be chosen and how is it chosen? The life Moses commands, as he has all through this corpus, is a life congruent with the will and purpose of YHWH as given both in the fabric of creation and in the commands of Sinai. That life consists in *loving YHWH*, which is a practice of holiness, and habits of distinctiveness that know life is directed toward and received from the inscrutable presence of YHWH in the midst of daily existence. That life consists, moreover, in *loving neighbor*, which is a practice of justice that grounds and promotes the entitlements of the neighbor, even at cost and inconvenience to self. "Love of God" in holiness and "love of neighbor" in justice constitute a life of relatedness that yields a sense of belonging in community and a gift of material prosperity in the land.

Moses says categorically, "choose." Joshua echoes Moses with the imperative "choose" (Josh 24:14-15). That imperative moves through the tradition that, in Christian purview, culminates in Jesus' summons to discipleship (see Matt 6:24, 25-33 and the entire Sermon on the Mount). Faith has to do with this life-or-death choice.

But of course the faithful keep choosing and rechoosing, keep choosing otherwise and then choosing again. The rhetoric of Moses is clean and simple. The reality of lived life is much more ambiguous, and so it was for Israel. Moses knows about the inescapable ambiguity, but that awareness causes no diminishment of the urgent rhetoric of choice.

THE OMINOUS FUTURE AS A MATRIX OF CALL (31:1-29)

The text of chapters 31–34 begins to look beyond Moses to the ongoing history of Israel across the Jordan into the land of promise. Chapter 31 is a meditation on that decisive transition in the memory and life of Israel. The transition is given as a *historical-geographical* move from landlessness to land across the Jordan. The transition is one of *leadership*, from Moses to Joshua. And the transition is a *literary* one from the founding traditions of Torah (Pentateuch) to the first canonical materials beyond the Torah in the book of Joshua. Given these various dimensions to the transition, it is no wonder that the text pays such careful attention to this turn in the life of Israel, a turn fraught with danger and possibility for Israel.

Exegetical Analysis

31:1-8: Israel is ready to cross the Jordan, at last to receive the land of promise. Moses, however, cannot go into the land and cannot lead Israel, for he has been prohibited by YHWH from going (v. 2; see 1:27; 3:26). The crossing is dangerous enough; it is even more so without Moses, upon whom Israel has relied so heavily. Moses must make provision and give assurances for this journey he himself cannot take. The assurance he gives is a theological one: YHWH will cross over as leader of Israel.

The assurance utilizes two stock phrases that Dennis J. McCarthy calls in turn an "Encouragement Formula" and an "Assistance Formula" (McCarthy 1971):

1. "Be strong and bold." (McCarthy translates "be brave and of stout heart.")
2. "YHWH will be with you."

YHWH will be, in time to come, whom YHWH has been for Israel in times past. YHWH is reliable and will not fail or forsake. The future will be safely governed by YHWH as has been the past. YHWH intends the land to belong to Israel and will forcefully act to secure it for Israel.

Along with the assurance, Moses must make provision for the reality of the new land. He does so by identifying and empowering Joshua to be his successor, to complete the work that he himself cannot do. Joshua has already been linked to Moses in traditions outside of Deuteronomy (Exod 17:8-16; Num 11:28) and in the book of Numbers is frequently cited (along with Caleb) as the embodiment of faithfulness who will represent and lead the new generation that is not burdened, like the old generation of Moses, with the recalcitrance of the wilderness (Olson 1985). The formula of encouragement is characteristically addressed to Joshua, for Joshua is the representative and embodiment of that post-Moses Israel that is called to enact the statutes of Deuteronomy in the land. It is Joshua who is under threat. Everything depends upon Joshua, for if his venture fails, everything Mosaic will have failed (Josh 1:5-7, 18).

31:9-13: Verses 9-13 constitute a distinct textual unit. But placed here, these verses provide for a regular liturgical exercise in the new land. Israel bets everything on the dramatic performance in liturgy of its distinctive identity as an antidote to the threats that will undo that identity. These verses have played a large role in scholarly hypotheses in the twentieth century concerning provision for the periodic public reading of covenant agreements, a provision common in treaty arrangements. There may be something in the analogue to other treaties; it is better, however, to take the text in its own context of anxiety and to see the great confidence that Israel invests in periodic liturgical enactment. Periodically, every seven years (see 15:1!), at the Festival of

Booths (see 16:13-15), Israel shall assemble to hear the Torah read again (see Neh 8:1-8). This meeting will be all inclusive of the community. Everyone shall be present, all Israel. The text displays concern for the children who must enter the peculiar world of Yahwistic covenant, and who do so by participation in the great liturgical event. The new land of promise is to be revisioned—generation after generation—as a different kind of land marked by covenant requirements as a condition of covenant blessing.

31:14-15: In verses 14-15, Moses brings Joshua to "the tent of meeting" where Joshua is exposed directly to the raw presence of YHWH and is thereby authorized as Israel's new leader. These verses are a continuation and completion of the initiative YHWH has taken toward Joshua in verses 1-8. The "tent of meeting" is the special place of presence and disclosure that is presided over by Moses (Exod 33:7-11). Thus Joshua is admitted to the place where only Moses can go, in order to give "sacramental" force to Joshua's new role. The text does not disclose what is said or done in the secret moment; it is important in any case that it is YHWH (and not Moses) who finally authorizes Joshua. Joshua is given the marks of authority previously monopolized by Moses.

31:16-18: The tradition of Deuteronomy offers a peculiarly self-conscious piece of theological anticipation as a rationale for the Song that is to follow in chapter 32 (vv. 16-22). What a sorry future it is! It is marked by "prostitution," that is, Israel will "shack up" with other gods, when its proper partner is YHWH only (v. 16; see Jer 2:20; 3:2). Israel will abandon loyalty to YHWH and violate covenant. This anticipation is generic and might refer to the judges or to the kings that are to come. Either way, trust in and obedience to YHWH will fail.

Thus verses 16-18 are a simple, unsurprising articulation of Deuteronomic theology: choose death . . . perish, the classical speech of judgment echoed so often by the prophets and narrated in the book of Judges.

There will, however, come a moment of honest reflection and self-awareness in Israel. Israel will have a moment of "recognition" (v. 17). That moment of recognition, moreover, will be interpreted by "this song," a reference to the "Song of Moses" to follow in chapter 32. That is, these verses are intended to frame and introduce the long poem of chapter 32, to give it context, and to identify its purpose. The song is a review of Israel's history that is shown to be a dreary story of endless rebellion and infidelity. Moses already recognizes Israel's sorry tale in this anticipatory articulation.

31:19: The primary purpose of the song, the text notes here, is to fix the blame for Israel's coming suffering. That is, the song establishes Israel's fault for the failed covenant with YHWH and thereby makes clear that YHWH is not at all at fault. YHWH is an innocent, faithful covenant keeper. This song will be sung and sung, and sung again, so that Israel in all its generations is kept aware of its cataclysmic failure as a covenant partner to YHWH.

31:20-22: The introduction of the song in verse 19 is followed in verses 20-22 that cannot resist, in anticipation, stating yet again the thesis of the song. The thesis is given in a series of indicting verbs:

eat . . . be full . . . grow fat . . . turn . . . serve . . . despise . . . break

Hints of this theme are already seen in chapters 6 and 8, but now it becomes the main point. The tradition knows that the very land that is the fulfillment of the promise is the land of abundance that will make Israel "fat and happy," complacent and self-indulgent, and finally indifferent to the conditions of covenant.

31:23: There is perhaps something ironic in the placement of verse 23. This single verse echoes the encouragement of verse 7, anticipates Josh 1:6-8, and urges Joshua to confidence in the promise that YHWH will accompany Israel in the dangers to come.

The word of YHWH to Joshua is a confident one. But it is set, in verses 16-22 and 29, in the midst of an acknowledgment of how wretched Israel will be in time to come. Joshua is to lead this recalcitrant, corrupt community in complete confidence in YHWH. What a mandate! Trust will defeat infidelity in the long run!

31:24-29: The way is now prepared for the song of chapter 32 that will tell the recurring truth about Israel and YHWH. But before the song, the narrative has one other strategy for guiding Israel in its ominous future (vv. 24-29). The Levites are, yet again, made custodians of the ark and of the Torah scroll it contains (see 10:8-9; 27:9; 31:9). The scroll is to be an abiding witness to Israel both of its covenantal commitments to YHWH's command and to its characteristic reneging on those commitments.

Theological and Ethical Analysis

The future is already at hand and the news is not good. One may wonder about such omniscience about the future, and resolve that issue by the critical judgment that the text that purports to be early is in fact a late retrospect after the events. Of course, but that critical judgment ought not to obscure the fact that those who practice sensitive moral discernment can indeed see what is in store for a community. They can see that an embrace of "folly" is irreversible even though, as Barbara Tuchman has seen, the warning signs may be everywhere (Tuchman 1984). The Mosaic Torah provides an angle of critical vision from which one can see the self-destructive habits to which the community, in its madness, is deeply committed. As a consequence the canonical tradition is shaped so that in this chapter all that will come in the historical account of Joshua–Judges–Samuel–Kings is in view (Fretheim 1983).

Deuteronomy provides for visible, highly authorized liturgical practices that are designed to call Israel back to its true self and away from its self-destructive insanity. Specifically this refers to the Festival of Booths, at which the Torah is read (vv. 9-13), and the abiding presence of the Torah (vv. 24-26); more generally for Israel it is the voice of "Holy Otherness" that endlessly subverts Israel's easy acceptance of its distorted life. One cannot overestimate the importance of such authorized, regularized truth-telling opportunities that are established in communities of madness, indifference, and complacency.

The future of the Torah community as anticipated here is one of continual failure, and corruption. This claim, so far removed from the affirmation of 30:11-14, pertains precisely and concretely to ancient Israel. The text refers to the coming judges and coming kings and coming deportation and termination of "the place" in Jerusalem. The concrete history of ancient Israel is held firmly under judgment by Torah, and nothing should detract from the concreteness of that reference.

Given the likely inadequacy of liturgical props for sustaining intentional Torah identity and given the dismal prospect for the life of Israel, this text focuses upon the crucial importance of leadership that is bold, confident, committed, and undivided in its passion.

This leadership—Joshua after the manner of Moses—is

- Torah based,
- addressed in encouragement,
- given assurance of YHWH's presence,
- given face-to-face access to YHWH's holiness,
- to reorganize the land in covenantal ways making the leadership role one of public engagement far beyond cultic management.

This leader, moreover, is to receive buoyancy from theological assurances in the face of a failed community. No doubt the expectation is too much, surely more than anyone could bear. And yet the text makes clear that the well-being of Israel depends upon leadership that is not defined by Israel's failure but by YHWH's fidelity. Thus it is leadership precisely for a community at risk and seemingly without adequate resources.

MASSIVE JUDGMENT, SURPRISING HOPE (31:30–32:52)

The poem of 32:1-43 constitutes a major statement of covenantal theology that has been anticipated in 31:19. It is almost surely an independent poem that has been secondarily placed here among the materials that mark the transition from the covenant commands of Deuteronomy to the covenant history beginning in Josh 1. The poem has on its horizon the entire history to follow in the corpus of Joshua-Kings.

The poem is framed by the narrative introduction of 31:30 that situates the song "in the assembly," and by the conclusion of 32:44-47 that reiterates the theme of "witness against" from 31:19. The narrative note of 32:48-52 is an independent unit, but shares with the poem the motif of "broken faith." Thus the poem and the narrative together attest to Israel's violation of the covenant that will become the *leitmotif* of history to follow.

The definitive study of the poem by G. Ernest Wright argued for a quite early date of the poem and, more important, identified its genre as a "prophetic lawsuit" that has most in common theologically and rhetorically with the speeches of judgment in the eighth-century prophets (Wright 1962). The discussion that follows is principally informed by Wright's analysis. As a "lawsuit speech," Moses' utterance is cast as a judicial case concerning broken covenant. The song establishes the generosity and reliability of YHWH and Israel's constant recalcitrance that refuses to trust and obey YHWH. Thus the song functions as a great theodicy concerning the history of Israel. It insists that all the troubles that have come upon Israel, which are to culminate in the destruction and deportation of 587, are warranted consequences of Israel's covenant violation. Only at the end of the song, in an unexpected turn, does the song move to an affirmation of YHWH's continued commitment to Israel in spite of its infidelity.

Exegetical Analysis

32:1-6: The introductory section of the poem issues a summons to listen and announces the main themes to follow (vv. 1-6). The situation of Israel, according to the seductions of chapters 6 and 8, is one of satiation and complacency. In a later context Israel is in despair about its life. Either way, in complacency or in despair, Israel lacks the insight and categories through which to understand its true situation. In verse 3, the poem states the subject matter of the name and greatness of YHWH. This is a deeply YHWH-centered poem, for it is precisely a disregard of or miscalculation about YHWH that has caused Israel—in complacency or in despair—to misperceive its life. Indeed, from the perspective of this tradition, Israel's life is perforce YHWH-focused; everything is skewed and misperceived if not definitively referred to YHWH.

Having announced the theme, verses 4-6 now provide a sweeping characterization of Israel's life with YHWH. Both parties are summarily identified:

> *YHWH:* perfect, just, faithful, without deceit, just, upright!

What a mouthful! Moses uses a rich, characteristic vocabulary to voice YHWH's utter fidelity.

> *Israel:* degenerate, false, perverse, crooked, foolish, senseless!

Another mouthful, in every syllable polemical and negative.

The presenting problem is how this God and this people could possibly interact. YHWH is the one who created, makes, establishes Israel, so that Israel is YHWH's creature, totally dependent upon YHWH. Israel, however, rejects that very status upon which its life depends. Verses 4-6 are a preliminary statement, as though to tell the jury at the opening of litigation what will be demonstrated for the court during the trial. Now the demonstration of concrete evidence begins.

32:7-14: First, the song explicates the claim of verse 4 that YHWH is faithful, just, and upright, that is, honors commitments and keep promises (vv. 7-14). It appeals to a very old vision that "at the beginning," the gods in convocation apportioned the peoples of the world among themselves, so that each god received a people as his or her own domain of governance and loyalty. The "High God," the one presiding over all the gods, in Deuteronomic vision, is none other than YHWH. In the meeting of "assigning peoples," this High God kept Israel as God's very own, thus making Israel the "special treasure" of YHWH (see 7:6; 14:2). At the outset the High God who could have had any people desired none other than Israel. "At the beginning," when other options were available, YHWH wanted only Israel. From that beginning point, Israel has been "the apple of YHWH's eye" (v. 10), the one on whom YHWH dotes.

That choice of Israel by YHWH left YHWH deeply obligated to be the God of Israel who would see to it that Israel prospered and enjoyed the good life in the land. Verses 10-14 are an offer to the cosmic court of evidence that YHWH has indeed been faithful in adhering to that initial choice and has given endless bounty to Israel. The evidence of YHWH's caring fidelity toward Israel basically follows the narrative recital of 26:5-9, focused upon love *in the wilderness* and well-being *in the land*. These verses are dominated by a rich series of verbs with YHWH as active subject: sustained, shielded, cared, guided, set, fed, nursed—all to Israel's great joy, well-being, and luxury.

32:15-29: In response to such overwhelming goodness, however, Israel has been ungrateful, unresponsive, and recalcitrant (vv. 15-18). Israel responded to YHWH stupidly! Israel's condition was one of satiation: fat, bloated, gorged. Israel was no longer needy and could not remember its dependence upon YHWH. This sorry condition expressed itself as the violation of the first commandment (5:7; 6:4-5). Israel embraced other loyalties and other ways of securing its own existence, not recognizing the crucial importance of the "father God" who sired or the "mother God" who birthed (v. 18). Israel refused the obedience and loyalty due YHWH for all of YHWH's goodness. The entire history of Israel is a sorry, sordid tale of stupid autonomy, of rejection of that odd relationship that gives Israel its life in the world (see Ps 106).

The indictment of verses 15-18, in predictable lawsuit form, is sure to be followed by a sentence (vv. 19-29). The same God who so generously created and embraced Israel is no patsy who will lightly accept disobedience. The God who has been "merciful" (see 4:31) is transposed into a "devouring fire" (see 4:24). YHWH will give as good as YHWH gets; Israel has made YHWH jealous, so YHWH will make Israel jealous (v. 21). Israel has abandoned YHWH, so now YHWH will abandon Israel. YHWH is deeply bound in loyalty to Israel, but that binding is not beyond recall. In rage at betrayal and infidelity, YHWH will put Israel at the mercy of "a foolish nation." That nation whom YHWH unleashes upon Israel is not identified. In the end, it is Babylon. But before that, in the long story of Israel in its unresponsiveness to YHWH, Israel is beset by many nations who come with fire and devastation, all of which is here understood as YHWH's anger.

The punishments now to come upon Israel are the implementation of covenant curses from chapter 28. What Israel is to suffer is not due to divine capriciousness, but on the basis of sanctions already known ahead of time: fire, hunger, consumption, pestilence, beasts, sword (see 28:20-22, 48-52). Israel deserves all of it, and YHWH will enact all of it.

In verses 26-29, however, there is a qualifying proviso. Israel deserves termination and YHWH is perfectly prepared and justified in terminating; but YHWH does not terminate. Because punishment stops short of termination, the poem reflects on the cause for the curbing of YHWH's rage and the restraint of covenant curses. When YHWH considered termination of Israel, YHWH feared that the watching nations—Egypt? Assyria? Babylon?— would imagine that they themselves had prevailed and defeated not only Israel but the God of Israel. Thus YHWH's restraint is not out of any love for Israel, but out of YHWH's own pride and reputation. YHWH did not want the watching nations to draw the wrong conclusion, either about themselves or about YHWH. As Num 14:13-16, Deut 9:28-29, and Ezek 36:22-33 attest, YHWH thinks not only of Israel's just deserts, but of YHWH's own reputation (glory) that inadvertently acts as a restraint on divine rage. The lawsuit has run its course in three stages:

1. YHWH's initial and constant goodness.
2. Israel's failure to respond.
3. YHWH's devastating judgment.

But there is more. There is "what comes next," and the poem continues (v. 29).

32:30-34: The poem makes an abrupt, nearly inexplicable turn (v. 30). The speech of judgment, which seemed like a last word from YHWH, is now completed. God's rage with Israel is exhausted. It turns out that YHWH's terminal rage toward Israel is provisional. In verses 30-33, YHWH turns attention away from alienated Israel to the more burdensome reality of the other nations (see v. 21), who imagine that they are initiators of their assaults on Israel (see Isa 10:8-14; 47:7-10). The truth is, as known in Israel's covenantal categories, that the other nations succeed in their exploits only because YHWH sanctions their success (see Deut 28:25, 36). In fact these nations, provisional instruments of YHWH, are repulsive. YHWH can have no enduring attachment to them, because they are abhorrent to YHWH. From that it follows that their capacity to abuse Israel is also provisional and cannot last.

32:35-42: As a consequence, YHWH has yet more to do (vv. 35-42). YHWH is the final arbiter of the future. The future will not be determined by Israel's sorry fate or by the arrogant autonomy of the nations, but only by YHWH. That is what it means for YHWH to assert that, "Vengeance is mine" (v. 35; see Ps 94:1-2). YHWH will act in complete and decisive freedom.

One aspect of that freedom is that the nations that seem so formidable will in fact "slip" swiftly (v. 35). They will not be able to sustain themselves, as is evident if one observes their "rise and fall." The other related but more important aspect of YHWH's freedom for the future is that YHWH will move effectively on behalf of Israel, acting in compassion and intervening decisively (v. 36). Now there is no more talk of Israel's failure or YHWH's rage against Israel. YHWH will boldly and decisively respond with an astonishing affirmation to Israel and a devastating rebuke to the arrogant nations (v. 39). *I* YHWH, even *I*, only *I*. It is YHWH who is the subject of all of the definitive verbs in the future, even as it was in the past (see vv. 7-14). There is no other god; there is no other effective agent. There is none who can challenge YHWH. There is none who can harm Israel (see Rom 8:31-35). YHWH is the dispenser of good and evil, life and death, and finally all parties must deal with YHWH.

32:43: It is no wonder that the poem ends in doxology, for Israel must respond in exultation that the inscrutable Mystery of all lived reality is mobilized on its behalf beyond all expectations and all its own merits (v. 43). Given such an assurance, praise is the only appropriate response. The opening lines of this doxology appeal to the cosmic court, as in verse 1, and celebrate YHWH's decisive, brutal action taken on behalf of Israel. After Israel knows about YHWH's commitment and compassion, Israel still must be reassured of YHWH's power to implement, and so one finds the language of "avenge, vengeance, repay, cleanse." All the enemies will be removed from the land in a "cleansing," and Israel will have room again for a covenantal life in the land.

32:44-47: The framing conclusion of the song in verses 44-47 attaches the song not only to Moses but also to Joshua, thus looking beyond the Jordan into the history of Israel in the land. Moses' final didactic comment in verses 46-47 summons Israel to pay attention to the song: It is your life! The rhetoric of Moses is reminiscent of 30:15-20. Israel can choose life, which is to live with reference to YHWH. All else is death.

32:48-52: This section supplies a fresh reason for Moses' exclusion from the land by making reference to Num 20:10-13; 27:12-14. Moses is indicted for not "keeping the holiness of YHWH," that is, not paying sufficient attention to YHWH's peculiar character and claims.

Theological and Ethical Analysis

This poem constitutes a major theological articulation that is representative of Deuteronomic theology and indeed of the primary themes of Old Testament faith. The poem turns decisively between verse 29 and verse 30, so that this hinge point is the place at which to marvel at the faith of Israel in its affirmation of the freedom of YHWH. The twofold structure of the poem portrays YHWH as (a) fully committed to a *quid pro quo* of obedience/blessing that pervades Deuteronomy and that is seen most clearly in 30:15-20, and (b) fully free to move beyond that symmetrical calculus to a more vigorous and surprising enactment of sovereignty.

The first part of the poem (vv. 1-29) is concerned to delineate the contrast of faithful God and faithless people that ends in judgment. The second part of the poem (vv. 30-43), still filled with brutalizing harshness toward the enemy, is an astonishing accent on YHWH's enduring commitment to Israel after Israel has given every reason for forfeiture of that relationship. The unexpected "news" of these verses is YHWH's inalienable devotion to Israel, a devotion that will cause the remaking of the world map on behalf of Israel and against autonomous superpowers. The poem bears witness to YHWH's sovereign capacity for both judgment and compassion, both of which are finally YHWH's free acts, even if evoked in turn by Israel and by the nations.

In relationship to the traditioning process, one may imagine that verses 1-29 look as far as 587 and the termination of Jerusalem and all that that devastation signifies. The poem continues, however, because the faithful community of Judaism persisted beyond 587 and continues to be sustained by YHWH. The poem looks beyond 587 to an enduring future for Judaism. It is possible, in Christian extrapolation, to see that the architecture of judgment and victorious compassion in this poem can be brought into contact with the Friday-Sunday mystery of faith. Friday in Christian tradition is a day of deep judgment and termination. That faith dares to assert that on Sunday all the indisputable facts of judgment are exploded in a new manifestation of YHWH's powerful freedom.

This poem is an insistence to Israel and to all others who attend to biblical tradition that YHWH is the key defining player in the life of the world. In modern times, as the church is more "user friendly" and "therapeutic," the notion of judgment seems remote, as though there were not an *answerability* (judgment) that is inescapable. In like manner, in a technological society that increasingly manages its own environment, the notion of life-giving *intervention* (rescue) seems unlikely. Thus the twinned themes of *judgment* and *compassion* collide seriously with the most elemental assumptions of contemporary culture. It is now a major theological burden to see what judgment and compassion might mean in the midst of a no-surprise, no-accountability, no-intervention, no-gift ideology.

A PEOPLE WITH AN ASSURED FUTURE (33:1-29)

This poem, commonly dubbed "The Blessing of Moses," is placed at the end of the book of Deuteronomy as Moses' last will and testament. Its placement suggests a canonical claim that the blessing functions in an anticipatory and efficacious willing of the future of Israel. A properly executed will does indeed cast an influential shadow over the future of a family. This utterance, attributed to Moses, intends not only to anticipate but to create Israel's future as a gift from YHWH.

The poem is framed by an introduction (vv. 1-5) and a conclusion (vv. 26-29) that attest to the massive power of YHWH that is to be mobilized in the future on behalf of Israel as a single, unified social entity. That is, the blessing is thoroughly Yahwistic, a declaration of YHWH's capacity to do the good for Israel that YHWH intends. Inside that frame, the utterance of Moses proceeds to pronounce specific blessings on eleven tribes of Israel, with Simeon being omitted (see Gen 29:31–30:34; 35:16-21). The blessings to the several tribes are characteristically this-worldly and material. The poem, in the context of a Deuteronomic expectation of exile, becomes an act of hope, asserting the conviction that YHWH's powerful blessing and providential resolve for goodwill finally overcome every historical circumstance of negation. The poem will concede nothing to the vagaries of history, not even the crises of 587, but affirms that Israel, into all future generations, is to be sustained and prospered by YHWH.

Exegetical Analysis

The poem begins with a doxological assertion that YHWH is on the move, coming up from the south, from Mt. Sinai where YHWH resides. YHWH comes with heavenly and earthly allies as a formidable invading power. Three quick claims are made in verse 4:

1. The presence of Israel in the invading force of YHWH is as a people of the Torah. Thus the poem, though not closely linked to the tradition of Deuteronomy, insists that Torah is the defining mark and primal resource of Israel.

2. YHWH comes as king over "Jeshurun." The later term is a pet name for Israel (in addition to vv. 5, 26, see 32:15 and Isa 44:2). The point to be accented, however, is that YHWH is coming as king. (See Buber 1967:121-35.) The divine king will come in power and great fearfulness to impose a royal will upon the entire world (see Pss 96–99).

3. The King presides over the united tribes of Israel. The vision of Israel is one unified people, united in loyalty to YHWH and in obedience to Torah. In verses 6-23, Moses proceeds to will to each tribe a future appropriate to its traditional character, a blessing for each tribe. Here I want to comment on only three of the particular blessings. (a) It is remarkable that Judah receives such a brief and undistinguished blessing (v. 7; see the contrasting extended blessing for Judah in Gen 49:8-12). Given the rise of the Davidic monarchy from the tribe of Judah, more coverage might be anticipated. Apparently this text reflects a perception of Israel in which the monarchy did not figure large, for YHWH as king need not defer to the tribe of David. (b) The blessing for the tribe of Levi is congruent with the Levites' role throughout the book of Deuteronomy, especially 10:1-8, 18:1-8, 27:9-14 (vv. 8-11). (c) It is noteworthy that Joseph receives by far the longest blessing (vv. 13-17). "Joseph" occupied the central hill country and was, for a long period, the core population of the covenant community. This is reflected in the mention of Ephraim and Manasseh, the two tribes regarded as the heirs of Joseph (v. 17; see Gen 48:8-22).

The blessing divides into two parts. First, there is a will that the land of Joseph should be fruitful and productive (vv. 13-16). The rhetoric aims at fullness and comprehensiveness, thus heaven-earth, above-beneath, sun-months (in Heb. "moon"), mountains-hills. The language is Israel's best rhetoric of productivity, of a fully functioning, abundant creation. The second part of the blessing concerns the political success and preeminence of Joseph (vv. 16b-17). It is anticipated that Joseph, in the territories of Ephraim and Manasseh, will be able to intimidate and overcome any who resist or impede its political purposes.

The conclusion of the poem returns to the themes of the introduction (vv. 26-29). YHWH is celebrated as incomparable, in a doxological appeal to Jeshurun, thus keeping YHWH's massive power mobilized on behalf of Israel.

The gifts of goodness and safety, abundance and preeminence make Israel unlike any other. Thus Israel as incomparable recipient is a perfect match for YHWH the incomparable giver:

YHWH: "There is none like God" (v. 26).
Israel: "Who is like you, O Israel?" (v. 29).

The *blessing* of verse 1 *(bĕrākâ)*, given by YHWH through Moses, makes Israel *blessed (ʾašrê)* in verse 29.

Theological and Ethical Analysis

This vigorous recital is unabashedly concrete. It concerns these tribes, and any theological extrapolation is derivative and must always be referred back to the particular. With that important awareness three themes are evident.

First, Israel's future—and the future of the world—is fully and beyond challenge in YHWH's hands. This poem is an assurance that YHWH knows what each tribe will need and will indeed supply it.

Second, it is characteristic but for that no less important, that the blessed state of Israel in time to come is thoroughly materialistic, consisting of the abundance of produce and the defeat of all enemies. The recovery of that material dimension of faith is, this text suggests, a major task facing theological interpretation.

Third, while the blessings concern the different tribes, each in its own particular context and environment, the unity of the tribes is also apparent (v. 5). It is not a far stretch to suggest that the vision of this text is a model for ecumenical pluralism, a vision that allows distinctiveness for the tribes but refuses to think of their separation. Finally the tribes constitute the one people of YHWH and share a common destiny (see Ezek 37:21-23). The reading of the will identifies the several tribes as "heirs" of the promises. The imagery of "heir" is taken up in the early church for the promises made by God and received by faithful people (Rom 8:16-17; Titus 3:6-8).

MOSES, BANNED BUT UNEQUALED (34:1-12)

This brief narrative account is a statement of closure. It brings the life of Moses to a close; it brings the report of Moses' parley "in the land of Moab" in the book of Deuteronomy to a close. Moreover, it brings to a close the Torah (Pentateuch), the most sacred and authoritative scriptures in Judaism. The purpose of this narrative chapter is to assert that the great founding events of Israel, identified with Moses, are now completed.

The chapter brings Israel—and the reader—to the brink of the Jordan. It plunges the reader into the dangerous historical process in the book of Joshua that will culminate in the land loss of 2 Kgs 24–25. It anticipates the leadership of Joshua and the deep conflict to be encountered in the land of promise, when Israel must live its faith in a circumstance of unrelieved ambiguity.

The narrative concerns the theme of the land of promise (vv. 1-5) and the death and celebration of Moses (vv. 6-12). This latter is interrupted in verse 9 with a reference to Joshua, for the purpose of establishing continuity in these events around the Jordan River that is a formidable boundary in the imagination of Israel. The river bespeaks both risky discontinuity and assured continuity between what has been under Moses and what will be under Joshua.

Exegetical Analysis

It is already established that Moses will not enter the land of promise. No reason for that exclusion is given here, but the verdict of YHWH reflects the keen irony characteristic in Israel's scripture. The great leader must leave his leadership task incomplete. In 1:37, 3:26, the reason for exclusion is "on your account," on account of Moses' contemporaries of the older, failed generation. In 32:50-51, reflective of Num 20:12-13, 27:12-14, a different reason for exclusion is given, based on Moses' own failure. The present narrative refuses to adjudicate between these two explanations, and has no interest in any justification for the exclusion.

What counts is the land, "the whole land." The book of Deuteronomy is about land, land promises, land temptations, land reception, land management, and ultimately land loss (Brueggemann 1978; Habel 1995). There is a possibility that the formula "show the land" is reference to a legal claim being established by survey, so that what Moses "sees" Moses can claim legally (Daube 1947:24-39). If that is the case, then through Moses, Israel now claims afresh the land long ago "seen" by Abraham.

With the land in this formulaic way now secure, the narrative of closure proceeds to focus on Moses (vv. 5-12). It reports his death and burial, his vigor, and Israel's grief, the normal ingredients for an ending to a formidable life. The transition of leadership is complete; Joshua will now do for Israel, in the new land, what Moses has done for Israel thus far. Joshua, however, must wait until "his book." For now the narrative turns its attention one more time to Moses to assure not only that Moses receives his just due in the memory of Israel, but that later generations in Israel will be aware of who Moses is and what he continues to mean in Israel (vv. 10-12).

In any case, these final verses identify two features of Moses that are distinctive and definitional. First, Moses knew YHWH face-to-face, as has no other. Moses has been permitted into the most awesome, dangerous presence of YHWH. (See Exod 33:11 on "face-to-face.") Such intimacy is unthinkable and acknowledged in Exod 33:20 as too dangerous. Nobody, not even Joshua in 31:14, enjoys such intimacy with YHWH's own holiness— nobody except Moses. The second, unparalleled claim about Moses is that nobody did "wonders" like he did (vv. 11-12). It is not said that the "wonders" derive from face-to-face access to YHWH, but such a connection may be inferred. In any case, verses 11-12 credit Moses, in a rich vocabulary, with signs and wonders, a strong hand, great displays of power. Such wonders are of course the substance of the entire Mosaic tradition. He enacted those wonders, sent from YHWH, in the land of Egypt, before Pharaoh, before Pharaoh's servants, before all Pharaoh's land, and before all the eyes of Israel. Moses confounded all things as they are in order to create a newness in the world. Nobody has ever done that, before or since!

It is conventional, in the long sweep of Deuteronomic history, to notice the parallel statement made about King Josiah at the end of the narrative:

> Before him there was no king like him, who turned to the LORD with all his heart, with all his soul, and with all his might, according to all the law of Moses; nor did any like him arise after him. (2 Kgs 23:25)

Nobody before, nobody after, like him. But of course Josiah, in this form, is a Deuteronomic "plant" in the narrative, a device whereby this theological history places a Moses-like figure at the end of the royal history in order to bracket and frame the entire account by the claims of Moses. Josiah is Moses who reappears in royal garb at the end of the story.

Theological and Ethical Analysis

The book of Deuteronomy ends as it began, with a focus upon the land (see 1:7-8). Deuteronomy is a meditation upon the new rule of YHWH that will create a safe, secure, prosperous place for

Israel in the world. It is this promise that is the propelling power of Zionist hopes in Judaism that have come to proximate fruition in the state of Israel. It is this same promise, moreover, that causes the church to pray daily for God's rule on earth as it is in heaven (Matt 6:10). Jews and Christians are people who await the earthly arrival of the full, good governance of YHWH. This chapter places the reading, believing community always again at the threshold of the coming kingdom. The believing community, like Moses, is not there, not admitted, but at the threshold, waiting. The same rhetoric is used in the inaugural utterance of Jesus, "The kingdom of God has *come near*" (Mark 1:15)—not here, but near, as near as can be seen and hoped for.

This tradition, at the end of Deuteronomy, takes great care in making the literary, theological move from "Torah" to "Prophets." The gap is as wide as the Jordan, between the ending of Deuteronomy and the beginning of Joshua, an immense canonical maneuver in the literature. Chapter 34 declares that everything originated is now completed. When the reader enters the Jordan and the land and the book of Joshua, Moses and Deuteronomy are finished. Fresh faith and fresh strategies are required under new leadership. The "new generation" of Israel represented by Joshua must take new form. This is "your little ones" (1:39) in "the next generation" (29:22) upon whom the tradition has had its hopeful eye. The discontinuity is clear, a discontinuity necessary if Israel is to have a life beyond recalcitrance. Thus the new generation does not need to pay forever for the failure of the old (24:16; see Jer 31:29-30; Ezek 18:2). At the same time, of course, the tradition insists that the new generation does not appear in history *de novo*. These are "your children" who must be fully inculcated into the story of wonders and into the demands of Torah that are the premise of life in the land. Thus the tricky relationship of new and old, of discontinuity and continuity, is much on the mind of this tradition, for the covenant is always "for all of us here alive today" (5:3), but also for "those who are not here with us today" (29:15). The memory is for the "grandchildren" who must be empowered and scripted by the tradition as they face their own venue of fidelity (see Exod 10:1-2).

It is precisely this rooted tradition that enables the facing of the problem and the demanding negotiation of continuity and discontinuity. The final form of the text is, in the end, power-fully contemporary for every generation that finds itself pondering old miracles, trusting old memories, heeding old commands, and always again entering new territory of promise (see Heb 11:39-40).

SELECT BIBLIOGRAPHY

WORKS CITED

Anderson, Bernhard W. 1999. *Contours of Old Testament Theology*. Minneapolis: Fortress Press.

Assmann, Jan. 1992. *Das kulturelle Gedächtnis: Schrift, Erinnerung, und politische Identität in früher Hochkulturen*. München: C. H. Beck.

Barton, John. 1979. "Nahum's Law and Poetic Justice in the Old Testament." JTS 30: 1-14.

Berger, Peter, and Thomas Luckmann. 1967. *The Social Construction of Reality. A Treatise in the Sociology of Knowledge*. Anchor Books, Garden City: Doubleday, 47-183.

Berger, Peter. 1990. *Sacred Canopy: Elements of a Sociological Theory of Religion*. New York: Doubleday.

Berry, Wendell. 1981. *The Gift of the Good Land: Further Essays Cultural and Agricultural*. San Francisco: North Point Press.

____. 1983. *Standing By Words: Essays*. San Francisco: North Point Press.

____. 1993. *Sex, Economy, Freedom, and Community: Eight Essays*. New York: Pantheon Books.

Betz, Hans Dieter. 1995. *The Sermon on the Mount*. Hermeneia. Minneapolis: Fortress Press.

Bird, Phyllis. 1997. *Missing Persons and Mistaken Identities: Women and Gender in Ancient Israel*. OBT. Minneapolis: Fortress Press.

Brown, Raymond. 1995. *The Sensus Plenior of Sacred Scripture*. Baltimore: St. Mary's University.

Brueggemann, Walter. 1978. *The Land: Place as Gift, Problem, and Challenge in Biblical Faith*. OBT. Philadelphia: Fortress Press.

____. 1982. *Praying the Psalms*. Winona, Minn.: St. Mary's College Press.

____. 1991. "The Commandments and Liberated Liberating Bonding" in idem, *Interpretation and Obedience: From Faithful Reading to Faithful Living*. Minneapolis: Fortress, 145-58.

____. 1994. "The Book of Exodus: Introduction, Commentary, and Reflection," *The New Interpreter's Bible I*. Nashville: Abingdon Press, 677-981.

____. 1997. *Theology of the Old Testament: Testimony, Dispute, Advocacy*. Minneapolis: Fortress Press.

____. 1998. A 'Exodus' in the Plural (Amos 9:7)," *Many Voices, One God: Being Faithful in a Pluralistic World*, ed. Walter Brueggemann and George Stroup. Louisville: Westminster/John Knox, 15-34.

____. 1998. "Faith with a Price." *The Otherside* 34, 4 (July-August, 1998) 32-35.

____. 1999. "Truth-Telling As Subversive Obedience, in idem," *The Covenanted Self: Explorations in Law and Covenant*, ed. Patrick D. Miller. Minneapolis: Fortress, 91-98.

____. 1999. "The Liturgy of Abundance, the Myth of Scarcity." *Christian Century*, 116, 10 (March 23-31) 342-47.

Buber, Martin, 1967. *Kingship of God*. Third edition. London: George Allen and Unwin.

Chaney, Marvin L. 1982. "You Shall Not Covet Your Neighbor's House," *Pacific Theological Review* 15 (Winter, 1982) 3-13.

Childs, Brevard. 1974. *Exodus: A Commentary*. OTL London: SCM Press.

____. 1985. *Old Testament Theology in a Canonical Context*. London: SCM Press.

Clarke, Erskine. 1979. *Wrestlin' Jacob: A Portrait of Religion in the Old South*. Atlanta: John Knox Press.

Coats, George W. 1968. *Rebellion in the Wilderness: The Murmuring Motif in the Wilderness Traditions of the Old Testament*. Nashville: Abingdon Press.

Cross, Frank M. 1973. *Canaanite Myth and Hebrew Epic: Essays in the History of the Religion of Israel*. Cambridge: Harvard University Press.

Crüsemann, Frank. 1996. *The Torah: Theology and Social History of Old Testament Law*. Edinburgh: T. & T. Clark.

Daube, David. 1947. *Studies in Biblical Law*. Cambridge: Cambridge University Press.

Dawn, Marva. 1989. *Keeping the Sabbath Wholly*. Grand Rapids: Eerdmans.

Dear, John. 1995. *Peace Behind Bars: A Peacemaking Priest's Journal from Jail*. Kansas City: Sheed and Ward.

Donner, Herbert. 1985. *"Jesaua lvi 1-7: ein Abrogationsfalls innerhalb des Kanons. Implikationen und Konsequenzen,"* Congress Volume: Salamanca, 1983, ed. by John A. Emerton. Supplements to *Vetus Testamentum*, 36; Leiden: E.J. Brill, 1985, 81-95.

Douglas, Mary. 1970. *Purity and Danger.* London: Routledge and K. Paul.

Ellul, Jacques. 1985. *The Humiliation of the Word.* Grand Rapids: Eerdmans.

Fensham, F. Charles. 1963. "Common Trends in Curses in the Near Eastern Traditions and *Kudurru* Inscriptions Compared with the Maledictions of Amos and Isaiah." ZAW 34 (1963) 155-75.

Fishbane, Michael. 1979. *Text and Texture.* New York: Schocken Books.

Fretheim, Terence. 1983. *Deuteronomic History.* Nashville: Abingdon Press.

Fukuyama, Francis. 1992. *The End of History and the Last Man.* London: Hamish Hamilton.

____. 1995. *Truth: The Social Virtues and the Creation of Prosperity.* New York: Penguin Books.

Gaiser, Fred. 1994. "A New Word on Homosexuality? Isaiah 56:1-8 as Case Study." *Word and World* 14 (1994) 280-93.

Gnuse, Robert. 1985. *You Shall Not Steal: Community and Property in the Biblical Tradition.* Maryknoll: Orbis Books.

Habel, Norman C. 1995. *The Land Is Mine: Six Land Ideologies.* OBT Minneapolis: Fortress Press.

Hallie, Philip. 1979. *Lest Innocent Blood Be Shed.* London: Michael Joseph.

Hamilton, Jeffries M. 1992. *Social Justice and Deuteronomy: The Case of Deuteronomy 15.* SBL Dissertation Series 136; Atlanta: Scholars Press.

Harrelson, Walter. 1969. *From Fertility Cult to Worship.* Atlanta: Scholars Press.

____. 1980. *The Ten Commandments and Human Rights.* OBT Philadelphia: Fortress Press.

Heschel, Abraham. 1962. *The Prophets.* New York: Harper and Row.

Hillers, Delbert R. 1964. *Treaty-Curses and the Old Testament Prophets.* Rome: Pontifical Biblical Institute.

Jacoby, Susan. 1985. *Wild Justice: The Evolution of Revenge.* London: Collins.

Joyce, Paul. 1989. *Divine Initiative and Human Responsibility in Ezekiel.* JSOTSup 51; Sheffield: Sheffield Academic Press.

Kaufman, Stephen A. 1978. "The Structure of the Deuteronomic Law." *Maarav* 1/2 (1978-79) 105-58.

Koch, Klaus. 1982. *The Prophets: The Assyrian Age I*. Philadelphia: Fortress Press.

____. 1983. "Is There a Doctrine of Retribution in the Old Testament?" *Theodicy in the Old Testament* ed. by James Crenshaw. Philadelphia: Fortress Press, 1983, 57-87.

Levine, Samuel J. 1998. "Unenumerated Constitutional Rights and Unenumerated Biblical Obligations: A Preliminary Study in Comparative Hermeneutics." *Constitutional Commentary* 15.

Levinson, Bernard. 1997. *Deuteronomy and the Hermeneutics of Legal Innovation*. Oxford: Oxford University Press.

Lifton, Robert J. 1993. *The Protean Self: Human Resilience in the Age of Fragmentation*. New York: Basic Books.

Lohfink, Norbert. 1981. "Distribution of the Functions of Power: The Laws Concerning Public Offices in Deuteronomy 16:18–18:22." *Great Themes from the Old Testament*. Chicago: Franciscan Herald, 1981, 55-75.

McBride, S. Dean 1973. "The Yoke of the Kingdom: An Exposition of Deuteronomy 6:4-5." *Interpretation* 27 (1973) 273-306.

____. 1987. "Polity of the Covenant People: The Book of Deuteronomy." *Interpretation* 41 (1987) 229-44.

McCarthy, Dennis J. 1971. "An Installation Genre?" JBL XC (1971) 31-41.

Miller, Patrick D. 1982. *Sin and Judgment in the Prophets: A Stylistic and Theological Analysis*. Atlanta: Scholars Press.

____. 1984. "The Most Important Word: The Yoke of the Kingdom." *The Iliff Review* 41 (1984) 17-30.

____. 1985. "The Human Sabbath: A Study in Deuteronomic Theology." *Princeton Seminary Bulletin* 6 (1985) 82-97.

____. 1990. *Deuteronomy: A Biblical Commentary*. Louisville: John Knox Press.

Moran, William L. 1963. "The Ancient Near Eastern Background of the Love of God in Deuteronomy." CBQ 25 (1963) 77-87.

Mullen, E. Theodore. 1993. *Narrative History and Ethnic Boundaries: The Deuteronomistic Historian and the Creation of Israelite National Identity*. Atlanta: Scholars Press.

Nelson, Benjamin. 1994. *The Idea of Usury: From Tribal Brotherhood to Universal Otherhood*. Princeton: Princeton University Press.

Neusner, Jacob. 1991. *The Enchantments of Judaism: Rites of Transformation from Birth to Death*. Atlanta: Scholars Press.

Noth, Martin. 1991. *The Deuteronomistic History.* JSOTSup 15; JSOT Press.

Oden, Robert A., Jr. 1987. *The Bible Without Theology: The Theological Tradition and Alternatives to It.* San Francisco: Harper and Row.

Olson, Dennis, T. 1975. *"nabalah*—A Term for Serious Disorderly and Unruly Conduct." VT 25 (1975) 237-42.

_____. 1985. *The Death of the Old and the Birth of the New: The Framework of the Book of Numbers and the Pentateuch.* Atlanta: Scholars Press.

_____. 1994. *Deuteronomy and the Death of Moses.* OBT Minneapolis: Fortress Press.

Philips, Anthony. 1970. *Ancient Israel's Criminal Law.* New York: Schocken Books.

Polanyi, Karl. 1957. *The Great Transformation: The Political and Economic Origins of Our Time.* Boston: Beacon Press.

Postman, Neil. 1986. *Amusing Ourselves to Death: Public Discourse in the Age of Show Business.* London: Heinemann.

Pressler, Carolyn. 1993. *The View of Woman Found in the Deuteronomic Family Laws.* BZAW 216; Berlin: Walter de Gruyter.

Schwartz, Regina. 1997. *The Curse of Cain.* Chicago: University of Chicago Press.

Stark, Rodney. 1996. *The Rise of Christianity: A Sociologist Reconsiders History.* Princeton: Princeton University Press.

Stern, Philip D. 1991. *The Biblical Herem: A Window on Israel's Religious Experience.* Brown Judaic Studies; Atlanta: Scholars Press.

Stulman, Louis. 1990. "Encroachment in Deuteronomy: An Analysis of the Social World of the D Code." JBL 109 (1990) 613-32.

Sweeney, Marvin A. 1996. "The Book of Isaiah as Prophetic Torah." *New Visions of Isaiah.* Ed. Roy F. Melugin and Marvin A. Sweeney. JSOT Supp. 214; Sheffield: Sheffield Academic Press.

Tillich, Paul. 1951. *The Protestant Era.* London: Nisbit and Co.

Trible, Phyllis. 1989. "Bringing Miriam Out of the Shadows." *Bible Review* 5/1 (February, 1989) 13-25, 34.

Tuchman, Barbara W. 1984. *The March of Folly: From Troy to Vietnam.* London: Joseph.

Washington, Harold C. 1998. "Lest He Die in Battle and Another Man Take Her: Violence and the Construction of Gender in the Laws of Deuteronomy 20–22," in *Gender and Law in the Hebrew Bible and the Ancient Near East.* Ed. by Victor H. Matthews et al. *Journal for the Old Testament Supplement Series,* 262; Sheffield: Sheffield Academic Press, 185-213.

Weber, Max. 1952. *Ancient Judaism.* Glencoe: Free Press.

Weinfeld, Moshe. 1972. *Deuteronomy and the Deuteronomic School.* Oxford: Clarendon Press.

_____. 1995. *Social Justice in Ancient Israel and in the Ancient Near East.* Minneapolis: Fortress Press.

Westermann, Claus. 1978. *Blessing in the Bible and in the Life of the Church.* OBT. Philadelphia: Fortress Press.

Wildavsky, Aaron. 1984. *The Nursing Father: Moses as a Political Leader.* Tuscaloosa: University of Alabama Press.

Willimon, William, and Stanley Hauerwas. 1989. *Resident Aliens: Life in the Christian Colony.* Nashville: Abingdon Press.

Wright, G. Ernest, 1962. "The Lawsuit of God: A Form-Critical Study of Deuteronomy 32." *Israel's Prophetic Heritage: Essays in Honor of James Muilenburg.* Ed. Bernhard W. Anderson and Walter Harrelson. London: SCM Press, 26-67.

COMMENTARIES

Clements, Ronald E. 1998. "The Book of Deuteronomy: Introduction, Commentary, and Reflections," NIB II. Nashville: Abingdon Press, 271-538.—An up-to-date theological exposition by one of the senior scholars in the field that has the special merit of drawing the text toward contemporary interpretive implications. The book is well grounded critically but serves the more practical and contemporary purposes of the series in which it appears.

Craigie, Peter. 1976. *The Book of Deuteronomy.* The New International Commentary on the Old Testament; Grand Rapids: Eerdmans.—This commentary, in a distinguished series, works through the text verse by verse and phrase by phrase. The author is a distinguished interpreter who pays attention to the larger purposes of the book and does not lose sight of those in the detail of the text.

Mayes, A. D. H. 1981. *Deuteronomy.* The New Century Bible; Grand Rapids: Eerdmans.—This commentary offers a rich bibliography and takes up, in turn, the several pericopes in the book of Deuteronomy. Focus is upon the important phrases and the astonishing weight that they are able to carry when understood in the context of the larger developing tradition.

Miller, Patrick D. 1990. *Deuteronomy*. Interpretation. Louisville: Westminster/John Knox.—This commentary by one of the most distinguished scholars in the field intends to deliver contemporary homiletical readings of the text. Particular attention is paid to the ways in which a critically understood book functions as a normative theological statement for ongoing theological reflection.

Thompson, J. A. 1974. *Deuteronomy*. Tyndale Old Testament Commentaries. London: Intervarsity Fellowship.—This commentary, from a somewhat more conservative perspective, carefully pays attention to the nuance and detail of the text.

von Rad, Gerhard. 1953. *Studies in Deuteronomy*. SBT 9; London: SCM Press.

____. 1966. *The Problem of the Hexateuch and Other Essays*. (New York: McGraw-Hill.

____. 1966. *Deuteronomy*. OTL. Philadelphia: Westminster.—This commentary is the normative classic in the field wherein this great German scholar developed his thesis about the convenantal shape of the book of Deuteronomy and the ways in which the text reflects the power and continuing contemporaneity of "preached law."

Weinfeld, Moshe. 1991. *Deuteronomy 1-11*. AB 5. New York: Doubleday.—Weinfeld, a distinguished Israeli scholar, presents what, upon completion, will no doubt be the reference commentary for a long time to come. The commentary reflects massive erudition and considers every imaginable nuance of the text as it is read in the context of the Ancient Near East, in which understanding it completely participates.

FOR FURTHER STUDY

Crüsemann, Frank. 1996. *The Torah: Theology and Social History of Old Testament Law*. Edinburgh: T. & T. Clark.—This book has quickly emerged as the classic in the field that provides a detailed critical reflection upon all the legal materials of the Old Testament. It is an accomplished reference work that focuses upon the policy implications and does not linger excessively over the particulars of any one text but looks at the impact and claim of all.

Harrelson, Walter. 1980. *The Ten Commandments and Human Rights*. OBT. Philadelphia: Fortress.—This book offered by a senior scholar in the field considers the ways in which the Ten Commandments function not only in the context of ancient Israel in the canon of the Old Testament but as a continuing source for social vision and social practice. A clue to the horizon of the book is the fact that it ends with a consideration of the Helsinki Human Rights Declaration with the suggestion that the contemporary issues faced in human rights are informed by and rooted in the initial enunciations of Mount Sinai.

Levinson, Bernard. 1997. *Deuteronomy and the Hermeneutics of Legal Innovation.* Oxford: Oxford University Press.—Levinson, a younger scholar, considers the way in which the legal traditions of Deuteronomy move from the older legal traditions of the book of Exodus but also move out beyond them. It is a study of the way in which legal interpretation is adaptable to circumstance. One may learn from here about the dynamic legal traditions in a way that contradicts all uncritical claims of "strict constructionism."

Lohfink, Norbert. 1981. *Great Themes from the Old Testament.* Chicago: Franciscan Herald.—This distinguished German scholar offers a variety of independent essays that are marvelously accessible and that are concerned with contemporary theological and ethical problems. For purposes of this commentary, the most important essay concerns the "separation of powers" that is reflected in the legal traditions of Deuteronomy. The author carries the matter of separation of powers into contemporary political questions of authority and participation.

McConville, J. G. 1984. *Law and Theology in Deuteronomy.* JSOTSup. Sheffield: JSOT Press.—This book is a study of the way in which the legal traditions of the book of Deuteronomy form a basis for the dynamic and developing theological interpretive tradition. The author understands the way in which the tradition is both rooted and open for rich interpretive possibility.

Miller, Patrick D. 1989. "The Place of the Decalogue in the Old Testament and Its Law." Interpretation 43, 229-42.—This brief discussion shows the way in which the commandments of the Decalogue have important interpretive trajectories implied in them that carry the ancient commandments into fresh ethical and moral issues.

Olson, Dennis. 1994. *Deuteronomy and the Death of Moses.* OBT. Minneapolis: Fortress.—This book is a creative monograph that considers the shape and force of the whole tradition of Deuteronomy and traces the way in which its accents revolve around the question of death. The author has moved away from a contemporary format and focuses on a single theological accent that permits a fresh interpretation of the whole.

Polzin, Robert. 1980. *Moses and the Deuteronomist: A Literary Study of the Deuteronomistic History.* New York: Seabury.—This book appeals to sophisticated literary theory and is interested in the way in which texts reflect tensions, contradictions, and conversations between various voices in the textual tradition. This book is part of a larger trilogy in which the dialogic force of the text is considered through a large portion of the canon.

Weinfeld, Moshe. 1972. *Deuteronomy and the Deuteronomic School.* Oxford: Clarendon Press.—This Israeli scholar has provided a classic study of the way in which the sapiential traditions of Israel are operative in the book of Deuteronomy and in its derivative historical narrative traditions. The book is an interesting alternative to the dominant tradition of covenant that is rooted in the study of von Rad and suggests that there is more than one possible way of identifying the informing tradition of the book of Deuteronomy.

INDEX